THE GOSPEL
IN THE OLD TESTAMENT

GOD BLESS YOU!

THE GOOD LIFE IN THE OLD TESTAMENT

R. Norman Whybray

T & T CLARK
A Continuum imprint
LONDON • NEW YORK

T&T CLARK LTD

A Continuum imprint

59 George Street
Edinburgh EH2 2LQ
Scotland

370 Lexington Avenue
New York 10017-6503
USA

www.tandtclark.co.uk

www.continuumbooks.com

First published 2002

ISBN 0 567 09855 X HB
ISBN 0 567 087212 PB

British Library Cataloguing-in-Publication Data
A catalogue record for this book is available from the British Library

Typeset by BookEns Ltd, Royston, Herts
Printed and bound in Great Britain by Biddles Ltd, Guildford and King's Lynn

*To my dear wife Mary,
whose interest means
continued encouragement*

Contents

Publisher's Preface

At the time of his sudden and unexpected death in 1998 Professor Whybray was working on a book to which he had given the title *The Good Life in the Old Testament*. His interest in the subject had been aroused by listening to a paper with the title 'God and the Good Life in Ancient Israel' read by Professor Bernhard Lang at the Summer Meeting of the Society for Old Testament Study at the University of Sheffield in 1996, a paper with which he strongly disagreed. Readers may be interested in the summary of the paper.

> This paper considered the religious dimension of the ancient Hebrews' good life from three perspectives. The *phenomenology of religion* reveals a universe that consists of several layers or perhaps concentric spheres at whose centre the human being stands encompassed and protected by divine forces. The deity who immediately touches the human individual is the personal god, while the Creator encompasses and cares for the entire universe. *Psychology* helps us understand some of the roots of the world view in early childhood experience. Psychology also explains how the divine dimension of the good life imposes itself on the human consciousness in what Hjalmar Sundén calls a structure-shift. Finally, the *anthropological* approach helps us to see how the good life is spoken of in religious, mythological terms — viticulture and arboriculture as a blessing vs. agriculture as a curse, and the forces of chaos as ever endangering but never abolishing the good life. This is why in the Hebrew Bible, in the words of Adolf Guttmacher, 'the joyous strain of existence bursts forth everywhere'. And this is why, in the words of William Robertson Smith, the ancient Israelites were at times 'well content with themselves and their divine sovereign' (The Society for Old Testament Study Bulletin for 1996, printed with permission).

It is perhaps significant that topics discussed in the workshops at that meeting included 'Health', 'Family', 'Learning' and 'Power', and the final session consisted of an Open Forum on 'The Quality of Life in Ancient Israel', at which questions about 'the definition of the quality of life and of the possibility and propriety of answering such a question on behalf of other people' were raised. All this certainly provided an important stimulus to Professor Whybray's work.

Professor Whybray had completed the first draft, but left little indication of the way he planned to revise it. The large amount of time and effort which he put into work on the project makes it clear that it meant a great deal to him, and his manuscript has now been prepared for publication by an academic editor with knowledge of the field. At no point have Professor Whybray's ideas been changed, even where it appears to the editor that he may well have had second thoughts when he worked through his manuscript. The text remains essentially as he left it apart from one feature: 'Summary' sections to the chapters on Job, Psalms and Proverbs were missing in the manuscript, and these have been added, following as far as possible the style of the other summaries. On the other hand, chapters on Obadiah, Nahum, Zephaniah and Habakkuk have not been produced, since their omission was deliberate, as Professor Whybray explains in his own Preface. Professor Whybray left no bibliography, and the list of books for further reading has also been compiled by the editor.

Norman Whybray was an exceedingly fine scholar who possessed a deep love and appreciation of the Old Testament. He told his wife that he anticipated that this would be his last book, and one reason for publication is to fulfil this wish. Even though it cannot be regarded as representing his considered views – for clearly he had planned a very thorough revision of the draft in accordance with his normal practice – we believe it presents a novel and interesting approach to the Old Testament and this is a second reason for publishing it.

Prefatory Note

This study is based on the Hebrew text as rendered by modern translations. In general quotations are taken from the New Revised Standard Version (NRSV), though in some cases I have preferred the Jerusalem Bible (JB) or the New English Bible (NEB). I have sometimes modified their renderings or supplied my own translation.

Where the chapter and verse numbering of the English Versions differs from that of the Hebrew I have followed the former. The order of the books as they appear in English translations has been followed, but four books – Obadiah, Nahum, Zephaniah and Habakkuk – have been omitted as they do not contain information about the good life.

1
Introduction: A New Approach

Old Testament scholarship has been changing in recent years. The approach which was dominant from the early nineteenth century to the present day aimed at reconstructing the history of ancient Israel. The Old Testament books were closely analysed and the 'sources' from which they had been compiled were separated out. It was held that these sources came from different periods and provided evidence for various stages in Israel's religious development. Interest has now shifted to the completed books found in the Hebrew Bible. Scholars have not rejected the labours of their predecessors as worthless, but they are now attempting to present the theology of those who produced the books as we have them. It is recognized that the theology will not necessarily be the same throughout the entire Bible, but the emphasis is placed upon each book as a completed whole rather than on the sources from which scholars claimed it had been compiled. The present study seeks to promote this type of investigation. It is no less a historical enterprise than the other, and no less worthy of serious pursuit.

It is to be taken for granted that there is nothing haphazard about the work of these final editors; that they worked with a definite purpose: to give encouragement to their contemporaries. While it is not possible to give precise dates to their work, it may be assumed that the time of the compilation of the books was a time when the Jews had already suffered the prolonged frustration of foreign domination, and needed to be given some hope of renewed freedom in the future.

This approach to Old Testament study is also of great importance for historians of biblical interpretation, since it is on these books in their final form that all subsequent theological interpretation was based until comparatively recent times, and still is based for the majority of readers for whom they have the authority of Scripture. To fail to take account of this fact and to treat the Old Testament simply as a collection of texts illustrating the progressive development of the religion of Israel is to ignore its importance as a body of literature that has had an incalculable effect on subsequent religious history.

It is not here contended that the study of the Old Testament in its final form is the only valid approach to it; only that it is one valid approach that has been wrongly neglected. If it is a valid approach it ought to be applicable to any topic that occupies a substantial role in the Old Testament books. It involves critical attention to the ways in which the material dealt with in each book has been managed and organized in order to imprint a particular notion of reality on the minds of the readers.

The topic here chosen to illustrate the method is that of concepts of the good life. This topic may appear bizarre and at best of secondary importance compared with the more 'spiritual' Old Testament concerns; but this is to underestimate the extent to which the ancient Israelites were affected in their daily lives by a longing for a more satisfactory mode of life that was constantly denied them, a longing that inevitably influenced their outlook on many things including their religious beliefs. No excuse, therefore, is needed for the choice of this topic.

The discussion of the topic as it appears in each book rather than on a thematic basis has been chosen partly in order to simplify the handling of the material; but it also has a further advantage. It makes it possible to demonstrate the variety of ways in which the topic is treated by different writers. It is not my contention that all the books underwent a single comprehensive redaction on the basis of a single set of principles, or that the individual redactors lacked imagination in dealing with their subject matter. This study has brought out the way in which each took into account the very different situations in which the nation found itself at different stages in its history, involving somewhat different concepts of the good life. For example, whereas Genesis depicts it mainly in a family setting, much of the material in the three books that follow is concerned with war, as also are the first half of Joshua and much of Judges. In those books that describe a period when Israel was engaged in fighting either for its existence or for its possession of Canaan, many of the aspects of the good life are necessarily muted, though in parts of Exodus and especially in Deuteronomy there are important collections of laws by which social and family relationships are to be governed and the conditions created in which the good life can be lived. Samuel and Kings, until the final chapters of Kings which describe the fall of the kingdom and the events that led up to it, depict once again a period of settled family life despite the many political upheavals, and offer numerous pictures of family and individual lives, giving the reader an insight into the actualities of living the good life, The Psalter, especially the laments and thanksgivings of individuals, conveys the experiences and aspirations of persons for whom the good life was especially associated with God's protective benevolence. The book of Job is an example of such an individual drawn on a larger scale, depicting a struggle for the good life in terms of a struggle against God himself. Qoheleth teaches that it is possible to live the good life provided that one is aware of the limitations that God has imposed on his human creatures, and of the inscrutability of God.

The term 'the good life' is not precisely a biblical expression. Its meaning, however, is clear to most English readers. In the Hebrew Old Testament each of the words 'good' (ṭôb) and 'life' (ḥayyîm) can convey separately a meaning not far removed from the double expression in English. 'Life' is commonly used metaphorically to signify a desirable state of affairs in contrast to an equally metaphorical 'death'. This is particularly true in Proverbs, which also uses such phrases as 'the path of life' (Prov. 2:19; 5:6) and 'a fountain of life' (Prov. 13:14; 14:27) in a similar sense. In Prov. 16:15 'life' appears in parallel with rāṣôn, 'favour (of the king)' and again in 8:35, where it is equated with the favour (again rāṣôn) of Yahweh. There it is included in a list of the rewards of humility together with riches and honour.

The other component of the phrase 'the good life', the adjective 'good' (ṭôb), can also stand in Hebrew with a virtually identical meaning. Its most significant occurrence in this sense is in the first chapter of Genesis, where God surveys his creation and pronounces, without any qualification, that it is 'good' or 'very good'. Though it is never paired with *ḥayyîm* it is sometimes used in connection with extended periods of time: there are 'good days' – that is, days of general rejoicing (as in 1 Sam. 25:8 (NRSV 'feast day'); Esther 8:17; 9:19, 22 (NRSV 'holiday')) and, in Gen. 41:35, 'good years', that is, years of plenty and prosperity. Each of the two words, then, independently denotes a desirable state of happiness and prosperity. It is this state of affairs, whether ideal or actual, which is the subject of this book.

It may be reasonably questioned whether it is possible for the modern investigator to discover from the Old Testament what the Israelites themselves held to be the components of the good life. The good life as portrayed in the Old Testament and the good life as the Israelites understood it may well have been different. The information that we have in the Old Testament has been selected, arranged, and supplemented at a late stage in order to present a particular interpretation. The writers of the books were presenting an ideal – their own ideal. Rather than attempting to recover the earlier material that the compilers incorporated in their books, or drawing on the evidence which archaeology provides from Israel's neighbours, the present study is limited to what can be discovered from the biblical writings themselves in the form in which we now possess them.

But how is the good life to be defined? What are its components? It may perhaps be described as a life of entire contentment with things as they are, the desire for which is a common feature of human mentality. Its component features probably do not vary greatly from one society to another. Perhaps the most fundamental of human needs is to live one's life in *security*. It has always been recognized that that need can never be fully met, for human life is commonly subjected to a variety of vicissitudes and finally and inevitably cut short by death. In the case of the ancient Israelites for whom there was no life beyond the grave, it was within their earthly span that they placed their hopes of a secure and peaceful life. Of these hopes, one that was of paramount importance was *security of place*. For them it was supremely important that they should possess a territory of their own in which they could live in safety from hostile attack or invasion.

The attainment and preservation of national security required that they should have the ability to defend themselves and their territorial possessions; and that involved some degree of *power*. Further, their land must be sufficiently fertile to produce an adequate supply of *food*. This was not always the case: there was a constant danger of famine in that part of the world. The precariousness of life with the possibility of serious illness or death by violence led the Israelites also to place great emphasis on *long life*, and especially on the ideal of a 'good old age' – a long life lived to the full in peace and prosperity.

Wealth and material prosperity are regarded in the Old Testament as a natural consequence of a virtuous life lived under divine blessing. Wealth, even though sometimes associated with wickedness or as a cause of unworthy ambition, is never regarded as intrinsically evil. Equally important for the good life was the possession of a *family*, and in particular of a male heir in each generation who would continue the line and so ensure, in some sense, the 'survival' of an individual in later generations. Yet another essential for harmonious communal living was the right of individuals to claim and obtain *justice*; and this in turn would normally be provided for in a body of *laws*.

A quality of mind conducive to the good life that is not always designated by name but was of great importance to Israelites was *wisdom*. Especially in the book of Proverbs wisdom is put forward as a goal to be pursued by individuals seeking a successful career: but it is also implicitly present in narratives about the achievements of certain exceptional individuals who through their wisdom greatly enhanced the well-being of the nation as a whole.

Despite the many hindrances to the good life, the Israelites on the whole possessed a very positive attitude towards life. Although it is only comparatively rarely that the Old Testament speaks specifically of the experience of *pleasure*, this positive attitude is everywhere apparent. It is significant that world-weariness and suicide were virtually unknown.

Finally, that all things are gifts from a benevolent *deity* is taken for granted throughout the Old Testament. It has been argued that the Old Testament in its final redaction exaggerates the extent to which Israelites in general took God into account in their daily lives. But in an age which made no distinction between the secular and the religious that is unlikely to have been so. In fact Israel does not appear to have differed essentially from the surrounding nations in this respect, although the distinctive monotheism with which it is credited by the final redactors is exceptional. But the idea that people could enjoy the good life without reference to the gods would have been unthinkable in the ancient world.

To sum up: although other items could no doubt be added, the following list contains what appear to have been the most prominent features of the Old Testament conception of the good life:

(1) security;	(7) family;
(2) a land to live in;	(8) justice;
(3) power;	(9) laws;
(4) food and sustenance;	(10) wisdom;
(5) a long life;	(11) pleasure;
(6) wealth;	(12) trust in God.

Several of these are closely linked, while in some books certain of them are lacking, but in the chapters which follow these are the features which will be especially looked for.

2
Genesis

This book serves as an introduction to the Old Testament in more than one way. One of its most important features is its depiction of the life of Abraham and his family as a model for the living of the good life. But the concept of the good life is already present in the opening chapter. The statements in that chapter that God was satisfied with what he had created and judged it all to be 'good' (*ṭôb*) or 'very good' must be regarded as paradigmatic for the whole book, or even for the whole Old Testament. But they raise the question, 'Good for whom?' Part of the answer to this question is obviously 'good for God'. God is pleased with what he has done. There is, however, an additional answer: 'good for the things that have been created'. In particular, this answer is applicable to those creatures to whom God had given control over the others: 'humankind' (*'ādām*), male and female. Their lives were thus 'good lives', pleasing not only to God but also to themselves. The next two chapters explain why that ideal situation was not permanently maintained. Nevertheless, the initial perfection of the creation, together with the further statement that human beings were made in God's image, would remain in the minds of the readers as a reminder of the good life that he had intended to be theirs, and which, however vaguely, they might aspire to be given once more.

Place and Security

Three themes pervade Genesis from beginning to end: the possession of a place to live; the possession of a family; and the divine blessing. All three were indispensable to the existence of that good life that human beings ardently desire but never fully and satisfactorily attain. They are closely linked, and often appear in one form or another in a single passage. The theme of *place* occupies a crucial position both

at the beginning and at the end of the book. Chapters 2–3
are already greatly concerned with the 'geographical'
location that God provided for occupation by the man
and the woman whom he created. He 'planted' a garden in
Eden, placed the man in it and provided it with abundant
water and a sufficiency of food. The account of the
subsequent expulsion of the man and the woman from this
garden (chapter 3) carries the implication that it had been
God's original intention that the garden should be their
permanent home: that they should never be obliged to leave
these idyllic conditions of life and become wanderers on the
face of the earth. This Eden tradition, though rarely referred
to explicitly elsewhere in the Old Testament, serves here to
remind the readers of God's benevolent concern to provide
this setting for the living of the good life.

This concern with place is again prominent, though in a
very different form, in the final chapters (37–50). At the
beginning of the story of Joseph, although it is stated that
his father Jacob had settled (*wayyēšeb*) in the land of Canaan,
he and his family were no more than 'resident aliens' (*gērîm*)
in that land, possessing no property rights. With Joseph's
sale into slavery in Egypt residence in Canaan comes to an
end, and the rest of the story is now centred on Egypt, the
country in which Abraham had once taken refuge for a time
during a famine (12:10–20). It would now seem that it was
Egypt which was to become the final place of residence for
Abraham's descendants. However, Joseph, despite the
immense power that he acquired in Egypt, remained aware
that this was not to be their final destination. They were
once more aliens in a land which was not theirs. Both Joseph
and his father Jacob insisted that they should be buried not
in Egypt but in Canaan (47:29–31; 49:29–32; 50:24–25), and
their wishes were carried out; Jacob's sons buried him in the
cave of the field at Machpelah (50:12–13), and Moses took
Joseph's bones with him when the Israelites left Egypt in the
Exodus (Exod. 13:19; cf. Josh. 24:32). In the final verses of
the book Joseph recalls the promise to Abraham that he and
his descendants would be given the land of Canaan. The
book thus concludes with an unmistakable expression of a
firm conviction that however Egyptianized the family may

have appeared to have become (50:26), Egypt was only an episode in their pilgrimage to the land of Canaan where their true safety lay.

The search for living-space as an essential condition of the good life is equally prominent in the rest of the book. The banishment of Cain after his murder of Abel from the 'ground' (*'ădāmâ*) which had consequently become infertile to him, to become 'a fugitive and a wanderer on earth' (4:12–14) suggests that for those who have been expelled from the garden the good life cannot easily be obtained. But it is with the coming of the Deluge (chapters 6–7) that 'a place to stand on' is most fully revealed as a necessity not only for the good life but for life itself. The solid earth was taken away altogether; and even those who survived death by divine grace were subject to the terrifying power of the sea which is the negation of earth and where there is literally 'no place': an unstable existence where there is no longer any point of reference. As the waters subside this remnant of humanity seeks anxiously for the restoration of 'place'; and only when their feet are on dry land again can they resume their activities of peopling the earth (9:1–3) and tilling the soil (9:20). Their descendants were to become nations that spread abroad through the earth, each to occupy its own place (chapter 10). In 11:1–9 an alternative version of this dispersion is given: humanity is represented as a single unit that wandered through the earth until they came on a place which seemed to them ideal for the establishment of a good life and a secure one; but as a consequence of this enterprise taken without God's consent and help they were dispersed throughout the world, deprived even of a common language.

It is against the background of this human craving for a good life based on the possession of a secure place in the world that the story of Abraham and his descendants takes its course. In 11:31 the phrase 'the land of Canaan' occurs for the first time. According to that verse Canaan was the goal of Terah's journey when he set out from Ur of the Chaldaeans, though he did not reach it but settled instead at Haran. It is not stated why he had wished to settle in Canaan. But throughout the rest of the book Canaan remains the place where Terah's descendants through Abraham suppose the good life to be found. In 12:1 Yahweh commands Abram to travel without any indication of 'the land that I shall show you'; but Abram interprets this mysterious command as meaning that he should go to the land of Canaan, his father's original destination.

The subsequent travels of Abraham, Isaac and Jacob within Canaan as recorded in Genesis were numerous and frequent. Abraham on his arrival 'passed through the land' (12:6). Later Yahweh commanded him to 'walk through the length and breadth of the land, for I will give it to you' (13:14–17). The patriarchs' subsequent migrations within the bounds of Canaan are intended to foreshadow an eventual occupation and possession of the whole, despite the fact that they themselves were never more than 'temporary residents' there. It is noteworthy that until the time of Joseph when they migrated temporarily to Egypt, whenever one of them was obliged for a particular reason to travel outside Canaan he always returned at last.

These foreign journeys were all journeys of necessity. Abraham was obliged to move temporarily to Egypt because of famine (12:11–20). Isaac was warned by Yahweh, despite another famine, not to go to Egypt but to remain in Canaan, and settled for a time, like Abraham before him (20:1–18), in the 'Philistine' city of Gerar, which counted as within the Canaanite borders (26:1–11). Abraham sent one of his servants to his relatives in Aram-naharaim (Mesopotamia) to obtain a wife for his son Isaac so that he should not marry a Canaanite, and the servant brought back Isaac's cousin Rebekah (chapter 24). Jacob's residence outside Canaan was of much greater duration; two reasons for it are given: it was either to avoid being killed by his brother Esau (27:42–45) or to obtain a non-Canaanite wife (27:46; 28:1–8). He also eventually returned, with Rachel and Leah, to Canaan (33:18).

The importance attached to place in Genesis is expressed no less emphatically, though negatively, with regard to those who did *not* receive the divine promise, for whom in consequence it was not deemed proper that they should inhabit the land of Canaan. Indeed, exclusion is as much a theme of the book as is promise. The first man and woman had been excluded from the garden; Cain had been condemned to be 'a fugitive and a wanderer on the earth' (4:12) and 'departed from Yahweh's presence'; after the human beings settled in Shinar and started to build a city and a tower to make themselves famous, God mixed up their languages so that they could not understand each other and they were scattered throughout the world (11:6–9). The Canaanites also were to be excluded from their ownership of the land, but not only they: even those members of Abraham's own family who were not in the main line of descent are regularly noted as having been expelled from Canaan or as having taken themselves off to live elsewhere. Abram's brother Lot chose to live in the plain of Jordan rather than in Canaan proper (13:10–12) and became the father of Moab and Ammon (19:36–38); Ishmael, Abraham's son by Hagar, migrated to the wilderness of Paran (21:21) and his descendants likewise (25:12–18). The territory of Laban the Aramaean, Rebekah's brother, is defined by treaty as being outside Canaan (31:44–54): Abraham 'sent away ... from his son Isaac' the children of his second wife Keturah, the mother of Midian, and also the children of his concubines, 'to the east country' (25:1–6). It is thus made clear that possible rival descendants of Abraham, Isaac and Jacob are in one way and another excluded from the promised land.

Power

It is already recognized in Gen. 1–11 that the exercise of power is an ineradicable component of human existence. In chapter 1 the report of God's creation of human beings is immediately followed by the command that they should 'fill the earth and subdue it' (kābaš) and rule (rādâ) over the animal creation; and this command is reiterated in 9:2 with the further statement that the animals should fear and dread their masters. This dominant status granted to the human race over the rest of creation is closely associated in both passages with God's blessing as well as being the source of material sustenance.

In the remainder of these chapters, however, it is made clear that power can be used wrongly and so become destructive of the good life, especially when it is used by human beings against others. The first murder, of Abel by Cain, is the earliest demonstration of the fatal possibility of using physical power to kill another human being On the other hand here and in succeeding chapters such inordinate use of power is frustrated by the irresistible power of God. Indeed, God had from the very beginning irrevocably set limits to the conditions in which the good life could be lived (2:16–17); and, when an attempt was made to breach those conditions, had imposed new and harsher conditions that made the full enjoyment of the good life impossible (3:16–24). Similarly in the story of the Tower of Babel (11:1–9) the ambition of human beings to 'make a name for themselves' – that is, to achieve power independently of God – met with failure because God used his power to disperse them and to prevent them from repeating the attempt. Admittedly the narrative records that on both occasions God was deeply concerned with the problem of such human aspirations to power (3:22; 11:6); but his ability to take decisive action to frustrate them is not left in doubt. The story of the Flood, though not specifically concerned with the question of human ambition, is the most complete illustration of the absoluteness of God's power and human powerlessness: this is a God who is capable of 'wiping out' (6:7; 7:4, 23) his whole creation because the human beings whom he had created have not pursued the good life that he had intended them to live.

In these chapters human power is sometimes exemplified in the founding of cities. It is probably significant that it is Cain who is first mentioned as having founded a city ('îr, 4:17). The immediate sequel of the establishment of city life was the development of the arts and crafts: animal husbandry, music and metalwork (4:20–22). These were all clearly conducive to the good life. But there again immediately follows (4:23–24) the boastful glorification by Lamech, a descendant of Cain, of murder and revenge – presumably also a mark of life in close communities. Finally human lust for power culminates in the universal determination to build a city and so 'make a name' — a phrase that suggests not just security but also seeking fame.

In the remaining chapters of Genesis this universal desire for power and both the good and the evil uses of power are shown in the lives of those who were to become the ancestors of the people of Israel. The power of God is evident throughout, guiding the lives of the human actors and preserving the family of Abraham again and again from the dangers that confronted it. Within this context, the exercise of human power took various forms. Power in the form of physical action is represented both negatively and positively. On the one hand the treacherous attack by Simeon and Levi on Shechem (chapter 34) is clearly deprecated by the author and is seen by him as also imperilling the good name and so the good life of the family in Canaan (v. 30); and the physical attack by the citizens of Sodom on the two 'angels' (chapter 19) graphically illustrates the general wickedness of that city that led to its destruction. On the other hand, Abram's military operation against the kings (14.1–16) is a manifestation of physical power that is clearly approved because its purpose was just; it led to Abram's receiving a blessing from King Melchizedek (vv. 18–20).

With the appearance of identifiable political entities such as the kingdom Egypt, political power comes to the fore. Joseph's dreams (37.5–11), in which he sees his parents and brothers bowing down to him, which his brothers interpret as an intention to reign (*mālak*) and to rule (*māšal*) over them, are seen in the light of subsequent events to be prophetic, but at the time disrupt family harmony and also result in Joseph's reduction to a state of total powerlessness. The subsequent events of the story are almost entirely concerned with the possession or lack of possession of political power. Joseph's rise to unheard-of power in Egypt shows the beneficial aspects of political power; he saves Egypt from famine and also uses his power to save his family from famine.

Power exercised within the family by one or more members over others is a constant theme in Genesis. It is used sometimes beneficially and at other times detrimentally.

Parental power was great: the parental blessing could be determinative of a son's success and prosperity (27:27–40); but the father also possessed the power of life and death over his children and close relations (38:24). However, the women of the family are represented as being not entirely without power. Sarah overruled her husband in the matter of Hagar (chapters 16 and 21); Rebekah made her own decision to marry Isaac (chapter 24); Rachel stole her father's household gods (teraphim) and later deceived her father when he came searching for them (31:19, 33–35).

But much attention is also given in Genesis to rivalry within the family, especially between brothers. Clearly the birthright or status of eldest son (běkōrâ) conferred authority as well as material advantage; but the story of the twins Esau and Jacob is one of continuous rivalry from the moment of their birth (25:21–26) although eventually they are reconciled (33:1–19). Fraternal hatred is also the theme of the story of Joseph (chapter 37), while in the last part of the story the positions are reversed with Joseph, though he was one of Jacob's youngest sons, exercising complete authority over his father and his brothers. These stories of the family of Abraham in their search of the good life suggest that while disputes over authority can lead to exile and misery, reconciliation between brothers can bring about the restoration of the good life.

Wealth and Sustenance

There is no glorification of poverty, or indeed sympathy with it, in Genesis. Wealth ensured a sufficiency or even superfluity of material sustenance, and was also a source of power. Apart from the periodical famines that drove Abraham (12:10), Isaac (26:1) and eventually Jacob and all his family to take refuge in countries where their livelihood would be more assured, Abraham's family is consistently represented as wealthy (13:2; 26:12–14; 32:5; 36:6–7). Those with whom they had to deal were prosperous landowners. Poverty is not a feature of Genesis. The family's wealth was evidently sufficient for its own needs, but also included a substantial surplus: Abraham was able to pay four hundred silver shekels for the purchase of the family burial place (23:1–16). Such wealth established the family's status in the eyes of the Canaanites, and enabled them to travel extensively throughout Canaan despite their alien position. Wealth, then, was for the author of the book a form of power which he never views with disapproval. It is taken for granted that it is conducive to the enjoyment of the good life, and its acquisition by both Jacob and Esau, who set out on their travels as poor men but ended as wealthy in their own right (30:43; 31:9; 32:13–15), is clearly regarded as estimable.

Family

The importance of family life is particularly stressed in the history of Abraham and his family; but the notion of the family is already established in chapters 1–11. It is, for example, exemplified in the frequent genealogies that link together the episodes of the primaeval history. The first mention of a family occurs in 2:18–24, where God creates woman as a necessary condition of human existence, saying 'It is not good that the man should be alone'. From that moment the destinies of the first man and the first woman are inseparable, both in good and evil fortune. Their relationship is further cemented by the birth of children (4:1–2). Eve becomes 'the mother of all who live' (3:20). In all that follows it is taken for granted that the succession of generations is a normal fact of human life. After the murder of Abel and the consequent banishment of Cain, Adam and Eve become the parents of another son, Seth, who is specifically stated to be a substitute for Abel (4:25), and Seth also begets a son (4:26). After the Flood which leaves only one family alive, the succession of generations is resumed (9:1), and Noah's descendants people the whole earth (9:18–19). But the fatal quarrel of the first pair of brothers stands as a warning of the consequences of a breach of harmonious relations within a family, and Cain's question 'Am I my brother's keeper?' (4:9), besides recording a murderer's denial of responsibility for his crime, was no doubt intended by the author to convey a more general message about mutual responsibility within the family – and also within the people of Israel, who regarded one another as 'brothers'.

The topic of family in Genesis is of course primarily exemplified in the stories of one particular family: that of Abraham. It is reasonable to suppose that the readers were invited to regard these stories as offering a model for future generations of Israelites, tempered by some warnings. The need to preserve the family line by obtaining a suitable male heir in each generation is a dominant topic. First, Abraham's concern (15:1–3) is allayed by divine assurance: Isaac rather than Ishmael will be his heir; but later Isaac is rescued from an apparently inevitable death as a human sacrifice (chapter 22). When he is grown the question of an heir arises again, and a trusted servant is despatched to Aram-naharaim to obtain a wife for Isaac from Abraham's own kin (chapter 24). Similarly his son Jacob journeys to Paddan-aram and marries his two cousins there, becoming the father of twelve sons. Thus in each generation a male heir is secured and preserved, not always without danger or uncertainty. Meanwhile other possible rivals (Ishmael, Lot, Nahor, Esau and their families, Abraham's family by his second wife Keturah) are removed in various ways from the succession by the providence of God.

Running through most of these chapters is the theme of the closely knit character and the impressive solidarity of Abraham's family – a solidarity comprising parents, sons and their wives, and brothers and sisters. Family concern begins already in chapter 12: although God's command to Abraham to leave his home and kindred is addressed to him alone, he interprets this command more widely, and takes with him his wife and his brother's son Lot, together with his personal household. Then, when it becomes clear on their arrival in the Negeb of Canaan that economic conditions necessitate a separation into two companies, Abram with great generosity leaves the best of the land to Lot (13:8–13). In a later generation a divided family is reconciled: Joseph's brothers confess their cruel treatment of their brother in the past (42:21–22) and are pardoned (45:5). Jacob's love for his

children is poignantly expressed in 42:36–38 and 43:14. In
43:7 Joseph enquires about the well-being of his father and
in 43:30 he weeps at seeing Benjamin again. In 45:4–8 he
comforts his newly found brothers by telling them that their
past treatment of him was part of God's plan to save the
whole family, and then sends for his father and brothers to
come to him in Egypt, providing them with the means to do
so. His evident concern for his father despite his acquisition
of great power is striking, and his further assurance of his
forgiveness and good will to his brothers after Jacob's death
is no less so (50:15–21). Family loyalty is also shown by the
wives: in chapter 31 Jacob's wives side with their husband in
defiance of their father Laban.

These relationships are characterized not only by loyalty
but also by affection. Several narratives speak of mutual love
between members of the family; others relate their piety
towards the dead. The cave of Machpelah, obtained by
Abraham at great cost to be a special burial place for Sarah,
became a family tomb in which Abraham himself (25:9),
Isaac and Rebekah (49:31) and Jacob (49:29–32; 50:13) were
also buried, an indication of strong family piety. Isaac was
greatly distressed at his mother's death (24:67); the two
estranged brothers Isaac and Ishmael combine to bury
Abraham (25:9); Esau and Jacob together bury their father,
Isaac (35:29). Jacob dies surrounded by all his sons (49:1;
49:33–50:1). These duties were far more than merely formal.
Abraham mourns and weeps for Sarah (23:2); Jacob refuses
to be comforted when he receives the report that Joseph has
been killed (37:29–35).

The intimacy of these family relationships is shown by
the frequent use of the verb to love ('āhab) to describe them.
Abraham's love for Isaac is made clear not only in v. 2 but
throughout the whole of chapter 22. Isaac's love for Rebekah
(24:67) and Esau (25:28), Rebekah's for Jacob (25:28) and
Jacob's for Rachel (29:30) are especially noted. In the story
of Joseph, Joseph's love for his father and for his brothers is
a recurring motif (42:24; 43:7, 27–30; 45:1–8; chapters 47–
50). These and other references attest the narrator's
intention to present Abraham and his family as a model
family despite internal quarrels. It is noteworthy that even

the hostility between Jacob and Esau ends in reconciliation. The story of the rape of Dinah (chapter 34) is presented with some ambiguity. Jacob condemns the actions of Simeon and Levi as endangering the safety of the whole family (34:30), and, according to 49:5–7, pronounces a curse on them; on the other hand, the two brothers responsible for the deed defend their action as necessary to preserve the honour of the whole family (34:31).

Life and Death

The first chapters of Genesis are much concerned with the issues of life and death. God gave life to the first human beings; but already in 2:17 we find him threatening the man with immediate death if he eats the fruit of the tree of the knowledge of good and evil. The snake tells the man and woman that the threat is an idle one: on the contrary, their lives will be enhanced, for as a consequence of eating that fruit they will 'become like God, knowing good and evil'. God's threat is only a ruse to frighten them. In this the snake was right: their disobedience does not in fact lead to their death.

But these chapters raise the question of human mortality. The question whether God originally intended human beings to be immortal has been frequently raised by subsequent interpreters, and it is difficult to know how the original readers would have understood the matter. But the text itself gives no reason to suppose that God had intended human beings to be immortal. On the contrary, God's soliloquy in 3:22 strongly suggests that this was not so. There God reflects that only if they eat the fruit of the other tree, the tree of life, would they live for ever; and he expels them from the garden to make sure that that will not happen. They will thus be permanently prevented from doing so, and will now be obliged to live 'all the days of their life' in conditions of hardship far removed from the idyllic life that they had lived in the garden (3:16–19). This scene is then immediately followed by the first human death, the murder of Abel (4:8).

Nevertheless, the lists of the descendants of Adam (5; 10; 11:10–30) attribute to certain persons lives of inordinate length, in some instances of 900 years. Though immortality has been ruled out, such longevity may have seemed to the readers to be appropriate for these giant-like figures, the 'men of old' (6:4). From the time of Terah, Abraham's father (he died aged 205), these figures are greatly reduced, but they are still much greater than the maximum number of years that were the lot of later human beings: Abraham lived for 175 years, Sarah 127, Isaac 180, Joseph 110. No explanation for any of these figures is given in the text: but these patriarchs also will have been seen as almost superhuman figures of a remote age.

Two notices about the age of patriarchs give an indication of the Israelite conception of a good life and of a 'good death'. Abraham 'died in a good old age, an old man and full of years' (25:8), and Isaac also died 'old and full of years' (35:29); each was 'gathered to his people'. These expressions, which may be coupled with Yahweh's promise to Abraham in 15:15, 'you shall go to your ancestors in peace; you shall be buried in a good old age', reflect the ideal of a happy, long and fulfilled life as well as a sense of family solidarity which extended even to the dead, whose lives would not be forgotten.

Law and Justice

Law, whether divine or human, is not a major theme in Genesis. Rather, the first human beings and then Abraham and his family are perceived as living under the direct providence of God, with whom they enjoy the privilege of direct communication. There is thus no need for particular laws. Human beings were expected to recognize and conform to certain principles of behaviour set by God – that is, principally, to know and respect the difference between righteousness and wickedness. God was perceived as both beneficent and severe. On the one hand he had created humankind and given them a freedom in which the good life could be lived; on the other, he punished wrong-doing with severity. His benevolence expressed itself in the form of promises and covenants – with Noah and with Abraham. There were, however, limits to human freedom. In 2:15–17 the permission to eat the fruit of the trees in the garden was restricted by a prohibition: the tree of the knowledge of good and evil was forbidden; and when that prohibition was disobeyed the ensuing punishment was extremely severe. Again after the Flood, in the context of the covenant with Noah when God permitted the consumption of animal flesh, the eating of the blood was forbidden (9:4). God forbade the killing of human beings by both animals and one another, and decreed: 'Whoever shed the blood of a human, by a human shall that person's blood be shed; for in his own image God made humankind' (9:5–6). The covenant that God made with Abraham was made conditional on the law of circumcision (17:9–14). These were the only laws, all restrictive, that God imposed on human beings in Genesis.

That justice and harmonious human relationships are essential elements in the good life is well recognized elsewhere in the Old Testament, but very little of this is explicitly reflected in Genesis. Very often it is left to the reader to conclude whether actions recorded in the book are regarded by the narrator as just or not; this is not always easy to decide. On 20:1–18, for example, the morality of Abraham's deceiving the king of Gerar about his marital status which put the lives of king and people in danger is not specifically questioned. Abimelech's reproach appears entirely justified, yet God does not condemn Abraham but appears to accept his excuse; he intervenes to put the matter right by accepting Abraham's prayer, warning Abimelech that Abraham is a prophet. Here one might almost be tempted to speak of God's moral blindness.

There is, however, one passage in Genesis in which the question of justice is explicitly discussed. This is Abraham's conversation with God in 18:22–33, a passage that is clearly on a different theological plane from the surrounding narratives. The question raised by Abraham in v. 25, 'Shall not the Judge of all the earth do what is just (ya'ăśeh mišpāṭ)' is ostensibly a question about *God's* justice and the result of the conversation is generally interpreted in this light; but it will probably have been recognized by the first readers that it is highly relevant to the question of human justice. Abraham here takes the high moral ground, demanding that God should conform to a concept of justice that he, Abraham, takes to be an accepted principle in human relationships, namely that the righteous (ṣaddîq) ought not to be condemned together with the wicked.

In the rest of the book the question of justice rarely receives explicit attention. This fact is reflected in the paucity of occurrences of the relevant terminology. The word mišpāṭ, so frequent in the prophetical books, occurs only three times in the whole book and only twice in the sense of 'justice'. Both of these occurrences are in chapter 18 itself. In v. 19, immediately before his conversation with Abraham, God states that he has chosen Abraham so that he may teach his household 'the way of Yahweh' in doing righteousness and justice (ṣĕdāqâ ûmišpāṭ). But in v. 25, as stated above, it is God's mišpāṭ that is in question.

There are thirteen occurrences of the words 'righteous' and 'righteousness' (derived from the root ṣdq) in Genesis, although NRSV translates them with a variety of English words. Eight are found in Abraham's debate with God over the destruction of righteous people along with the wicked in Sodom (18:17–33). Apart from these, Noah is twice said to be 'righteous' (6:9; 7:1); after Tamar has pretended to be a prostitute and has become pregnant with Judah's son in order to fulfil the demands of the levirate Judah declares that she is more 'in the right' than he is, because he had refused to give her his third son Shelah (38:26); Abimelech claims to be 'innocent' after he had taken Sarah because both Abraham and Sarah had said they were brother and sister (20:4); and Jacob says that he had acted honestly in his dealings with Laban over the sheep that he should receive as his wages (30:33). It is probable that the statement that God counted Abraham's faith as 'righteousness' (15:6) is the theological comment of the compiler of the stories.

Another word that relates to human relationships is ḥesed, which occurs eleven times in Genesis. In 21:23, 24:49 and 47:29 it refers to loyal dealings between Abimelech and

Abraham and between Laban and Abraham, and to Joseph's faithful carrying out of Jacob's deathbed wish not to be buried in Egypt. Elsewhere, apart from the six places where it applies to Yahweh's 'steadfast love' or the kindness of the 'angels' to Lot, it has the sense of kindness (20:13; 40:14). Such loyalty and kindness contributes to harmonious human relationships that are conducive to the good life.

Wisdom

The noun *ḥokmâ*, 'wisdom' and its cognates *ḥākām*, 'wise' and *ḥākam*, 'to be wise' are almost unknown to Genesis. Of the three, only the adjective *ḥākām* occurs, three times and in the same chapter. In 41:8 it denotes the official 'wise men' of Egypt, in v. 33 it occurs in Joseph's advice to Pharaoh to appoint a wise administrator, and in v. 39 it refers to Joseph as the one so appointed. The only other term in Genesis with a similar meaning is the verb *hiśkîl* (3:6).

The failure to employ the terminology of wisdom is somewhat surprising, since the story of Abraham's family could be described as a 'success story' involving the employment of what would ordinarily be called wisdom. Elsewhere, especially in the book of Proverbs (e.g. Prov. 3:13–18) it is wisdom that gives the key to success and happiness in life and so is an important element of the good life for the individual. In Genesis there are numerous examples of such human wisdom although the term itself is lacking. Although the material success of Abraham's family is attributed to divine guidance, and although in secular terms it might be put down to an astonishing amount of good luck, the actions of members of the family are in fact often examples of the application of wisdom in the sense of practical intelligence or shrewdness.

The first reference to wisdom in Genesis occurs in 3:6, where on the assurance of the snake that the fruit of the forbidden tree would not cause immediate death but that eating it would make her 'like God, knowing good and evil' The terms are not necessarily to be understood in the moral sense of what is good or evil in itself. Rather 'good and evil' are what is useful or harmful for human beings. Eating the fruit of the tree gives them the ability to know what will be advantageous to them and what will harm them, and so makes them 'wise'.

In the story of Abraham and his family it may be said that they exhibited the truest wisdom in obeying God's commands, which went hand in hand with his promises and his guidance and protection, ensuring their preservation from generation to generation and their material prosperity. This is illustrated in a number of incidents. The story begins with Abraham's obedience to God's initial call (12:4) and continues in 15:6 with his profession of faith and his circumcision of himself and his household, again following God's command (17:23–24). His unquestioning obedience to God's command in 22:1–3, however, was an act of faith rather than of wisdom, as he was unaware of the eventual outcome. But Jacob's setting up of the pillar at Bethel (28:18) could be called an act of wisdom in that it was done in the hope of continuing divine guidance, as was also his putting away of 'foreign gods' (35:2–4).

Often, however, the wisdom exhibited by members of the family was a simple shrewdness not stated to be prompted by God but exemplifying the gift of 'knowledge of good and evil' conveyed on humankind – in other words, the independent choice of an advantageous course of action. So both Abraham and Isaac passed off their wives as sisters (12:10–20; 20:1–18; 26:1–11), actions that in the end increased their prosperity. It is Jacob, however, who was the great deceiver: he steals the blessing from Esau (chapter 27) and deceives Laban (30:29–43). In 31:19 Rachel deceives her father; in 37:31–36 Joseph's brothers deceive Jacob. In chapter 38 Tamar deceives Judah. Finally in chapters 42–44 Joseph deceives his brothers and so contrives to meet his long lost brother Benjamin. On these incidents, in which members of the family exercise their shrewdness in order to obtain an immediate advantage or to escape from a dangerous situation, the author makes no comment, either approving or condemnatory. In the context of the whole narrative, however, it is evidently intended that the readers should understand these incidents as fulfilling God's intentions for the preservation and prosperity of the family.

Joy and Pleasure

Hebrew narrative generally is reticent in its references to the emotions experienced by its characters; the emphasis is mainly placed on actions rather than emotions, and Genesis is no exception to this. Sometimes, however, it is remarkably successful in suggesting emotions indirectly. In chapter 22, for example, the statements in vv. 1 and 2 that God *tested* Abraham are sufficient in themselves to suggest Abraham's intense grief in being required to sacrifice his son, though the statement that Isaac was his only son and that he loved him makes this more explicit The story of Hagar in chapter 21 records both Abraham's distress or displeasure at the probable fate of Ishmael and, more poignantly, Hagar's despair. Jacob's distress on learning of Joseph's presumed death (37:33–35) is also explicitly depicted; and in the story of Joseph the brothers' fear when they find the money and the cup in their sacks is recorded (42:28; 43:18), as also are Joseph's emotions when he meets Benjamin and when he makes himself known to his brothers (43:30; 45:1–3).

The pleasurable emotions (joy and pleasure), which are generally regarded as essential components of the good life, are only rarely made explicit in these stories. One of the best indications of such feelings is the use of the word *ṭôb*. The concept of the 'good' is applied to God himself in the opening chapters of the book. The statement in 1:31 that everything that he had made was very good immediately follows the description of the creation of humankind and the permission given to them to use the vegetable and animal creation as food, showing God's concern for their well-being and happiness. In 2:18 this concern is further shown in his creation of woman, since he has reflected that it is 'not good' that the man should live alone.

In later chapters the word *ṭôb* is frequently used of material sustenance in the form of cattle and crops. Chapter 27 with its reference to Isaac's preference (*'āhab*, 'to love') for a particular dish is a clear indication of human pleasure, and also of a certain refinement of taste. The word *ṭôb* was also applied to other forms of positive appreciation: Rebekah (24:16; 26:7) is described as physically attractive. Other aspects of an appreciation of the good life to which the adjectve *ṭôb* is applied include the fruit of the tree (3:6) which was delightful or desirable to the eyes (*neḥmād*) as well as being good to eat and able to confer wisdom; to gold (2:12), to a dowry (*zēbed*, 30:20) and to land (49:15). The expression 'a good old age', used with regard to Abraham (15:15; 25:8), signifies a full and happy life; this is confirmed by the use of the phrase 'in peace' (*běšālôm*).

The writer of Genesis uses the verb 'to love' fourteen times. Abraham loves Isaac (22:2); Isaac loves Rebekah (24:67) and Esau (25:28), while Rebekah loves Jacob (25:28); Jacob loves Rachel (29:18, 30), while Leah hopes that by bearing six sons Jacob will begin to love her (29:32); Hamor, the Canaanite, loves Dinah, with disastrous consequences (34:3); and Jacob loves Joseph (37:3, 4) and Benjamin (44:20).(The other three references are to Isaac's love of savoury food!) At the end of the book Jacob dies in peace, surrounded by his twelve sons who are to become the twelve tribes of Israel. So the good life was achieved for Abraham's family.

God

All these things are presented as due to the benevolent care of God, without whom there could have been no good life, or indeed any life at all. It was God who had created the human race and set them in the marvellously fertile garden; who had made the woman to be the man's helper and companion; who had created the human family and given them the gift of children; who after their rebellion and consequent punishment had given them a new beginning with Noah; who chose Abraham, made a covenant with him and gave him an heir; who guided and presided over the succeeding generations and preserved them from many dangers; who blessed them and promised to give them the possession of the land of Canaan, to make them a great and numerous people who would be a blessing to all peoples; and who finally brought them together as a united family ready to become a nation looking forward to the fulfilment of his promises.

However, in the early chapters of the book (1–11), the readers are made aware of another aspect of the divine nature. Here humanity is almost entirely treated as a single entity. The story is one of their repeated rejection of their Creator's good intentions for them, a state of affairs which provoked God to react with extreme severity. The good life that he had designed for them was already impaired when he excluded them from the garden and condemned them to face the rigours of the world outside. Eventually, when they had become depraved beyond endurance, God regretted that he had created them (6:7) and determined to exterminate them by means of a great Flood; only Noah and his family were spared. Even then their rebellious nature came to the fore again when Noah's descendants once again increased in numbers and they attempted to make themselves independent of God, who was obliged to restrict their growing power, dispersing them into separate groups whom he made incapable of acting any longer as a single unit.

Yet even in these chapters there are signs of God's forbearance and of a concern for the well-being of the human race. He spared the lives of Adam and Eve despite his threat that disobedience would bring death on them, and also spared the murderer Cain. Despite the state of total corruption into which humanity had fallen he refrained from total destruction of them. After the Flood he recognized that 'the inclination of the human heart is evil from youth' (8:21), renewed his blessing on the human race in the persons of Noah and his sons, and made a covenant with them in which he promised never again to send a flood to destroy the earth. But it was with the choice of Abraham that he made a definitive new beginning; from chapter 12 to the end of the book it is the positive side of God's nature that becomes and remains dominant.

Summary

We may conclude that it was an aim of the compilers of the final form of the book of Genesis to offer to its readers a picture of the good life as lived by their remote ancestors, but also to give them a realistic indication of the impediments to it owing to an innate human tendency to sinful rebellion against what God had intended for it. For later generations – perhaps particularly those that had experienced the loss of the good life both nationally and individually – these narratives constituted both a warning and an encouragement for the future. Security, possession of the land, material prosperity, wealth, a long life, justice, power, wisdom and happiness were all blessings that they longed to possess or to possess in greater measure. The picture presented by Genesis is fundamentally a positive and optimistic one.

3
Exodus to Numbers

References to the good life are far less frequent in these books than in Genesis. The family of Abraham has become a numerous and strong people (Exod. 1:7); and for the most part the accent is now on corporate life rather than on the family or the individual. Moreover, this is a people on the march, in a transitional state between Egypt and Canaan the land of God's promise, living a precarious and dangerous life – though one that had its own lesson to teach to a later generation which was also living in insecurity.

Nevertheless, amid the hardships and austerities of life in the wilderness and the vicissitudes of the people's bouts of obedience and disobedience to God and Moses and the imposition of dire penalties for their disobedience, it is yet possible to find some aspects of the good life in their thoughts and aspirations. Prominent among these were the longing for place and security.

Place and Security

These books frequently recall the promise to Abraham and his heirs that they would achieve the secure and unquestioned possession of the land of Canaan (Exod. 3:6–8; 6:2–8; 32:13; Lev. 26:42; Num. 32:11). But now for the first time both the land and its future occupation are envisaged in detail. Its marvellous fertility is described: it is a good land 'flowing with milk and honey' (Exod. 3:8, 17; 13:5; 33:3; Lev. 20:24; Num. 13:27; 14:8; 16:13, 14). But this was to be enjoyed in the future, not immediately. The mass of the people after the report of the spies were fearful that far from being a place of security the land would be a place of danger from the present, powerful and presumably hostile population (Num. 13–14).

The process by which the Israelites were to obtain possession of Canaan, left quite vague in Genesis, is described for the first time in these books. Yahweh would fight against the present occupants of the land and to exterminate them (Exod. 23:23–33; 34:11–16). In contrast to Genesis where relations with the Canaanites were almost without exception harmonious, war has become an essential means of obtaining the good life, and already in the wilderness Israel resorted to war against other peoples (Exod. 17:8–13; Num. 21:3, 23–25; 31:1–47). In Num. 32 in preparation for the invasion of the land Israel is instructed to prepare for war.

Leviticus takes the future occupation of Canaan for granted. The law of 14:34–57, for example, begins with the introductory clause 'When you come into the land of Canaan which I give you for a possession ...'. The same assumption is made by the rules for the observance of the land's 'sabbaths' and the arrangements for the allocation of tribal lands, cities of refuge, etc. (Num. 33:5–35:15). Enjoyment of the land, however, was to depend entirely on obedience to the divine commandments mediated through Moses. If Israel obeyed these they would enjoy every kind of blessing and prosperity, and God would make his dwelling among them (Lev. 26:3–13); but disobedience would lead to crop failure, disease, death and other terrible afflictions (Lev. 26:14–39). There could be no good life without Yahweh's approbation.

In these books the concern for place is thrown into sharp relief by the new situation in which the nation finds itself. The texts draw a complete contrast between Egypt and Canaan, Israel's past and future homes. In Gen. 12–36 most of the action takes place in Canaan which, although Abraham and his family have no territorial rights there, is paradoxically the very land of promise; moreover, the resident Canaanites, though no doubt due to be eventually expelled, are hospitable rather than hostile. Somewhat similarly, the Egypt of Genesis, where the final chapters of that book are set, does not have the negative character that it has in the later books; on the contrary, it is the place where Joseph rose to prominence and where his family was welcomed.

For Exodus to Numbers, on the contrary, Egypt has become the most sinister of places, the place of Israel's oppression and slavery, from which Yahweh delivered them (Exod. 1–15). Yahweh brought Israel out of Egypt miraculously into the wilderness to serve him there (so Exod. 20:2; 29:46; 32:11; Lev. 11:45; Num. 15:41 and many other verses). It is true that in the wilderness the people sometimes complained that they had been safer and better off in Egypt and that they wished that they had been left there, or even wished to return there (Exod. 14:10–12; 16:2–3; 17:3; Num. 11:4–6, 18–20; 21:5); these incidents, while illustrating the rebelliousness with which Moses had continually to contend, also illustrate the people's desire for a place where they could live securely. In their minds Egypt still had strong positive attractions, and despite the continued assurance given to them that Canaan was their promised destination (e.g. Exod. 3:8; 33:1), the featureless wilderness in which they were now forced to wander, which was for them 'no place' at all, had a greater and grimmer reality than the land 'flowing with milk and honey' that had been promised to them.

However, a means was found to create in the wilderness itself a special 'holy place' (Exod. 25:8) where Yahweh would come to dwell among his people and where they could communicate with him and he with them (Exod. 29:43). This was the Tabernacle (*miškān*), also closely associated with the 'Tent of Meeting', which the people constructed according to the pattern (*tabnît*) that Yahweh communicated to them (Exod. 25:9). The Tabernacle plays a central role in the life and worship of Israel, especially in Exodus (from chapter 25) and Numbers. The people carried this portable 'place' or temple with them during the remainder of their journey to Canaan, assuaging their desire for a permanent place, and ensuring that even in the empty wilderness there was a specific centre which was the source of divine guidance.

Despite this assurance, Israel in the wilderness was not allowed to fall into complacency. Their situation was far from secure; the fullness of the good life remained unattainable, and it was their sense of insecurity that was the cause of their frequent complaints and revolts against the leadership of Moses. The hostility of neighbouring tribes added to their physical hardship; and the terrifying and sometimes death-dealing anger of God at their lack of faith and other shortcomings, which finally expressed itself in the exclusion of that entire generation from attaining its goal, the land of Canaan, was an even greater peril. They were condemned all to die without entering the land: only the next generation would do so (Num. 14:26–35; 32:10–13). Ironically, that exclusion was due to the people's refusal to believe that the land was theirs for the taking.

Power

In Exod. 1–15 power is a dominant motif. In Moses' confrontation with Pharoah the issue is whether it is the seemingly omnipotent king of Egypt or Yahweh the God of Israel who possesses the greater power. But the deliverance of Israel from slavery through the exodus from Egypt and the crossing of the Sea also put power into the hands of the people of Israel, changing their way of life completely from one of powerlessness as an enslaved people to one in which they had the freedom to determine their own destiny – a new form of power that could be used to their ultimate advantage and so to the development of the good life, but which if wrongly used could bring about their destruction.

The new situation is already foreshadowed in the statement in Exod. 1:7 that the Israelites 'multiplied and grew very strong so that the land of Egypt was filled with them', and with the new Pharaoh's reaction to that situation (1:9–14). The narrative then becomes an account of a contest between two opposing forces (those of the God of Israel and the Pharaoh), with Moses and the Egyptian magicians as their agents. The plagues, the exodus and the miracle at the Sea finally establish that invincible power is on the side of Israel; the destruction of the firstborn of Egypt and of the Egyptian army show that the Egyptians are in fact power-less. The Israelites depart from Egypt with the Egyptians' gold and silver in their hands (11:1–3; 12:33–36).

From that time and throughout the remainder of these books it is Moses who, as God's representative, exercises the power of leadership over Israel. He is the recognized leader,

commander in war and diplomat, and the unique commu-
nicator of Yahweh's commands to the people, who promise
obedience (Exod. 24:7). His role is to promote the well-being
of the people – that is, to enable them as far as possible to
enjoy the good life – and he performs that task with
complete consistency. He alone is privileged to speak with
God face to face (Exod. 33:11) and to see his glory, though
not his face (Exod. 33:17–23). When his authority is
questioned, God dramatically authenticates it (Num. 12:1–
15). On one occasion it is recorded that when angered by
the people's rebelliousness God proposed to disinherit them
and to make Moses the founder of a new people, more
powerful than they, in their place (Num. 14:12).

However, Moses' own relationship with God does not
always run smoothly. On occasion Moses does not hesitate
to confront God and dares to oppose him, even succeeding
in persuading him to change his mind and postpone or
cancel the punishment that he has proposed for them. In
these incidents Moses appears as a fearless hero-figure, using
his authority to frustrate God's anger (Exod. 32:7–14; Num.
11:10–15; 14:11–25). He even threatens to abandon a task
that has become too heavy for him, asking for death (Num.
11:15). Nevertheless, however great Moses' power may
seem to be – even over God – the ultimate power is God's,
and Moses himself is excluded, with the rest of the exodus
generation, from entering the land of Canaan (Num. 20:9–
12).

Despite these incidents there is no doubt that these books
present the power of God, whether mediated through
Moses or not, as the force that led the people of Israel
through the dangers of life in the wilderness towards the
good life that he had promised to them in the land 'flowing
with milk and honey'.

Wealth and Sustenance

Not surprisingly, the stories of Israel's long sojourn in the
wilderness are greatly concerned with the supply of food
and water. It was the lack or insufficiency of these basic

commodities that were the chief subject of the people's complaints to Moses (Exod. 15:22–25; 16:3; 17:1–7; Num. 11; 20:2–13). Quails and manna were miraculously provided to meet these needs (Exod. 16), and it is recorded that the provision of manna continued for forty years until the entry into Canaan, where there was a sufficient supply of ordinary food (Josh. 5:11–12).

But Exodus and Numbers also record the people's inordinate lust for food; and this had to be punished. Despite the oppressive conditions of their life in Egypt the Israelites had preserved memories of the succulent food that they had eaten in Egypt (Exod. 16:3; Num. 11:5). They were now taught the consequences of greed (Exod. 16:19–20; Num. 11:33). These are not the only passages in which God's concern for the Israelite diet is shown: according to Lev. 11 he gave them through the mediation of Moses the rules which defined those creatures whose flesh they were permitted to eat and those which were unclean and so forbidden – rules still observed in Jewish communities.

The authors of these books were at pains to portray the Israelites of the wilderness period as well provided with material possessions. Like the family of Abraham in Genesis, they were not impoverished immigrants. According to Exod. 12:38 they took with them great numbers of cattle when they left Egypt, though their own numbers were so great (Exod. 12:37) that these were evidently insufficient to satisfy their need for food. But according to Exod. 12:33–36 they also possessed large quantities of other material possessions of silver, gold and jewellery that the Egyptians had heaped on them at their departure, an action triumphantly described as the 'plundering' of the Egyptians. Their wealth can be assessed by the list of valuable articles which they freely gave for the manufacture of the Tabernacle, its ornaments and its service (Exod. 25:1–7; 35:20–29; 38:24–25; Num 7:2–88).

Family

In contrast with Genesis, the family in the restricted sense of parents, their children and close relations – brother, sister,

uncle, etc. – plays little part in these books. This is not due
to an authorial intention to dismiss it as a significant feature
of the life of Israel in the wilderness. What is depicted now is
the life of a whole people understood as 'brothers'. The
family of Abraham on whose preservation and well-being
the very existence of which the later Israel had depended
had become so numerous that no single family was
responsible for the nation's destiny. All the families in Israel
were now joint heirs of the covenant and promises. No
doubt the birth of a firstborn son remained an event of the
first importance in every family; the incident of the
daughters of Zelophehad (Num. 27) shows that the question
of family inheritance was still a major concern. The name of
an individual's father is frequently stated. But the central
question dealt with in these books is no longer the survival
of a particular family but the survival of a whole nation. In
some of the later Old Testament books the fate of an individual family will once again be of the first importance (for
example, in the book of Ruth); but for the present it is the
national situation which is to the fore.

The only family that is singled out in these books is that
of Moses. This exceptional treatment is due to his exceptional importance as sole leader of the nation; his family
background needed to be recounted as part of what is in
some respects the life-story of a hero. Just as in Genesis the
divine preservation of the individual patriarchs was essential
to the survival of the ongoing family of Abraham, so Moses'
preservation as a baby from the murderous intentions of the
Pharaoh was essential to the survival of the 'family' of Israel.
So an account is provided of Moses' early years: the parents'
concern to hide their newborn child by concealing him in the
bulrushes; their acquiescence in his adoption by Pharaoh's
daughter; then his forced flight as a young man to the land
Midian, his marriage to Zipporah and the birth of his son
Gershom are duly recorded.

But beyond this even the family life of Moses is hardly a
major concern in these books. The names of his sons
Gershom and Eliezer are only mentioned in passing (Exod.
2:22; 18:3, 4). Nothing is said about his possessing an heir in
the sense in which this is so important in Genesis. His wife

Zipporah reappears in only two incidents, the mysterious occasion when Yahweh 'tried to kill' him (Exod. 4:24–26) and the statement in Exod. 18:2 that he 'sent her away' together with her two sons. According to Num. 12:1 it is recorded that he married a second time – a Cushite woman, a marriage to which his brother Aaron and his sister Miriam objected.

The only members of Moses' family who play significant roles in these narratives are Aaron and Miriam. Aaron was associated with his brother in many activities beginning with Yahweh's appointment of him as Moses' spokesman (Exod. 4:14–16) and was responsible for the making of the golden calf (Exod. 32). Miriam, simply referred to as Moses's sister, was responsible for watching over the infant and suggesting that his mother should nurse him for Pharaoh's daughter (Exod. 2:4–9). Described as a prophetess, she led the women out to dance and sang a victory song after the crossing of the Sea (Exod. 15:20–21). Later she joined Aaron in opposing Moses and was punished with leprosy (Num. 12:1–15). Her death and burial are recorded in Numbers 20:1. Yet the relationship of Aaron and Miriam to Moses is not stressed. In general Moses is presented as a solitary figure, the true father of his people; and this relationship took precedence over his family life in the narrower sense.

Longevity

The concept of 'dying in a good old age' like Abraham and his family is entirely absent from these books. On the other hand, much is said about the people's concern about health and about their survival in the wilderness. Their complaints about the insufficiency of their supply of food and their fear of extermination by enemies (Num. 14:2–4) testify to this. But the deaths of large numbers in punishment for disobedience together with God's decree that the present generation should die in the wilderness (Num. 14:26–35; 32:10–13) make it clear that the good life in its aspect of a 'good old age' is not a main topic of these books. Health and life were not to be taken for granted but were granted as a special favour and were dependent on obedience to God's will.

Justice and Law

These three books contain the most extensive collection of laws in the Old Testament. All are presented as imposed on the people by God in connection with a covenant that they have made with him, in a few instances through his direct command (e.g. in the Decalogue, Exod. 20:1–17), but mainly through the mediation of Moses acting as God's spokesman. Many of these laws are concerned with the priesthood and sacrificial offerings; but others concern justice – that is, the equitable treatment of individuals by others irrespective of rank, status or origins (Lev. 19:15; 24:22; Num. 15:16).

The body of laws comprising Exod. 20–23 contains many items whose purpose is to promote and ensure harmonious relations between individuals within the community. These chapters begin with the Decalogue or Ten Commandments (Exod. 20:2–17). These, in addition to admonitions concerning duties towards God, include a command to honour one's parents and prohibitions of certain crimes against society: murder, adultery, theft, malicious perjury and coveting the possessions of others. In the chapters following, legislation about these and other matters relevant to the maintenance of the good life is listed, sometimes with greater detail: the treatment of Hebrew slaves and of resident aliens, involuntary manslaughter, violence against parents, kidnapping, the regulation of disputes, mutual responsibility with regard to property, loans to fellow-Israelites and the taking of bribes. Similar legislation is found in some other chapters of Exodus and Leviticus.

The administration of these laws necessitated the establishment of a legal system with judges and the examination of witnesses (Exod. 21:22; 23:2–3, 6, 8). The position of chief judge was allotted to Moses, and his decisions, made under divine direction, were regarded as definitive; but other judges were appointed to assist him in judging minor cases (Exod. 18:13–26). These books thus depict a society in which the good life – in this case, justice for every individual – was to be assured.

Wisdom

The root ḥkm with its derivatives ḥākam, ḥākām and ḥokmâ is employed in Exodus to contrast the ineffectiveness and failure of the Egyptians with the ability of the Israelites under Yahweh's guidance. In Exod. 1:10 a form of the verb is used to denote a political strategy: Pharaoh in consultation with his people proposes a scheme for the suppression of the increasingly troublesome Israelites: 'Let us deal prudently with them.' But this policy of oppression followed by the murder of all Israelite male babies failed: 'The more they were oppressed, the more they multiplied'; and the life of their future leader, Moses, was saved. The final consequences of that failure were the disaster of the plagues with the death of all the Egyptians' firstborn children, the destruction of the Egyptian army in the Sea, and the release of Israel from slavery. The point is made succinctly in 10:7 by the blunt comment of Pharaoh's officials to Pharaoh: 'Do you not yet understand that Egypt is ruined?'

In Exod. 7:8–12 the incompetence of the Egyptians is demonstrated at another level. Pharaoh summons his 'wise men' together with the Egyptian sorcerers and magicians to show that they are able to perform a magic trick equal to the feat performed under God's direction by Aaron. All their staffs were turned into snakes; but Aaron's snake swallowed up those of the Egyptians. This demonstration of the superior power of Israel's God over heathen magic arts was a presage of the future successes of Israel.

The only other references to wisdom in these four book occurs towards the end of Exodus. God tells Moses that he has filled the men who are to make Aaron's vestments with a 'spirit of wisdom', so that they will have 'wisdom of heart'. Wisdom here is practical ability (cf. NRSV 'all who have ability, whom I have endowed with skill', Exod. 28:3)). The skilful women who span the coloured yarn and wove fine linen are also described as being 'wise of heart' (Exod. 35:25), and the same term is used of other 'skilful ones' (lit. 'wise men') in Exod. 35:10, and 36:1, 2, 8). God filled Bezalel with 'divine spirit' and with wisdom (NRSV 'skill'), while he and Oholiab are filled with 'wisdom of heart' (Exod. 35:35). For the author there was apparently no essential distinction between political and practical ability, both of which he termed 'wisdom' (*ḥokmâh*). While the 'skill' of the Egyptians had failed to stop the Israelites, the latter achieved success in their work because God had conferred their skill on them. The making of the Tabernacle and of the priestly vestments was not a matter of small importance. The Tabernacle was the symbol of the presence of God among his people and even his temporary dwelling-place (Exod. 25:8) as he guided them on their journey; and the priests, who wore the sacred vestments when they carried out their duties, were the persons who daily made atonement for the people's sins, without which they would have perished. Thus God's gift of the 'spirit of wisdom' to those engaged in these activities was essential to Israel's very existence.

Joy and Pleasure

One might suppose that the events described in Exod. 1–15 would have offered to Israel the greatest occasions for rejoicing that that nation experienced in the course of its history. Their God Yahweh had shown himself to be more powerful even than the mighty Egyptian empire; and this power had been exercised wholly on behalf of his chosen people, whom he had set free from slavery through the miracles of the plagues and the crossing of the Sea. In these chapters it was as a saviour that Israel knew him, and joy might be expected to be their dominant emotion. Yet these books make very few references to this emotion.

It is true that the victory songs of Moses and Miriam in Exod. 15 might well be regarded as expressions of joy. Yet it is recorded that when Israel 'saw the great work that Yahweh did against the Egyptians' at the miracle of the Sea it was fear rather than joy that they experienced: they 'feared Yahweh and believed in Yahweh and in his servant

Moses' (Exod 14:31). Joy in these books is almost entirely restricted to rejoicing at the festival of Booths or Tabernacles, when it is specifically enjoined on the people as reminding them of Yahweh's great deeds on their behalf (Lev. 23:40; Num. 10:10). Nor is there any mention of private joy.

It is fear rather than joy that is the principal emotion attributed to Israel throughout these books. This fear of Yahweh is sometimes best interpreted as awe, but also frequently as sheer terror (e.g. at Sinai, Exod. 20:18–20). Another dominant concept is that of holiness, which for Israel involved the requirement of meticulous obedience to the commandments promulgated at Sinai. Israel was to be a kingdom of priests and a holy nation (Exod. 19:6), and is reminded that it is to be holy because Yahweh is holy (Lev. 19:2). Israel's mood in the wilderness is sober rather than exultant, even before it learns of Yahweh's decree that none of the present generation will, after forty years' hardship, be permitted to enter the promised land.

God

It was in Egypt that Israel first learned the name Yahweh and that he was identical with the God of their ancestors Abraham, Isaac and Jacob. At the same time he declared his intention to free them from their slavery and to lead them to the land of Canaan (Exod. 3:16–18; 6:2–8). (This revelation had already been made to Moses in Midian (3:1–8)). The chapters that follow describe how he carried out the first of these intentions: he led the people out of Egypt and they recognized his as their saviour. But it was a wilderness to which he first led them; and the immediate destination was Sinai.

The experience of Yahweh as saviour of his people was a partial revelation of his true nature. In Jewish tradition the significance of the events at Sinai is no less than that of the exodus from Egypt, for it was at Sinai that Yahweh established Israel as his own people and bound them in obedience to himself by the giving of his laws and by a covenant. The earlier chapters of Exodus (before chapter 19) give no hint of

what was to come: Moses had demanded that they should
be allowed to go and worship their God on a mountain in
the wilderness; but they had no notion of what that would
involve.

The God who reveals himself at Sinai is the supreme
sovereign who regulates his people's lives down to the last
detail and demands total obedience as the condition of the
good life. He assures the people of his steadfast love for
those who love him and obey his demands (Exod. 20:6) and
promises to make Israel his 'treasured possession out of all
the peoples' (Exod. 19:5). But he remains unpredictable. He
sometimes forgives offences, but can also be implacable and
destroy those who offend him. He sometimes shows himself
to be amenable to persuasion, as when after the incident of
the golden calf he allows himself to be induced by Moses to
abandon his threat to destroy the whole nation (Exod. 32:7–
14). On the other hand he was implacable when he condemned Moses, who had led the people throughout their
travels, to die in the wilderness and not have the satisfaction
of leading them into the promised land of Canaan (Num.
20:12; 27:12–14). Total obedience to him is the only key to
the good life in these books; but the situation of Israel is
always precarious in face of Yahweh's undisputed power
either to bless or to punish.

Summary

Whereas in Genesis Abraham and his family enjoyed many
aspects of the good life even though God's promise of the
land still remained to be fulfilled, these books taken together
describe a situation in which their descendants, now become
a nation, suffer many hardships. Under Moses, Yahweh's
servant, they are set free from an initial slavery and
oppression; but on leaving Egypt they find themselves in an
inhospitable wilderness, threatened with the hostility of
neighbouring tribes and often saved from starvation only by
special divine intervention. At Sinai they encounter Yahweh,
who takes them as his special people and gives them his
laws, which set out the conditions which would make the

good life possible for them. Although he becomes their guide in their travels and provides them with the Tabernacle as a symbol of his presence, there follows a tale of consistent disobedience and rebelliousness against him and his servant Moses which frequently results in severe punishment, culminating in Yahweh's decision to exclude the exodus generation from taking possession of the promised land of Canaan. The freedom that was given them through the miraculous events of the exodus and the defeat of the Egyptian army at the sea has been tragically misused, and the good life has been denied to them. These books, while celebrating Yahweh's power and his desire for his people's welfare, will have served as a warning to later generations that the good life is attainable only by faithful obedience to his laws.

4
Deuteronomy

Deuteronomy presents a complete contrast with the three previous books in its depiction of the good life. The people of Israel are still waiting to enter the land of Canaan from which their elders have been excluded (1:35–40); but now the focus is on the immediate future. This is a picture of how things will be when the people are settled in the land: a picture of a peaceful life for the obedient. The elements of the good life are set out in great detail. In particular, all the blessings that Yahweh promises to confer on Israel are presented in 28:1–14. (Here and in some other places in the book the people is addressed in the singular ['thou'], a form of address that is applicable either to the nation considered as a single entity or to the individuals within it.) These blessings will be enjoyed by all who obey God's commands; the much longer list of vv. 15–68 portrays the disastrous fate of the disobedient, from whom Yahweh will withdraw his gift of the good life.

Security, Power, Sustenance, Wealth

In 28:1–14 the reiterated promise of the land satisfies the need for a permanent place of abode. The specific mention of both cities and the countryside confirms that Israel will have possession of the entire land. If it is obedient it will also receive power: the people will defeat their enemies, and the other nations will be afraid of them. The soil will be fertile, and there will be abundance of rain. Israel will also enjoy an abundance of food from crops and fruit, and will gather the surplus into barns. They will derive wealth from the great fertility of their cattle; and their families also will increase, so that their survival will be assured. In short, they will be successful in all their undertakings: they will be 'the head, and not the tail' (v. 13).

The list in the second half of the chapter of the curses that will fall on the disobedient is equally instructive. It sets out the things that Israel most feared, and so by contrast throws further light on their notions of the good life. The consequences of these curses are depicted in such horrific terms that the readers would recoil in horror from them. They comprise the negation of all the positive features of the preceding list: the loss of land and security, the failure of crops, the loss of animals, defeat and conquest by enemies. But they also add further items: death-dealing disease, dire poverty, starvation and even the horrors of cannibalism.

Another pointer to the notion of the good life in Deuteronomy is the use of the word *ṭôb*, a word that occurs nearly thirty times – an indication of the buoyant tone of the book as a whole. The occurrences of this adjective are confined mainly to the hortatory and promissory parts of the books – to the Prologue (chapters 1–11) and chapters 28–30; in the central corpus of the laws (chapters 12–26) there are only five occurrences (12:28; 19:13; 23:6, 16; 26:11). The word is used in several distinct ways, including well-being in an unspecific sense of general prosperity (e.g., 6:24; 10:13; 19:13; 26:11; 30:9; in 23:6 the Israelites are commanded *not* to seek the prosperity of the Ammonites and Moabites), and moral rectitude (1:39; 6:18; 12:28). In ten cases it qualifies the noun 'land', as well as to the 'good' cities and houses in Canaan (6:10; 8:12). In addition to the adjective the verb *ṭôb* occurs twice (5:33, 'if you would live and prosper' [it may go well with you], and 15:16 'he fares well with you' [of a slave who does not wish to be given his freedom]), and the related verb *yāṭab* nearly twenty times (e.g. 4:40; 5:16; 12:25; 22:7; 28:68; 30:5, often in the phrase 'to inquire diligently', 13:14; 17:4; 19:18).

Whereas in the books already discussed the references to the land of Canaan were generalized and lacking in detail, suggesting a mysterious unknown, eagerly anticipated but still remote, in Deuteronomy it is described in detail, perhaps on the grounds that as the Israelites approached it they would have acquired a more precise notion of it from the peoples with whom they had come into contact during their journey. These details were of course familiar to later generations for whom possession of the land lay in the past.

The familiar formula 'the land which he swore to your fathers to give you' characteristic of Exodus and Numbers is now supplemented by a new formula, 'the land which Yahweh your God *is giving you* as an inheritance' (4:21), suggesting that its conquest is now imminent. The land with its properties and contents is most precisely described in 8:7–10:

> For Yahweh your God is bringing you into a good land,
> a land with flowing streams
> and waters welling up from the deep in valleys and
>   hills,
> a land of wheat and barley ...
> a land where you may eat bread without stint,
> where you will lack nothing,
> a land whose stones are iron
> and from whose hills you may mine copper.
> You shall eat your fill and bless Yahweh your God
> for the good land that he has given you.

The emphasis here is on the abundance of the food produced by the lush fertility of the land, but also on its provision of the means to fashion the tools and other artefacts necessary for a settled and civilized life.

Another passage, 6:10–11, stresses that Israel will not need to labour as pioneers forced to undertake the back-breaking toil of cultivating a barren wilderness (contrast Gen. 3:17–19). They will find a land 'ready-made' to provide them with an 'instant good life', abandoned by the ousted population for them to occupy; it is described as

> a land with great and fine cities that you did not build,
> houses filled with all kinds of good things
> that you did not provide,
> rock-hewn cisterns that you did not hew,
> vineyards and olive groves that you did not plant.

Here tribute is paid – grudgingly – to the superior civilization of the Canaanites, who during their occupation of the land had provided all these things for themselves and had

lacked nothing of the good life. It was they who created all
that Israel was about to enjoy.

It might be possible to detect a note of triumphalism or
even of *Schadenfreude* in this passage, were it not for the
fact that the enjoyment of all these benefits is made wholly
conditional on faithfulness to Yahweh. The passage
continues:

> Take care that you do not forget Yahweh
> who brought you out of the land of Egypt,
> out of the house of slavery.
> Yahweh your God you shall fear,
> him you shall serve,
> and by his name alone you shall swear.
> Do not follow other gods ...
> Because Yahweh your God who is in your midst is a
>   jealous God,
> the anger of Yahweh your God would be kindled
>   against you
> and he would destroy you from the face of the earth.
> (6:12–15)

This motif runs through the whole of the book. It draws an
absolute distinction between the way in which the good life
is to be enjoyed by Israel and the way it was practised by
the Canaanites, who had attributed it to their own gods
(6:14; cf. Hos. 2:5) and were therefore now to be dis-
possessed. This is summed up in Moses' final words in
30:19–20:

> Today I have set before you life and death,
> blessings and curses.
> Choose life ... that you may live in the land.

Life and death are here to be understood literally. Disobedience to Yahweh will not only deprive Israel of the
good life; it will deprive them of life altogether.

The use of the verb 'to choose' (*bāḥar*) in a command to
Israel occurs only here in the book. In 23:16 the slave who
has run away from his master is to be allowed to remain in

the town where he chooses to live. Apart from these two occurrences, the subject of the verb is always Yahweh: he chose Israel to be his people (7:6–7), he chose Israel's future, and sole, place of worship, the place where he would 'put his name' (12:5, 11, 14, 18) he chose Israel's future king (17:15), and he chose the tribe of Levi (18:5) and the priests for their respective functions (21:5). The use of this verb in the phrase 'choose life' is therefore particularly significant. It shows that it is a free choice that Israel is to make. To 'choose death' is a real possibility which presages what was actually to occur in Israel's later history, and its consequences are set out in the curses of chapter 28.

Choosing life involved 'loving Yahweh your God, obeying and holding fast to him; for that means life to you and length of days' (30:20). To love God and to obey him are closely connected in Deuteronomy. That loving God can be commanded may seem strange; but it describes one side of a mutual relationship. It is because Yahweh has loved and loves Israel that he chose Israel and bestows the blessings of the good life on them (4:37; 7:13; 23:5). This is, however, one side of a loving relationship; and so, as Yahweh loves Israel, so must Israel love him. This love expresses itself in obedience, like the obedience of a child for its loving parents. But the concept of love, though it involves the keeping of the laws set out in the code of chapters 12–26, includes more than that.

Law and Justice

An outstanding feature of the laws of Deuteronomy is a concern for the practice of justice within the community of Israel. An equitable relationship between individuals and between individuals and society is seen as an essential aspect of the good life. This is also stressed in the legislation of Exod. 20–23; but the laws of Deuteronomy are fuller and more systematic – a blueprint for the creation of an integrated and well-organized society living in the land which is shortly to be theirs.

The overriding importance of justice for Israel's life is

summed up in an emphatic command of those who are to be appointed to judgeships: 'Justice, and only justice, you must pursue, so that you may live and occupy the land that Yahweh your God is giving you.' In other words, if the judges appointed by the people do not make it their sole aim to mete out fair treatment to individual Israelites who come before them, Israel will have forfeited the right to occupy the land. This verse comes at the end of a passage (16:18–20) which calls for 'judges and officials' who will 'render impartial decisions regarding the people'. Such decisions are defined in negative terms: judges must resist all attempts that may be made to influence their decisions by bribery or other immoral means. It is taken for granted that it would be their natural inclination to judge cases fairly; but this is a warning not to succumb to temptation to act otherwise.

The laws of Deuteronomy have been described as humanitarian, and this could certainly be said of some of them. But the majority of those that deal with relations between individuals are concerned with society as a whole: towards the creation and maintenance of a harmonious community within which individuals can live in peace and enjoy the benefits of the good life in the land which they are about to enter. These laws are mainly concerned with four areas of life: human rights, property, honesty and relations between the sexes.

'Human rights' is a modern term. These laws are mainly concerned with the status and rights of the individual Israelite who is a member of the chosen people. However, the 'stranger' or resident alien (gēr) is not forgotten. To a considerable extent he is to share the same privileges as the Israelites among whom he lives. They are to love him because Yahweh himself loves them, and because Israel is to remember that it once lived as an alien in Egypt (10:18–19). These 'strangers' are to be given a share in the Sabbath rest (5:14), the rejoicing at festivals and other cultic occasions (16:11; 26:11–13) and, together with orphans and widows, the right to glean after the harvest (24:19–21) and to the wages that are due to Israelite labourers (24:14). They are not to be denied the right of appeal to the courts for justice (24:17; 27:19). Because Israel was commanded to care for the alien in these ways, observance of these laws was as much a condition of the good life for Israel as was obedience to those laws which directly concerned the Israelites themselves.

1. Human rights

In the laws concerning Israelite citizens the protection of the rights of individuals occupies an important place. A fundamental right to personal freedom is asserted by the law against kidnapping (24:7) which impose the death penalty on persons who seize, enslave or sell into slavery a fellow-Israelite. Another threat to personal freedom which was evidently by no means unknown in ancient Israel was the imposition of the death penalty on the innocent family of a convicted criminal – a practice presumably acceptable at an earlier time. This is forbidden in 24:16. This law does away with the notion of corporate guilt and establishes the principle of the sole responsibility of an individual for his actions (cf. the discussion between Yahweh and Abraham in Gen. 18:23–33).

The notion of a united society whose concept of the good life included a special concern for persons whose social and economic situations would otherwise exclude them from it is expressed in a number of laws in Deuteronomy. Chief among these are the poor, together with widows and orphans. It is interesting to observe, however, that the continued existence of a class of the very poor ('ebyôn) was not regarded as detracting from the good life of the people as a whole. The recognition in 15:11 that 'the poor will never be lacking in the land' is a realistic assessment of an inevitable situation. These laws are legislation for relief of the poor, not a programme for the elimination of poverty. The same reaction to poverty is found in Proverbs. In the passage under consideration (15:7–11) the presence of the poor within Israel's borders is invoked as an incentive for the demand that those who are able to do so should provide from their own resources the means to meet their basic needs.

Similar considerations of compassion motivated the demand that employers should pay the wages of their labourers regularly (24:14–15). Courtesy must be shown by those who make loans when they collect pledges: they must not enter the debtor's house but must wait outside, and if the debtor is so poor that he has to pledge his cloak, this must be returned to him at night so that he may sleep in it (24:10–13). Other classes of persons whose special rights are protected include the firstborn sons of fathers with two wives, whose right to inherit must be protected (21:15–17) and men called for military service, who are to be exempted on compassionate grounds (20:5–7).

2. Property

Slaves were considered the property of their owners. But the laws concerning slaves are drawn up in the interests not of their owners but of the slaves as persons. Chapter 15:12–18 prescribes the amount of time that an Israelite slave can be held in slavery and the need for generosity when the time comes for his release, and also with the procedure to be followed in the case of a slave who does not wish to be released because he loves his master. Chapter 23:15–16 restricts the powers of the owner still further with its surprisingly liberal provision, rare in the ancient world, that an escaped slave is not to be returned to his owner but should be received with kindness by those to whom he has fled for protection.

In other respects, however, there is a strong affirmation of the rights of property owners. The surreptitious moving of boundary stones to augment the size of one person's fields at the expense of another person is strictly forbidden (19:14). This practice was equally forbidden in neighbouring countries; in Israel, however, where the land had been allotted to Israel by God (e.g. 12:10) there was a special reason for the prohibition (cf. the protest of Naboth, 1 Kings 21:3). There is also a provision that anyone who sees a neighbour's livestock straying or in trouble, or finds a neighbour's possessions knowing them to be lost should return them to his neighbour (22:1–4).

3. Honesty

The good life depends on honest dealings between fellow-Israelites. In the Decalogue (5:19; Exod. 20:15) theft is forbidden in general terms, and various forms of theft are dealt with in specific laws. The duty to return lost property and the prohibition of moving boundary stones are examples of these. The requirement of impartial administration by the judges is an example of a general emphasis on the importance of honest dealing. The prohibition of cutting a neighbour's standing corn is a further law against theft (23:25). A clear example of dishonest commercial practice is the possession of false weights (25:13–16); this is specifically condemned as an 'abomination to Yahweh'.

4. Relations between the sexes

The laws concerning relations between the sexes are naturally biased towards the husband and the woman's father, but they attempt to deal fairly with issues that commonly arise. Thus the laws in 22:13–21 are designed to protect the rights of both husband and wife when the question of the wife's virginity has been raised. Deuteronomy 22:22–29 deals with adultery and rape, and make distinctions between rape in the open country, where the woman is defenceless, and rape in the town, where it is held that she could have shouted for help. Rape of an unbetrothed virgin is punished by a payment to her father. Chapter 24:1–4 shows that a husband who divorced his wife had to give her a 'certificate of divorce', but the law is primarily concerned with forbidding the remarriage of a divorced woman to her first husband; and 25:5–10 deals with the brother of a childless widow who refuses to marry her, in this case shaming rather than a judicial punishment being decreed. It might be claimed that they maintain the rights and legitimate interest of those concerned, without which the possibility of the good life would be endangered.

5. The judicial system

Many of the laws mentioned above could not have been enforced without an organized judicial system. Without this, crime and injustice would have been unchecked and the good life at risk. In the wilderness the chief judicial office had been filled by Moses with some help from subordinate judges (Exod. 18:13–27); but now Moses prepares for the future when Israel will have entered the land and taken possession of it after his death. He sets out in some detail the arrangements for a permanent system. It is presupposed that Israel will have a king (17:14–20); but he will himself be subject to the laws listed in this book. He must study and obey these laws, but no actual power is assigned to him. The judicial power will be in the hands of judges and officials appointed by the people in each tribe and town (16:18–20), though these must submit disputed questions to the higher authority of the priests, who will make the final decisions on Yahweh's behalf (17:8–13). Chapter 18:15–22 also speaks of prophets who will speak in Yahweh's name. The relationship between these functionaries is unfortunately not clear.

Other laws are concerned with the judicial process itself. In 19:15–21 the principle is established that the testimony of a single witness in a lawsuit or trial is insufficient to establish the truth, and that three, or at least two, are required for a reliable judgement to be made. As has been noted above, 24:16 established the further principle that only the person convicted of a crime should suffer the death penalty, his family being deemed guiltless. Unintentional homicide is dealt with by the establishment in various parts of the country of cities of refuge to which the person concerned can flee and live in safety (19:1–10). Chapter 21:1–9 concerns the case of a corpse whose murderer is unknown. Those who live nearby who might be suspected of the murder are exculpated if they take an oath of innocence. Finally, the question of the severity of punishment in the form of flogging is settled: it is limited to a maximum of forty lashes to ensure that the recipient does not die (25:1–3).

There is, however, a negative side to the concept of the

good life in Deuteronomy. It can be placed in peril or even made impossible by the polluting presence of sin in the community. This must therefore be purged or eliminated in order to preserve the purity and integrity of the nation. The process of purgation is defined by the use of the verb *bi'ēr* 'to consume, remove' in the formula 'so shall you eliminate the evil from your midst' (or 'from Israel'). This formula occurs ten times in Deuteronomy in connection with a range of crimes: false prophecy (13:5); idolatry (17:7); disobedience to the priests (17:12); murder (19:13; 21:9); false testimony (19:19); disobedience to parents (21:21); premarital unchastity (22:21); adultery (22:22); and kidnapping (24:7). In every case but one (the malicious witness, 19:19) the crime carries the death penalty, but this exception casts a slight doubt on the supposition that the purging of the nation from impurity is achieved by the execution of the offender.

This concept of a nation whose integrity must be protected by the ruthless elimination of polluting sin makes it clear that for Deuteronomy the good life is not something that the people make for themselves and that God then stamps with his approval, but that it is completely dependent on God's control. This is not only implied in the laws but is made endlessly explicit in the hortatory introductory chapters, where the very possession of the land is made conditional on obedience to the divine laws conveyed to the people by Moses (so, e.g., 4:1–2). The danger of incurring God's displeasure is also illustrated by the warnings against being led into idolatry by the peoples of the land, and in the commands to destroy the latter (7:1–6; 12:2–3, 29–32; 20:10–18).

Family and Pleasure

It is perhaps not surprising that very little is said in Deuteronomy about pleasure. The main references to joy are in connection with public worship when the people are to express their gratitude for the benefits conferred on them. As had been mentioned above, a number of laws regulate certain aspects of family life, but the only reference to its enjoyment occurs in 24:5, where the newly married man is to be excused military service and any other public duty for a year so that he can remain at home 'to be happy with the wife whom he has married'. This goes beyond the similar law in 20:7, where the reason is that the man may die in battle before he has consummated the marriage and his betrothed wife become the wife of another man. The use of the verb 'to love' (*'āhab*) is mainly restricted to Yahweh's love for Israel and Israel's duty to love him. There are, however, significant exceptions. The slave who refuses his freedom declares that he loves his master and his household (15:16), and it is expected that a man will love his wife, even though this is set in the context of a man preferring one wife to another (21:15–17). It should also be noted that Yahweh loves resident aliens as well as the Israelites, and provides them with food and clothing (10:18). The society depicted in Deuteronomy is a disciplined and regimented one in which there will be great material prosperity provided that God's laws are obeyed, but in which private pleasure is not singled out. There is not even any specific mention of personal enjoyment by the king (17:14–20), who is to avoid a life of luxury, live modestly, and diligently read his copy of the laws and obey them. If he does these things he is assured that his descendants will long reign over Israel.

Wisdom

Wisdom is regarded in Deuteronomy as essential to the good life of the nation. It is especially understood as a necessary qualification for individual leadership. It is stated in 34:9 that Joshua, who was to lead Israel into the land of promise, was 'filled with the spirit of wisdom' by the laying on of Moses' hands. It is thus presumed, though not stated in the book, that the leadership of Moses had been blessed with the same gift. (The same phrase is used in Isa. 11:2 of the future king.) This verse looks to the future, anticipating the occupation of the land under Joshua's leadership. But the topic of wise leadership already occurs in the first chapter, in which Moses recalls how when the people were assembled

at Horeb he had selected wise leaders from each tribe in
order to lessen the burden of responsibility borne by himself
(1:9–15). In this way the book presents the whole of Israel's
sojourn in the wilderness as governed by wise leadership
now to be continued under Joshua.

But in this book God-given wisdom is also extended to
the whole people. Although in chapter 32 they are castigated for their lack of wisdom in not recognizing the
benefits that God has conferred on them, in 4:6–8 they are
characterized as being potentially a great nation because
their possession of Yahweh's laws has made them a 'wise
and discerning' one. They are assured that if they obey those
laws in the future they will excite the envy of other peoples.

God

In Deuteronomy as in the three preceding books the good
life is entirely dependent on the keeping of the laws of
Yahweh communicated to the people through the medium
of Moses. The way in which the people are to live when
they take up residence in Canaan is regulated in great detail,
and their existence is made conditional on their obedience.
Yahweh's first requirement is that they should worship him
and him alone, rejecting all temptation to worship the gods
of the Canaanite peoples, all traces of whom with their
idolatrous practices must be eliminated. The Tabernacle
(*miškān*) signifying God's presence, which had accompanied
Israel in its journeys, is now to be replaced by a single place
of worship: 'the place that he will choose out of all your
tribes as his habitation to put his name there'. There they are
to assemble 'to bring their offerings, to eat the sacred meals
in his presence, and to rejoice before him' (chapter 12). The
fear of his presence, so prominent in the earlier books, has
been removed. Deuteronomy does not describe in detail
their mode of worship, which had already been specified
earlier.

But although the place that Yahweh will designate as the
sole place of public worship is constantly referred to as
central to the lives of the people, their life is to be centred on

him in all their doings. They are 'a people holy to Yahweh your God; it is you Yahweh has chosen out of all the peoples on earth to be his people, his treasured possession' (14:2). In the opening chapters of the book they are reminded of all that he has done for them in the past, and assured of his love for them (4:37; 7:13). In return, they must love him (11:1). This love, which is to be expressed above all in obedience, is prescribed with especial emphasis in 6:5: 'You shall love Yahweh your God with all your heart, and with all your soul, and with all your might.'

Summary

Deuteronomy is above all a book of anticipation. The promised land is now almost within Israel's grasp; only, in its new life in the land Israel must be scrupulous in carrying out Yahweh's demands, which are intended for its own good. Although the people are warned that the good life – and indeed life itself – will be wrecked if they forget Yahweh or refuse to live as he wishes, the destructive side of his nature, so prominent in Exodus and Numbers, does not appear in this book. It is essentially a book of hope: a blueprint for the future life of the nation. With its emphasis on the relationship between Yahweh and his people as one of mutual love, it presents an ideal picture of the nation as God intended it to be.

5
Joshua and Judges

These two books, unlike Deuteronomy, present an unsettled picture. Despite the promises of an unimpeded occupation of the land of Canaan followed by the tranquil enjoyment of the good life, and despite the narration in the book of Joshua of the conquest of the land, both books are dominated by virtually continuous fighting in wars both international and internecine. In addition, the development of the good life was hindered by criminal behaviour. The warnings of Deuteronomy frequently went unheeded. It is therefore not surprising that little mention is made of its peaceful amenities; rather, both books may be regarded as portraying failures to procure its attainment.

Place and Security

The main features of the book of Joshua are the conquest of the land of Canaan and its distribution among the Israelite tribes, carried out under the leadership of Joshua, Moses' appointed successor. At the beginning of the book (1:2–4) Yahweh addresses him in terms reminiscent of his promise to Abraham in Gen. 15:18–19 and again to Israel in Exod. 23:31 and Num. 34:3–12, defining the boundaries of the land which he is to grant and specifying that 'every place that the sole of your foot will tread upon' will be theirs. After the account of the conquest it is recorded that this promise is carried out. It is further promised that 'No one shall be able to stand against you all the days of your life' (1:5). Some passages, however, (e.g. 13:2–6, 13; 16:10) indicate that there were exceptions: that Israel was not always successful.

Although the conquests made under Joshua's leadership were mainly effective, Israel's security was not in fact achieved in the period covered by Joshua and Judges. The latter book records that after Joshua's death the Israelite tribes were attacked by outside enemies. Their successes or failures in self-defence depended on their loyalty or disloyalty to Yahweh at different times, and on several occasions they suffered foreign domination. In addition there were internal struggles described in Judg. 9 and 20; and terrifying acts of violence committed by Israelites against their fellow-Israelites are recorded (Judg. 8:16; 9:22–25; 18:14–26; 19:22–30). The picture presented in the final chapters of Judges is one of political chaos and social unrest: 'There was no king in Israel; everyone did what he pleased' (17:6; 21:25; cf. 18:1; 19:1). In the earlier chapters there had been a succession of 'judges' during whose activity 'the land had rest'; but this 'rest' was never lasting; it was always succeeded by a period of defeat and other trouble before a new judge took charge.

Power

Power in Joshua and Judges takes the form of military success, whether against the previous inhabitants of Canaan or against other nations who after the conquest attempted to invade the land. This power was entrusted to the leaders of the nation; first Joshua and then the 'judges' who succeeded him. The activities of these judges were of two kinds: they included the military conquerors (Ehud, Deborah, Gideon, Jephthah) but also unmilitary leaders (Judg. 10:1–5; 12:8–15) of whose judgeships few details are given, but who seem to have promoted the good life in their regnal periods of peace and tranquillity.

Sustenance

It is not surprising that scant attention is paid in these books to some aspects of the good life. But the fertility of the land and its capacity to produce an adequate source of food are clearly taken for granted. Although on the first day of their arrival the Israelites ate only unleavened cakes and parched grain described as 'the produce of the land' (Josh. 5:11), food

appropriate to the Passover season, the following verse
abruptly states that the supply of manna had suddenly
ceased, and they began to partake of the full produce of the
land — the crops planted by the Canaanites — in the ensuing
year.

The phrase 'a land flowing with milk and honey' (Josh.
5:6) recalls earlier descriptions of Canaan (e.g. Exod. 3:8). A
number of incidental details provide a partial picture of
material abundance: Jael, not an Israelite but living in the
land, gave Sisera milk to drink from a standing supply (Judg.
4:19); in Judg. 13:19 Manoah offered a kid to the angel.
Several passages in Joshua (especially in chapter 21) refer to
pastures (migrāšîm) which were distributed among the tribes,
where they could graze their cattle.

Health and Longevity

Bodily health is not specifically mentioned in these books,
though the longevity of national leaders when stated almost
equals that of the patriarchs of Genesis or of Moses: Caleb
lived to be 85 or more (Josh. 14:10–11) and Joshua 110
(Josh. 24:29). Gideon, like Abraham, died in an unspecified
'good old age' (Judg. 8:32).

Family

The crucial importance of the provision of heirs to ensure
the continuation of the nation while avoiding contamination
by foreign marriages with pagans is recognized in various
passages in Joshua and Judges concerning family life. On the
one hand, intermarriage with the survivors of the former
inhabitants of the land was strictly forbidden (despite the
command to exterminate them) and Joshua declared that
Yahweh would not continue to drive out these nations, but
they would become 'a snare and a trap for you, a scourge on
your sides and thorns in your eyes, until you perish from
this good land that Yahweh your God has given you' (Josh.
23:12–13). This was a concern that appears in various books

of the Old Testament from Genesis onwards. On the other hand, the final chapter of Judges reports the extreme measures resorted to in order to ensure the survival of the tribe of Benjamin by providing the men of that tribe with 400 virgins from Jabesh-Gilead, so that 'a tribe may not be blotted out from Israel'. The chosen people must survive; but it must survive uncontaminated.

Among the few passages in Judges (there are none such in Joshua) depicting family life there are two that speak of the intimate relations between mothers and sons: these are the stories of Samson and of Micah. The importance of the role of mothers is also reflected in the phrase 'a mother in Israel' applied to Deborah in 5:7. This striking phrase, which occurs only once elsewhere in the Old Testament (2 Sam. 20:19, where it is presumably intended to allude to the importance of the city of Abel) evidently alludes to Deborah's authoritative role in the events that follow in the chapter. Behind this metaphorical usage there clearly lay a contemporary view of mothers in general as persons of high status and authority within their families. Its occurrence here at the beginning of the poem was no doubt intended to make a contrast with the poignant picture of the bereaved mother of Sisera at the end (vv. 28–30). While the latter verses are an example of Israelite *Schadenfreude* and imply no friendly feelings towards this woman, the description of the mother anxiously but also proudly awaiting the return of her son from battle rings true. Israelite mothers also will have been awaiting the return of their sons from the same battle. The situation of the mother forced to remain at home when her sons are exposed to mortal danger, but waiting to comfort them and if possible share in their triumphs must have been a feature also of Israelite experience; but it also has a universal quality. Here this is recognized as one of the roles of mothers of sons in their efforts to promote the good life.

The stories of Micah and Samson depict the roles of mothers somewhat differently. Both are set in the last part of Judges and so at a time when Israel was more or less settled in the land but lawlessness was rife (17:6). Judg. 17:1–4 depict a son and his mother who forgives the son's theft of a large sum of money. Some episodes in Judg. 14 concern both the father and the mother of an impetuous and uncontrollable Samson, who insists on marrying a Philistine girl despite his parents' warning but refrains from telling them about his exploit in killing a lion with his bare hands, and also from telling them the secret of his riddle.

One of the most striking features of Judges is the prominent role ascribed to women. These include Deborah, Jael, Sisera's mother, the anonymous woman who killed Abimelech by dropping a millstone on his head (9:53–55) and Jephthah's daughter (11:34–40). Of these, three (Deborah, Jael and the anonymous woman) are strong-minded women who perform deeds of valour that men by themselves are incapable of performing; they are saviours of Israel, and as such to be regarded as having contributed to the good life by saving the nation from its enemies or from tyrants. Abimelech, however, represents the more conventional point of view: he disdained to be killed by a mere woman (9:54). Another woman who may be mentioned here, although she had nothing to do with family life and was a Canaanite, is Rahab the prostitute (Josh. 2; 6:17, 22–25). Hers is a unique case, for she alone of all Canaanites is singled out to escape the Israelites' destruction of the Canaanite cities; because she hid the Israelite messengers sent to spy on Jericho she was granted permission together with her family to live unharmed among the Israelite people.

Jephthah's daughter, on the other hand, is quite different, though equally courageous. She is an extreme example of the obedient daughter, totally subservient to the demands of the head of the family. Nothing, however, is said in that story of any contribution to the good life that she may have made by self-sacrifice. Somewhat similarly neither the 400 virgins who were 'given' to the Benjamite men nor the young women of Shiloh whom they were encouraged to abduct (Judg. 21) were consulted about their fate – though their marriages served the good life in that through them the tribe of Benjamin was saved from extinction.

The story of Samson (Judg. 13–16) is concerned with another type of woman, who whether unwittingly or deliberately led the hero into actions that were destructive of relations with Israel's neighbours and so harmful to Israel's good life. Although these episodes are elements in a story that may have been intended as a hero-story, Samson's sexual proclivities and especially his predilection for Philistine women were productive of increased hostility between Israel and the Philistines. At the beginning of chapter 14 relations between the two peoples are depicted as relatively harmonious; Samson's visit across the border of Timnah (14:1) is treated as unremarkable, and both Israelites and Philistines were present at the wedding feast (14:10–18). But when his Philistine wife was persuaded to reveal the secret meaning of his riddle, he attacked and killed thirty men of the town. And when his wife was given to another man (14:20) he set fire to the Philistine's standing crops. A further adventure with a Philistine prostitute led to further conflict. Finally Samson's liaison with Delilah led to his downfall. This story of a hero destroyed by a scheming woman was surely intended as a warning to the readers.

Law and Justice

The books of Joshua and Judges are quite different in their representation of Israel's attitude towards the law. In Joshua, as in Deuteronomy, it is the law of Moses recorded by Moses in the book of the law that Joshua warned the people to disobey at their peril (1:7–8; 8:30–35; 23:6). The only variation of this command occurs in 24:25–26. This passage speaks of a new covenant made by Joshua with the people at Shechem, when new statutes and ordinances were made which Joshua recorded in 'the book of the law of God'. Joshua, despite some lapses, is essentially the book of an obedient people who thus secured for themselves the possibility of a good life. No reference is, however, made to specific laws; it is presumed that the laws of Deuteronomy are known to the people.

The concept of law in Judges is quite different. The word Torah never occurs in this book, although the phrase 'the commandments (miṣwôt) of Yahweh' occurs twice (2:17; 3:4). But these commandments are now regarded as belonging to the past, when Moses delivered them to the ancestors ('fathers') of the present generation. It is stated that since then Israel had become apostate and disobedient. In fact the central part of the book (2–16) is devoted to an account of periodical apostasy ('doing evil in Yahweh's sight') when Israel abandoned Yahweh and his worship, alternating with periods when 'judges' arose to save the people from the disasters that Yahweh had inflicted on them in the intervening periods. It is asserted in 2:17–19 that they did not even listen to their judges but relapsed when each judge died.

Judges, then, is the story of a lawless and disobedient nation. According to the final chapters of the book (17–21) it lapsed still further into chaos when there was no king and everyone did as he pleased (17:6; 18:1; 19:1). The final verse of the book (21:25) accurately summarizes the situation. There is no sign in the book of the elaborate machinery of Deuteronomy setting up a system of courts of law. But this is also true of Joshua. Crimes like that of Achan who 'troubled Israel' (Josh. 7) and the 'outrage' at Gibeah (Judg. 19–20) are dealt with summarily and drastically, with no possibility of appeal or pleas in mitigation. There is, however, a difference here between the two books. In Joshua there is a single accepted leader appointed by Yahweh who assumes the responsibilities of judge. It is he who equitably distributes the land to the tribes with due consideration for particular cases (1:12–15; chapter 21) and who establishes cities of refuge for unintentional homicides as commanded in Deuteronomy (Judg. 20). However, in Judges Israel is depicted as a nation not yet fully settled in the land, with justice dispensed on a rough and ready basis.

Wisdom

It is perhaps significant that the word ḥokmâ, 'wisdom', does not occur at all in either of these books. The only occurrence of the root ḥkm is in Judg. 5:29, where it is used ironically. The 'wise women' (ḥakĕmôt) attending on the mother of Sisera prove not to be wise at all: they give their mistress an assurance of her son's victory in battle which proves to be

entirely false. It is probably implied that these women possessed a recognized status as 'official' advisers comparable to
that of Pharaoh's 'wise men' (Exod. 7:11). It may be implied
that on the other side the Israelites possessed an effective
wisdom that gave them victory; but the text says nothing of
this.

God

The book of Joshua recounts Yahweh's fulfilment of his
long-delayed promise to give his people possession of the
land of Canaan. But in chapter 24 Joshua, on the eve of his
death, summons the tribes and warns them about the true
nature of this God who has led them so far. He begins by
reporting words spoken to him by Yahweh for the people to
hear. In this speech Yahweh recapitulates the entire story of
the benefits that he had conferred on them and their ancestors from even before his call of Abraham. He thus
reminds them that their settlement in Canaan was the climax
of his care for them. The people reply with a renewed vow
that they will serve Yahweh. To this Joshua makes an
entirely unexpected warning: 'You cannot serve Yahweh,
for he is a holy God.' He then elaborates this statement by
specifying what will happen to them if they fail to carry out
their vow. He tells them: 'He is a jealous God; he will not
forgive your transgressions or your sins. If you forsake
Yahweh and serve foreign gods, then he will turn and do
you harm, and consume you' (24:19–20). Despite this
warning, a covenant was made by which the people pledged
to serve Yahweh. A stone was set up which would 'be a
witness against you, if you deal falsely with your God'.

In fact, the consequence of God's displeasure had already
been demonstrated, notably in the case of Achan, whose sin
in stealing objects dedicated to Yahweh following the
capture of Jericho led to Yahweh's causing Israel to be
defeated in their first attempt to capture the city of Ai
(chapter 7). But it is in the book of Judges that a pattern of
sin and punishment becomes evident. The book records that
whenever Israel 'did evil in Yahweh's sight' – especially in

worshipping other gods (10:6–16) – Yahweh sent external enemies to attack or even dominate them. But these incidents demonstrate Yahweh's mercy as well as his anger. Despite Joshua's warning that Yahweh would not forgive the people's sins, he showed mercy on them, raising up a leader to rescue them and to give them a period of tranquillity when they appealed to him.

The final chapters of the book illustrate yet another aspect of Yahweh's nature: his withdrawal of his presence. After the demise of the last saviour-judge he raises up no more, and lawlessness ensues. The book ends with a comment about the lack of a king – the need for a new kind of divinely appointed leader who would give stability to the nation is expressed.

Summary

Joshua describes the Israelite conquest of Canaan and its allocation to the tribes; Judges relates Israel's behaviour after it settles in the land. Materially the land offered all the opportunities for the living of the good life. But the book of Judges is in the main a story of lost opportunities. The nation falls into apostasy again and again, is punished by invasions by external enemies, and is rescued by a merciful Yahweh only to forget him once more. When he finally withdraws his presence, social and moral chaos ensues, and the need for a strong and permanent leadership is felt. The early readers would have drawn a lesson from these books about the necessity for grateful obedience to their redeemer.

6
Ruth

This book is set in the time of the judges (1:1). But it has little in common with the book of Judges: it is the story of a family living in a small Judaean town. The lives of these people are entirely peaceful, quite unaffected by the tremendous political and military events of the period, of which there is no mention at all. This is a story of two women who succeeded in overcoming severe disadvantages to achieve the good life in full measure. The final verses (4:17–22) in which the heroine, Ruth, is identified as an ancestress of King David perhaps provide a clue to the author's purpose; but the book is a charming story in its own right depicting love and generosity between members of a family, wealth and power rightly used, and a happy ending under the blessing of Yahweh.

Place and Security

When the two widows Naomi and her Moabite daughter-in-law Ruth migrated to Bethlehem in Judah after a long residence in the neighbouring country of Moab they were unprotected strangers without means of support and uncertain of their welcome. They were obliged to take advantage of the laws of Lev. 19:9–10 and a Deut. 24:19–21 to glean what they could from the remains of the barley harvest then in progress. But a fortunate chance meeting with the wealthy farmer Boaz changed their fortunes. Boaz showed great kindness to Ruth and also to Naomi, and the security and status of the two women was finally secured when he took Ruth as his wife.

Power, Wealth and Sustenance

If Ruth is the heroine of the story, Boaz is the hero. He was a member of the landowning class (*'iš ḥayil*), employing young men who were then getting in the harvest under the supervision of one of his household servants (2:6). He was evidently a person of importance in the town. No mention is made of any higher authority; local decisions were made or ratified by the elders sitting in the gate, the traditional place for such activities. Boaz's authority is indicated by the somewhat peremptory way in which he addressed the person with whom he had business to contract, and by the manner in which he appointed a committee of ten elders to sit with him to witness a formal declaration (4:1–6). His nature was quite unlike that of Nabal, another wealthy landowner (1 Sam. 25:2–11), who is described as 'brutish and mean' and who treated with contumely David and his followers who had approached him as strangers in need with a polite request. Boaz is represented as a model of kindness and generosity, a man who used his position to give material assistance to two distressed women, concerned himself with the matter of Naomi's former property, and gave his protection to the widowed foreigner Ruth by taking her as his wife.

Old Age

The author treats with especial sympathy the ageing Naomi. Her situation at the beginning of the story is even more pitiable than that of Ruth. As an elderly widow who has been deprived of the support of both husband and sons, she at first sees herself as totally without hope – too old to find another husband and to have a second family. She complains bitterly that Yahweh has treated her harshly (1:20–21). But as the story proceeds she experiences the double fortune of having a daughter-in-law who attaches herself to her, loves and cares for her and shares her life, and who is to her 'more than seven sons' (4:15), and an equally caring son-in-law who had from the outset been concerned for Ruth's welfare, had praised her for leaving her own native land and remaining with her mother-in-law, prayed for God's blessing on her, and protected her while she was gleaning in his fields

(2:8–16). In the end the women declare that Yahweh, who Naomi had once declared had made her life bitter, had now fulfilled her life by providing her with a grandson (4:14–15). The climax of the story is reached when Naomi takes her baby grandson in her arms and the women exclaim, 'A son has been born to Naomi!' (4:17).

Family and Law

The book is essentially the story of a family. According to Israelite law it was the duty of members of the family to care for the welfare of other members who were in distress by taking certain steps to relieve them. First, in the case of a person who was forced by poverty to sell ancestral land, it was the duty of the nearest relative (the $g\bar{o}$'$\bar{e}l$) to intervene and redeem that property, restoring it to its former owner (Lev. 25:25). Second, in the case of a wife whose husband had died without issue and so left her unprotected, it was the duty of the deceased husband's brother to marry her (Deut. 25:5–6). However, if the brother did not wish to perform this duty he had to declare so in public. The widow was then entitled to disgrace him, spitting in his face and removing his sandal (Deut. 25:7–10).

These laws, which were originally separate, had evidently fallen into disuse, as had the practice of removing a sandal and handing it over to the contracting party to confirm a commercial transaction, and the author found it necessary to explain the latter to his readers (4:7). His making the one law dependent on the other is not attested anywhere else in the Old Testament. It also appears that Boaz was not in fact Naomi's closest relative; there was a closer relation, to whom Boaz first addressed himself. Having announced that he was purchasing Naomi's property he insisted that the purchaser would be expected to marry Ruth. When the nearest relative declined the proposal because his own inheritance might thereby be damaged, Boaz as now the nearest kinsman declared himself to be Ruth's bridegroom (4:1–10).

It is not clear what the first readers of the book would

have made of this somewhat complicated account of legal procedures which were at least partly archaic. But they will surely have been impressed by this demonstration of the importance of the due observation of the law for the good life of a God-fearing community.

Wisdom

Although Ruth's success is attributed to the action of Yahweh who rewarded her for her kindness to Naomi (2:20; 3:10; 4:11, 14), the author makes it clear that Naomi, Ruth and Boaz all acted with wisdom. As soon as Naomi learned Boaz's identity she laid her plans. Knowing that he was her relative and so a potential *gō'ēl*, she encouraged Ruth to stay close to him while she was gleaning and then to surprise him when he was in a contented mood (3:1–4). He cautioned her to conceal her knowledge. Boaz's actions on the following day were motivated by his intention to take the other kinsman by surprise. But this human wisdom won the approval of Yahweh, who blessed the marriage.

Joy

Among the books of the Old Testament Ruth stands out as a happy book. It is a story of two loving women who found unexpected happiness. There are no villains, and no obstacles occur to prevent this outcome. The story has some resemblance to a fairy tale: 'they all lived happily after'. From the moment when Naomi identifies Boaz as her kinsman and, shaken for the first time out of her despondency, invokes a blessing on Yahweh 'who has not withdrawn his kindness from either the living or the dead' (2:20), the narrative proceeds to its joyful climax. The prayers of the women at the betrothal of Boaz and Ruth for their happiness and for the family that they will found (4:11–12) are more than fulfilled when their son is born, and Naomi's joy is also complete when the women exclaim that a son has been born to Naomi.

God

But this is no fairy tale. Although the characters are portrayed as using their own wisdom to secure a happy outcome, the author stresses again and again that it is Yahweh who has brought about these events, and that he has done so in answer to prayer. Already in 1:8 Naomi prays that he will show kindness to Ruth, and in 1:16 Ruth vows that she will adopt Naomi's religion as her own and become worshipper of Yahweh. Boaz prays that Yahweh will reward Ruth for her care of Naomi (2:12), and again invokes Yahweh's blessing on her because she has chosen him and not a young man (3:10). In 2:20 Naomi recognizes that it is Yahweh who has provided Boaz as a *gō'ēl*. In chapter 4 the elders and all the people at the gate who witnessed the betrothal pray for Yahweh's blessing on the union of Ruth and Boaz and the women also thank him for his provision of a *gō'ēl* for Ruth. It was clearly the intention of the author to demonstrate to his readers that Yahweh cares for those who faithfully serve him and rewards them for their faithfulness.

Summary

The book is an idyllic tale portraying the good life as lived in a small community in faithfulness to Yahweh. It shows how the wealthy and influential can use their position for good, caring for the distressed and the elderly, giving them the security they need with the support of good laws. It also advocates sympathy towards non-Israelites driven by circumstances to take up residence in Israel. Though it attributes the attainment of the good life entirely to the benevolent action of Yahweh it also encourages people to use their wisdom to help themselves. In presenting Ruth as the ancestress of the glorious King David it attests the supreme rewards of lives lived in obedience to the moral demands of Israel's God.

7
Samuel and Kings

These books are a history of the Israelite people from the time of Samuel to the fall of the kingdom to the Babylonians. Unlike the books of Joshua and Judges they present a picture of a people securely settled in its own land and enjoying its amenities. These circumstances made possible a fuller treatment of the lives of families and individuals and so of the extent to which they were able to achieve the good life. But with few exceptions the information provided is confined to a relatively small class of socially and economically privileged persons, who controlled the life of the nation: kings, royal officials and a small class of independently wealthy families. It was this ruling class that possessed the leisure to enjoy the material good things of life. The situation of the mass of the people and particularly those who suffered from exploitation is mentioned only peripherally; and, despite the existence of the laws, justice for individual citizens was not always done. There was, however, also a class of prophets or 'men of God' whose activity from time to time succeeded in alleviating the plight of the oppressed.

Place and Security

These books may be said to tell a single story with regard to the place − that is, the land − that had been provided for Israel by Yahweh's benevolence. This is a story of three parts: first, a period of relative insecurity especially due to foreign hostility; second, one of security and triumph under David and Solomon; and third, the gradual loss of control over the land ending with its total loss and exile. The first part is not unlike the book of Judges in that it tells of oppression by the Philistines and Ammonites, interrupted briefly by the victories of Saul, the first king, and his son Jonathan, followed by Saul's disgrace (1 Sam. 15) and then the hopes engendered by the rise of David but ending in total disaster with the death of Saul and his sons on Mount Gilboa (1 Sam. 31), when the land appeared to have been irretrievably lost to the triumphant Philistines.

The books of Samuel begin, however, with a picture of a settled life in which there is as yet no hint of disruption: no hostile enemy or danger to disrupt the enjoyment of the good life. The family of the Ephraimite Elkanah (1 Sam. 1) was not itself entirely free from domestic conflict, but here was a pious Ephraimite accustomed to pay a regular annual visit to an established shrine at Shiloh administered by an established family of priests, to worship and sacrifice to Yahweh. Travel across the country does not seem to have been attended by any dangers, and although there is no mention of a national political leadership, the chaotic state of affairs described in the final verse of Judges, when 'everyone did what was right in his eyes', appears not to have persisted. This chapter speaks of a secure and orderly society.

Power, Wealth, Sustenance

This situation was completely changed when the Philistines invaded the country and inflicted a crushing defeat on the – apparently national – Israelite troops (1 Sam. 4), entailing the loss of the Ark of the Covenant of Yahweh: 'The glory has departed from Israel' (4:21). The good life had departed with it. The situation was saved temporarily by Samuel, who had then become the acknowledged Israelite leader; but when in his old age Samuel appointed his sons as 'judges', these became corrupt and perverted justice. The elders then assembled and demanded a king 'to rule over us'.

The chapters that follow (8–12) are concerned with the urgent desire of the people for the restoration of the good life of the nation in terms of their national security. These chapters raise the question of the desirability of a monarchical system: whether it was the way to achieve security, and whether it was best that Israel should become a nation 'like other nations' rather than remaining the 'people holy to Yahweh, your God', 'chosen out of all the peoples of the earth to be his people' as Moses had taught (e.g. Deut. 7:6).

Nowhere else in the Old Testament is this question, on which the entire history of the nation was to depend, so fully discussed. This was the fundamental question about the nature of the good life for Israel.

Samuel's speech in 1 Sam. 8:11–18 in which he warned the people of the consequences that would follow their appointment of a king is a realistic description of a people living under an absolute monarch 'like all the nations'. It is significant as a negative account of the good life: that is, it lists significant features of the good life that would be suppressed. It will have been interpreted as an accurate prediction of certain features of the reign of Solomon (1 Kings 3–11), and is in pointed contrast to the prescription of the conduct of an Israelite king made in Deut. 17:14–20. The author of Samuel appears to have had some knowledge of the behaviour of kings of other Near Eastern monarchs of the time.

A most important feature of Samuel's speech concerns the *land* – that is, the land that Israel now possessed in freedom. A king, if they set him over them, would take for himself the most productive of their fields, vineyards, olive groves, herds, flocks and work force and a tenth of the produce of what remained to them (vv. 14–17) and make them plough and harvest *his* land – a significant adjectival suffix. Worse, he would establish a new superior social class of royal officials (literally, 'servants') to whom he would grant donations of those estates, but who would be personally answerable to him (vv. 14, 15). He would also take the young men and women to be his employees (vv. 11, 13), and the people would be no more than slaves (v. 17). So the people would no longer have unfettered possession of the land and its produce in freedom. They would vehemently protest against their treatment but to no avail (v. 18). This new regime would amount to a complete reversal of what Yahweh had done for his people in giving them absolute possession of the land and indeed in making them his special people.

Samuel was overruled. The new king, Saul, fulfilled the people's hopes in that he fought their battles for them, though he ultimately lost the land to the victorious

Philistines. In one respect, however, he fulfilled Samuel's
prediction of the evil consequences of a monarchical system:
in reproaching his 'servants' for their supposed disloyalty in
protecting his adversary David, he referred to the fact that
he had rewarded them with the gift of fields and vineyards
as well as promotion as military commanders (1 Sam. 22:7).

The second part of the story, the reigns of David and
Solomon, is one of mainly continued prosperity. As king
first of Judah and then of all Israel, David fully restored
Israel's possession of the land and enjoyed 'rest from all his
enemies round about' (2 Sam. 7:1). His foreign conquests
gave the people an unexampled sense of security, and the
promise of a lasting dynasty (2 Sam. 7) appeared to confirm
a secure future. The rebellion of Absalom, however, showed
that even this could be threatened. Absalom for a time 'stole
the hearts of the people of Israel' (2 Sam. 15:6) and it is made
clear that many were dissatisfied with their present lot
(2 Sam. 15:12). The further rebellion of Sheba (2 Sam. 20)
was an uprising of the northern tribes which threatened the
political unity of the country.

The account of the reign of Solomon, as far as the secure
possession of the land is concerned, is a mixed one. The
emphasis is on Solomon's unexampled power, wisdom and
wealth, which are said to have been the envy of other
nations. It is clearly a source of pride for the author, who
insists that 'Judah and Israel lived in security (lābeṭaḥ), each
man under his vine and his fig tree all the days of Solomon'
(1 Kings 4:25) and that they were as numerous as the sand
by the seashore (4:20, fulfilling the promises made to
Abraham and Jacob, Gen. 22:17; 32:13). This was confirmed
by the visiting Queen of Sheba in 10:8, but is counteracted
by other events, that no reader could miss, especially as they
mainly occur at the close of the history of Solomon in
chapter 11 – first by Solomon's prayer on the completion of
the temple, which envisages the possibility of various
misfortunes, including exile, if the people sinned (8:33–53)
and then by Solomon's giving twenty Galilean cities to
Hiram king of Tyre in payment for his services (9:11–13).
That puts a question mark against Solomon's alleged great
wealth and also, more important for our present concern,

constitutes the first diminution of the territory of Israel since the time of David. Even more ominous for the future of a good life for the people was Yahweh's declaration in 11:9–13 that because of Solomon's apostasy he would take the kingdom away except for a single tribe, even though this would not occur in Solomon's lifetime. This is followed by notices about the activities of three 'adversaries', Hadad, Rezon and Jeroboam who rebelled against Solomon's rule (11:14–40), of whom one, Rezon, actually 'ruled over Aram'. Another, Jeroboam, left Solomon's service and fled to Egypt to make more trouble, having been assured by the prophet Ahijah that Yahweh would indeed carry out his intention to take the kingdom away from Solomon's son. The stage was thus set for the division of the kingdom narrated in the following chapter. The disintegration of the kingdom had begun.

The dissatisfaction of many of the people of Israel with the Davidic monarchy which had already become evident during David's reign came to a head with the successful revolt of Jeroboam against Solomon's successor Rehoboam (1 Kings 12:1–20). The author anticipates the permanence of the division of the kingdom in 12:19 when he concludes his account of Solomon's reign with the comment that 'Israel (that is, the northern tribes) has been in rebellion against the house of David *to this day*', and adds that 'There was no one who followed the house of David, except the tribe of Judah alone'.

One of the main grievances against Solomon was his use of forced labour (*mas*) to build the temple and other buildings in Jerusalem and elsewhere. There is a discrepancy in 1 Kings about this. Although 1 Kings 9:15–22 asserts that Solomon did not conscript Israelites to do this forced labour and did not enslave them but conscripted only the remnants of the native peoples who had been left in the land when Israel had conquered it, it is stated in 1 Kings 5:13 that he conscripted 30,000 men 'out of all Israel' for the work, forcing them to labour in shifts of one month out of three. The reader would realize that this obligation would have seriously impeded their agricultural work and consequently their livelihoods. Their resentment is confirmed by the fact that when Rehoboam stupidly sent Adoram, his minister in charge of forced labour, to negotiate with the rebels they stoned him to death (1 Kings 12:18). A further cause of resentment may have been Solomon's division of the kingdom into twelve districts, each with an official deputed to provide the huge supplies required by the royal household (1 Kings 4:7–19), though the author makes no comment on the hardship that would have been caused by this system. However, there is sufficient in the text of Kings to show that Israel under Solomon was not free to live the good life in its land and enjoyed no true security there.

The remainder of the books of Kings recount a progressive loss of the land and a concomitant hardship for the people both of northern Israel and Judah. These chapters tell of frequent wars, first between the two kingdoms (1 Kings 15) and then with neighbouring states; especially there was intermittent war between northern Israel and Aram (1 Kings 15:18–22; 20; 22; 2 Kings 6–7; 13). More than once Israel was defeated and humiliated. In 1 Kings 14:15 the prophet Ahijah had prophesied that Israel would be exiled 'beyond the Euphrates'. The suffering of the people as a result of these wars is exemplified in the horrific story of the famine caused by Aram's siege of Samaria (2 Kings 6:24–31). The constant upheavals due to a series of internal revolutions in which the king was assassinated by a usurper who then seized power testified to internal instability and progressive weakness in which the northern kingdom eventually became a prey to the power of Assyria, resulting in its eventual annihilation (2 Kings 17).

The kingdom of Judah eventually suffered the same fate, succumbing first to Assyria and then to Babylon. First, however, it had to endure an invasion of Jerusalem by Egypt, when it was forced to pay tribute to Necho, the Egyptian king (1 Kings 14:25–27). Later Hezekiah was forced to pay a very large tribute to Sennacherib of Assyria (2 Kings 18:13–16), although the author records a miraculous deliverance when the Assyrian king had to withdraw from his threatened siege of Jerusalem (2 Kings 19:35–36). In Manasseh's reign Yahweh's intention to destroy Jerusalem and Judah was announced by prophets (2 Kings 21:12–15).

After the death in battle (or by assassination) of Josiah (2 Kings 23:29) Judah became a vassal state under Babylonian dominance, but attempts to rebel against this resulted in fierce reprisals, culminating in a first exile, in which many of Jerusalem's inhabitants were deported to Babylon (2 Kings 24:14–16) and a second, when there was a further deportation of all but the poorest citizens (25:11–12) and Jerusalem and the Judaean state were destroyed.

What opportunities did the ordinary people of Israel have to live the good life during the period of the monarchy? As will be suggested below, the intermittent wars and consequent deprivation do not appear to have made this by any means totally impossible. Nevertheless, as far as living in security in the land is concerned, the biblical text mentions the existence of considerable impediments, especially towards the end of the period. First, it is unlikely that the able-bodied men were exempt from military service, and this would have had a detrimental effect on their livelihoods, similar to that caused by Solomon's forced labour (see above). Further, the cost of military activity would have fallen on the people in the form of taxation, and heavy taxes would have been exacted in order to enable the vassal kings to pay the large sums demanded by foreign rulers. This is especially mentioned in 2 Kings 23:33–35, where Pharaoh Necho imposed tribute 'on the land' to the amount of a hundred talents of silver and one of gold, and taxed the population in order to meet the demand. We may compare the thousand talents of silver paid by Menahem to Pul of Assyria, which he extracted from the well-to-do ('al kol-gibbôrê haḥayil) at the rate of 50 shekels a head, in fact no doubt provided by their tenant (2 Kings 15:19–20), and the even greater amount of 300 talents of silver and 30 of gold paid by Hezekiah to Sennacherib (2 Kings 18:14). These are very large amounts for a people dependent on their agricultural labour.

Famine was no stranger to ancient Israel (1 Kings 17:1; 2 Kings 4:38). But famines could also be caused deliberately by enemy action. Besides that occasioned by the siege of Samaria (see above) there was another during the final siege of Jerusalem (2 King's 25:3). These last, it seems, were a particular hazard for those living in fortified cities in war time because then it was impossible to bring in provisions from outside; conditions would have been less severe in the countryside. But wars brought other misfortunes. There was considerable loss of life not only of the combatants but also of civilians when Assyian or Babylonian troops sacked the cities of Judah.

The author of Kings says nothing about what must have been the hardships suffered by the deportees on their journeys to their new locations, or about their conditions after their arrival. But it may be presumed that the author understood these hardships, combined with the total loss of the native land, as occasioning a state of despair. It is true that the final paragraph of 2 Kings (25:27–30) records a mitigation of the lot of the imprisoned former king Jehoiachin: but at most this action by Evil-Merodach may be regarded as symbolic of the possibility of a brighter future rather than an indication of any 'good life' that might have been enjoyed by the deportees as a whole in the present.

Power

Except in their worst times (as described in the book of Judges) the Israelites had always had strong leaders whom they regarded as endowed with divine authority: Moses, Joshua, the 'judges'. These leaders had had power and the people had acknowledged it: power especially to save Israel from its enemies and so to make the good life, to some degree at least, a possibility. At the beginning of 1 Samuel they were without a leader until the appearance of Samuel. When Samuel was old they were again without leadership (1 Sam. 8:1–3); and they demanded the appointment of a new national leader. It may thus be said that at that point such political power as remained resided in the hands of the people as a whole, but that, with their elders or tribal leaders they voluntarily handed it over to a new kind of leader who for the first time was called 'king' (*melek*).

Samuel immediately recognized that the word 'king'

signified an entirely new kind of leadership for Israel, and warned the people that whatever military success a king might achieve to the people he would arrogate to himself other powers which would not give to Israel that good life which they desired (1 Sam. 8:10–18). The author relates that Samuel was overruled by Yahweh, who had initially refused the people's demand as being tantamount to a rejection of his own kingship (8:7) but ended by accepting it (8:22). It is emphasized that it was the people (*hā'ām*) who had both demanded and obtained this new kind of authority over themselves. It was evidently assumed, although this did not occur with the first king, Saul, that kingship was a dynastic institution and that Jonathan would succeed his father (1 Sam. 20:31) – although this would be subject to the good behaviour of the people and, it is implied, of the king (1 Sam. 12:25).

During the reigns of David and Solomon power was entirely in the hands of the king. But as has been suggested above, the extent to which this power was exercised in promoting the good life for the people of Israel is not clear. David was successful in securing peace for the nation, as Yahweh promised (2 Sam. 7:9–10) when he also promised that his dynasty would be established for ever (vv. 12–16). David is credited in 2 Sam. 8:15 with administering justice with equity; and there are stories that he swore to punish a rich man who had stolen a poor man's property (2 Sam. 12:1–6) and to protect a widow's son who had committed manslaughter (2 Sam. 14:4–11), though in both cases his royal power was exercised in an impetuous manner and he was easily duped. According to 2 Sam. 24:17 he expressed pity for his people; but his misuse of his power in the murder of Uriah (a foreigner, but a loyal servant) does not suggest a consistent care for his subjects. Further, his temporary abandonment of his kingdom during the rebellion of Absalom (2 Sam. 15–19) shows how precarious was his real hold on power.

When we come to the reign of Solomon (1 Kings 3–11) there is little in these chapters that speaks of positive consequences for the good life enjoyed by the people of Israel apart from some very general statements about his good governance (3:9–14, 28) and 4:20, which simply asserts how happy they all were. The whole account is one of Solomon's self-aggrandisement and love of display – the splendid buildings including his own palace built with slave labour (6–7; 9:20–23), the flattery of the visiting Queen of Sheba, the taxation of the people to supply the enormous demands of himself and his court (4:7, 27–28), his enormous personal wealth (e.g. 10:25) and so on. Although the author was clearly impressed by all this and appears to have derived a certain pride from it, there can be little doubt that he also voiced a strong criticism of the accumulation of such power in the hands of a single potentate. In fact he deliberately depicts Solomon as behaving precisely in the way that Samuel had predicted when he warned the people of the way in which the king whom they had asked for would behave (1 Sam. 8:10–18) to the detriment of the interests of the people. This king was a far cry from the leadership that Israel had enjoyed under Moses, Joshua and the judges. The author also depicts Solomon as failing to act as a leader who would fight their battles. Solomon fought no battles, and in 1 Kings 11 it becomes clear that he ended by endangering the political independence that David had obtained and had appeared to have ensured.

The story of the rebellion of the northern tribes under Jeroboam (1 Kings 12:1–16) which led to the division of the kingdom is illuminating with regard to the concepts of the powers of the kings over their people, and also sheds light in particular on the extent of the power exercised by Solomon in the previous reign. The plea of the rebels in 12:4 refers to the 'harsh service' (*'ăbōdâ qašâ*) and 'heavy yoke' (*'ōl kābēd*) imposed regularly on Israel by Solomon, a yoke that they demanded should be lightened. If Rehoboam agreed to this they would 'serve' (*'ābad*) him as they had served his father. When Rehoboam consulted those who had held office under Solomon how he should answer their demand, they, recognizing the reality of the situation, advised him to 'be a servant' (*'ebed*) and to 'serve' (*'ābad*) them, and to 'speak good words' to them, so that *they* would be *his* servants in the coming days.

This passage uses the words 'servant' and 'serve' in two quite different senses, even in the same sentence. Obviously the two senses cannot be absolutely contradictory. Rather, they suggest a *reciprocal* relationship between king and people implied in the context which has the form of a bargain ('If . . . then'). This is not the language of leadership and allegiance employed in the preceding Old Testament books; but it does imply a recognition of mutual responsibility, if not a sharing of power. Each side is to have an obligation to the other. The proposal of the rebels is rejected by Rehoboam, who accepted the advice of the 'young men', in harsh and even insulting terms. The people have *no* rights and no power; the king's power is absolute. Rehoboam, following his father, had completely accepted the concept of kingship practised by the monarchs of the great powers of Mesopotamia and Egypt, and so lost altogether his power over the northern tribes, who — so the author implies — are determined to adopt a concept of royal power more in keeping with the older Israelite traditions.

The revolution of the northern tribes which led to the foundation of an independent northern kingdom obviously involved a transference of political power, the kingdom of Judah being the smaller and lesser of the two residual states (1 Kings 12:20). With this division both states became more vulnerable to foreign aggression. Although at an early stage there was continuous warfare between Judah and Israel in which the former attempted unsuccessfully to regain control over the north (l Kings 15:6, 16–24), there was later some reconciliation between the two. Some incidents, however (e.g. 1 Kings 22:2–4), make it clear that Israel was the dominant partner.

The history of both states until the final extinction of Israel by Assyria (2 Kings 17:5–6) and of Judah by Nebuchadnezzar of Babylon (2 Kings 25) is primarily the history of their kings (though see below). In Israel, however, there was no real dynastic continuity: no king succeeded in founding a dynasty that extended for more than four reigns, and some founded no dynasty at all. Eight of its kings died by assassination by usurpers who then succeeded to the throne, and in the final years of the weakened state such assassinations were increasingly frequent. There is no evidence that these kings, often of a military kind, implemented the promise of less oppressive rule which had characterized the original revolt against Rehoboam. In Judah also the kings were not immune from struggles for power. Three of them were assassinated (2 Kings 12:20; 14:19; 21:23). Whether these assassinations were the result of widespread popular dissatisfaction is not clear; but in contrast with northern Israel the people (or the 'people of the land') in each case preserved the continuity of the Davidic dynasty by appointing the son of the assassinated king to succeed him. This 'king-making' suggests that, at any rate in such crises, the Judaean people had retained some degree of political power, which, however, they exercised in loyalty to the dynasty.

In both kingdoms the text of Kings records some important exceptions to the otherwise unrestricted power of the kings, although this did not necessarily involve the ordinary people. One of the most significant episodes is that concerning the foreign-born queen Jezebel, wife of Ahab king of Israel (1 Kings 16:31). She is presented (1 Kings 19:1–3; 21; 2 Kings 9) until her murder by the usurper Jehu (2 Kings 9:30–37) as the real ruler of Israel throughout the reign of Ahab. She is credited with the murder on her own initiative, though supported by her husband, of the prophets of Yahweh (1 Kings 18:4, 13; 19:1–3) and of causing even the great prophet Elijah to flee for his life (1 Kings 19:3), and of promoting the interests of a large number of prophets of Baal and Asherah (1 Kings 18:19). Most significantly, according to 1 Kings 21, she dominated her husband, taunting him with weakness (v. 7) and arranged without his help the execution of Naboth in a story which is significant also for another reason: Naboth's refusal to sell to Ahab the vineyard that he had inherited from his ancestors is one of the few incidents that reveal that there still remained at that time Israelites who resisted the absolutist claims of the kings and defended their ancestral rights – a vestige of the ancient traditional freedoms of the Israelite people.

The story of Jezebel and Naboth is also interesting in that it presents the picture of a wife who is the dominating partner in a marriage. Another example of this is 2 Kings 4:8–37, where it is the wife who takes the initiative and overrules her husband. Whether this was a common situation in the lives of the ordinary people – the wife in question is described as a 'great lady' (or possibly a 'wealthy woman', *'iššâ gĕdôlâ*) and so presumably as belonging to the upper class – is not known, but it was evidently a reality in the time of the kings. Another instance of a powerful, and ruthless, woman is the story of Athaliah, the granddaughter of Omri, who seized the throne of Judah by assassinating the royal family (2 Kings 11:1).

Another group of persons who exercised power, and sometimes political power which limited that of the kings, especially at certain critical moments, were the prophets of Yahweh. The first half of 1 Samuel is dominated by the figure of Samuel and the prophet Nathan plays a significant role at a point in David's reign. The books of Kings relate that in the northern kingdom several prophets were politically influential, especially Elijah and Elisha, while in Judah the prophet Isaiah is a prominent figure in the reign of Hezekiah. However, although the activities of some of the prophets occupy a prominent place in the narratives and they are to some extent treated by the authors as figures of heroic stature, it is made clear that they always acted as spokesmen for Yahweh, who was the hidden but real ruler of the kingdoms and able to set up kings and destroy them and finally to bring the kingdoms to an end. These books are not straightforward political histories; the politics are always intertwined with the religious lessons that the authors were concerned to inculcate.

The role of Yahweh's prophets was exercised by a combination of direct intervention in political affairs through prophecies, later fulfilled, of future events. The first of the major prophets, Samuel, exercised complete power over Israel before the inauguration of the monarchy and also over the fate of the first king. It was he who anointed Saul (1 Sam. 10:1) and then announced his rejection (1 Sam. 15:26), and who anointed David to succeed him (1 Sam. 16:13). Elijah, having been responsible for the coming of a devastating drought, ordered Ahab to arrange a contest on Mount Carmel which resulted in the murder of the prophets of Baal (1 Kings 18) and denounced Ahab and Jezebel for the murder of Naboth, correctly prophesying their deaths (1 Kings 21:17–24; 22:34–36; 2 Kings 9:30–36). The usurper Jehu was anointed by a young prophet sent by Elisha (2 Kings 9:1–6).

Some prophets served as advisers to kings. Elisha advised Jehoram of Israel on military strategy (2 Kings 3), on the question of the treatment of the visiting Aramean general Naaman (2 Kings 4) and again on the treatment of some Aramaean prisoners (2 Kings 6). It was also he who secured the victory of Joash on one occasion (2 Kings 13:14–19). In Judah, Isaiah was the trusted adviser of Hezekiah (2 Kings 19–20), and Josiah consulted the prophetess Huldah about the finding of the Book of the Law in the Jerusalem temple (2 Kings 22:14–20) when he also received from her a prophecy of the coming fall of the kingdom only mitigated by an assurance that he himself would not live to see it.

Such prophetical engagement with political decisions cannot be properly described as power-sharing by the kings, nor did it necessarily promote the aspirations of the ordinary people to the good life. But it does indicate that kings in whose hands lay the security and fate of the nation were not always capable of taking effective action during crises. In any case, from the moment when Assyria appeared on the international scene with demands of tribute in the person of Tiglath-pileser, known to Kings as 'Pul', in the reigns of Menahem of Israel (2 Kings 15:19–20) and of Ahaz of Judah (2 Kings 16:7–9) respectively, real power passed from the Israelite kingdoms, which then became no more than client states first of Assyria and then of Babylon – as vassals paying tribute or as attempting abortive rebellions against these great powers. Only king Josiah of Judah was able to take advantage of Assyria's collapse and to renew control of parts of northern Israel, as is implied in 2 Kings 23:4–23, but he met an ignominious end (2 Kings 23:29–30) and his successors never possessed genuine power again.

A class of Israelites (not to speak of foreign slaves owned by Israelites) without any power even over their own lives was of course that of slaves ('*ebed*, plural '*ăbādîm*). The comparative paucity of reference to slaves in Samuel and Kings suggests that slavery was taken for granted in Israel as

in other ancient civilizations. But little is said in Samuel and
Kings about the treatment of slaves; whether it was harsh or
humane. Debt slavery (2 Kings 4:1–7) may have been a
common practice; this is suggested in other Old Testament
books. The pursuit and capture by their owner of runaway
slaves (1 Kings 2:39–41) must have been legally permitted; it
is not for that in itself that Shimei is condemned and
executed in that passage. Shimei was presumably comparatively wealthy (1 Kings 2:36), and owned more slaves than
those who absconded. Ziba, who is described as 'servant'
('ebed') of the house of Saul, had his own slaves, who were set
to work together with his own sons to farm Mephibosheth's
estates (2 Sam. 9:10). Samuel's warning that the king whom
the people had demanded would make slaves of them (1
Sam. 8:17) suggests that such a fate was something that they
particularly feared.

Wealth and Sustenance

The accounts of the kings of Judah and Israel, whose reigns
cover almost the whole of the books of Samuel and Kings,
are provided with – mainly unfavourable – final summary
appraisals; in almost none of these (Manasseh, 2 Kings 21:16
is a notable exception) is there any reference to their
contribution to or conduct detrimental to the well-being of
their people. The authors of these books were mainly concerned with the religious proclivities of the kings and
sometimes for their notable achievements in the political and
military realms.

   Not surprisingly, the kings with their entourage of court-
iers and officials possessed great wealth as they possessed
supreme power, though only in the account of the reign of
Solomon is this especially stressed. But little is said in
Samuel or Kings about the economic condition of the mass
of the people. There is, however, a number of stories about
families of what appear to have been moderate means that
enabled them to give modest feasts and to travel about the
country. Occasionally there are specific references to the
poor and the wealthy which point to an awareness of a

distinction between classes. Words meaning 'poor' (*rāš*) or 'the poor' (*dal, dallâ*) occur several times. In 1 Sam. 18:23 David at the beginning of his career modestly claims to be 'poor and insignificant' (*rāš wĕniqleh*) – though his father has in fact been able to send suitable provisions to his brothers in the field and a gift of ten cheeses to their military commander (1 Sam. 17:17–18). The poor as a specific class in Jerusalem are mentioned in 2 Kings 24:14 and 25:12 as capable of working only as agricultural labourers and therefore left behind when the Babylonians took the remainder of the population of Jerusalem into exile. Nathan's parable (2 Sam. 12:1–6) provides a single example of the arrogant treatment of a very poor man by a wealthy one by the theft of the former's chief possession and means of livelihood, an act which the king judged to be worthy of death. In 2 Kings 4:1–7 there is a reference to the practice of debt-slavery whereby a destitute woman's children would have been sold to a creditor in default of payment of a debt had it not been for a miracle performed by Elisha.

There was equally a class of very wealthy people. Nabal (1 Sam. 25:2) is described as a wealthy owner of many sheep and goats and one who also behaved arrogantly to persons whom he judged to be mere vagabonds, and the 'great woman' of 2 Kings 4:8–37 was evidently a woman of ample means. The possession of slaves mentioned occasionally is an indication of at least moderate wealth.

Various incidents and situations described in these books show that the distinction between rich and poor was obliterated in times of crisis. Famine and drought, causing poor or non-existent harvests, affected all classes; they are mentioned with some frequency. (2 Sam. 21:1; 24:13; 1 Kings 8:35; 17:1; 18:2), and sometimes lasted as long as three years (2 Sam. 21:1; 1 Kings 17:1 cf. the threat in 2 Sam. 24:13). Famine was also caused by the siege of cities by foreign armies (2 Kings 6:25; 7:4; 25:3) and could even reduce the population to the practice of cannibalism (2 Kings 6:25–31). Other calamities affecting the population as a whole were the forced labour imposed by Solomon, which hindered the harvesting of the crops, the perhaps frequent oppressive demands of creditors (2 Kings 4:1–7) and excessive taxation due to demands for tribute by Assyria (2 Kings 15:19–20), Egypt (2 Kings 23:33–35) and probably Babylon. No doubt the necessity during the later monarchy to maintain an army to defend the country against foreign aggression will also have necessitated heavy taxation. In earlier times the Philistine oppression reduced the population to a state of poverty and misery (1 Sam. 13:6, 19–22). All these circumstances will have affected seriously the possibility of a good life for Israel at certain periods.

Health, Old Age and Death

Nothing is said directly in Samuel and Kings about good health, although three royal personages are said to be exceptionally handsome. It is noted that Saul was an exceptionally handsome young man (*bāḥûr wāṭôb*), taller and more handsome than any other (1 Sam. 9:2); that the boy David was 'of fresh complexion, with fine eyes and good looking' (*'admônî 'im-yĕpēh 'ênayim wĕṭôb rō'î*, 1 Sam. 16:12); and that Absalom was praised for his good looks, was physically unblemished, and had an abundant head of hair (2 Sam. 14:25–26) – all signs of robust health. In the cases of Saul and Absalom these qualities are mentioned in order to make a contrast with their ignominious deaths.

The authors make special mention of persons who lived to a very great age. Eli died at the age of 98, though feeble and blind (1 Sam. 4:15); Barzillai at 80 claimed to have lost interest in pleasure (2 Sam. 19:31–39), but may have lived longer, as his death is not noted. The age of David at his death is not stated, but he was greatly enfeebled (1 Kings 1:1–4), having reigned for 40 years (1 Kings 2:11). It is stated of Asa that in his old age he was 'diseased in his feet' (1 Kings 15:23).

References to illness and premature death in Samuel and Kings, not surprisingly, frequently concern kings or other royal persons, and also involve the activity of prophets or 'men of God'. Prophets were regarded by the authors as having special powers either of healing or the ability to predict or announce the healing or the death of the persons afflicted. The premature death of a king was sometimes seen as divine punishment for his apostasy or other sins. Thus the death of David's first child by Bathsheba after a brief illness was announced by the prophet Nathan as punishment for David's sin (2 Sam. 12:13–19). The reason for the unconventional behaviour of David during the child's illness and after his death (vv. 20–23) is not given by the author and so remains obscure, but the incident, which is unique, probably reflects some contemporary questioning about the proper attitude towards illness and death, especially the death of children. Certainly the whole episode reflects a belief that the sin of parents could be visited on their children. This is also reflected in the story of the death of Jeroboam's son Abijah, prophesied by the prophet Ahijah (1 Kings 14:1–18).

According to 2 Kings 1:2–17 King Ahaziah of Israel died as Elijah had prophesied as punishment for his apostasy in enquiring of Baal-zebub the god of Ekron rather than of Yahweh whether he would recover from an injury; and according to 2 Kings 8:29–9:26 King Joram of Israel was killed in battle because of his father Ahab's murder of Naboth, following the earlier word of Elijah; and Jezebel was murdered by Jehu for the same reason (2 Kings 9:30–37). The curious incident of 2 Kings 8:7–15 when Hazael murdered his master King Ben-hadad of Aram and succeeded him on the throne of Aram with the apparent encouragement of Elisha is presented as the belated fulfilment of Yahweh's command to Elijah in 1 Kings 19:15.

But prophets also possessed powers of healing, both of kings and of other sick persons. In these incidents the authors describe the methods of healing employed – a fact which, although these cures are at least to some degree represented as miraculous, may perhaps suggest a genuine medical concern. In 2 Kings 20:1–7 the prophet Isaiah healed King Hezekiah of Judah partly by conveying to him Yahweh's promise of a cure, but also partly by applying a fig poultice to his ulcer. In 2 Kings 5:1–19 Naaman, the Aramaean general, was cured of leprosy by following Elisha's recommendation to bathe in the river Jordan; in 1 Kings 17:17–24 Elijah revived the apparently dead son of the woman of Zarephath by a combination of prayer and stretching himself on the body of the child three times; and in 2 Kings 4:18–37 Elisha revived the child of the woman of Shunem by similar means, having failed, however, in a first attempt to achieve this by sending his servant to lay his master's staff on the child's face.

The relevance of these data about health, old age and death to the good life in Israel in the time of the monarchy is not easy to assess. But it may be observed that longevity, though probably exceptional, was regarded as enviable and not entirely unattainable; that in some cases (at least in that of David), despite the infirmities brought on by old age, death came at the end of a successful life which was estimated as having brought benefits to the people as a whole; and that robust health in young men was held to be a mark of manliness and leadership. Life, however, depended on faithful obedience to the known will of Yahweh, and his prophets, acting as his servants, could hold the keys of life and death. While there are no instances of the practice of 'medicine' except in the context of divine sanctions, and the notice of King Asa's foot disease in his old age as a simple statement of fact suggests that in most cases there was no attempt at a remedy, there appears to have been at least an interest in the mechanics of healing. The premature death of even such an excellent king as Josiah (2 Kings 23:29) was evidently regarded as inexplicable and as an instance of the inscrutability of the divine will, especially since the prophetess Huldah had prophesied that he would die 'in peace'. The various references to a general or particular shortage of food, even starvation, and 'plague' at certain times, whether as a result of natural causes or of human activity, indicates that the good life was, at least at times, far from being universal.

Family

There is a sense in which the family – that is, the succession of sons to their fathers' position as the head of the family – is the principal theme in the books of Samuel and Kings. In the case of succession to the throne the entire account of the political history of Israel depends on this principle. The most prominent example of this is of course the matter of the succession to the throne of David, which occupies a large portion of 2 Samuel and the first chapters of 1 Kings. This theme is first announced in 2 Sam. 7:11–17, when Yahweh promises through the prophet Nathan that David's 'house' will be established for ever – that the throne will always be occupied by his descendants. The contrary fate of the 'house' of Jeroboam, first announced by the prophet Ahijah (1 Kings 14:7–14) is also an important theme. In the chapters that follow, the question of the passing of the royal succession from father to son or the absence of that succession is a topic with which the authors of the books of Kings are continually concerned. At an earlier time before the establishment of the monarchy the fall of the 'house' of Eli, the priest at Shiloh, excluding his descendents from succeeding to the office of priesthood is similarly announced by a 'man of God' to Eli (1 Sam. 2:27–36) a prophecy later repeated to the child Samuel in 1 Sam. 3:10–14. The authors of these books duly report the fulfilment of these and similar prophecies. All these stories reflect the importance to the people of Israel in general of the principle of the succession of sons to their father as heads of the family.

More directly relevant to the picture of the good life in Israel is the fact that these books contain a considerable number of stories of family life and relationships between the members of families and also represent a wide spectrum of social and economic classes. They are stories of a kind that is almost entirely lacking in the books so far considered in this study. There may be two reasons for this: firstly, that these are the first of the Old Testament books considered which depict a people living – as far as possible – a settled life in their own land pursuing their accustomed occupations; and, secondly, that several of these stories involve the activity of prophets, who play an important part in the course of events, particularly at certain times. But it is particularly interesting to note that there is a distinct difference in this respect between the books of Samuel on the one hand and of Kings on the other: the great majority of the family stories and allusions occur in the books of Samuel. This may indicate that the family was a special interest of the authors of Samuel; most of Kings is more concerned with what may be called the *political* history of the nation.

There are six stories, all in the books of Samuel, which concern *fathers and sons*. The first two relate the activities of the sons of Eli (1 Sam. 2:12–17) and of Samuel (1 Sam. 8:2–3). Both are unedifying. The sons of each of these successive leaders of the nation were corrupt; and each led to eventful consequences: the first – it is implied – was the cause of the disastrous defeat of Israel by the Philistines and the loss of the Ark and to the death of Eli (1 Sam. 4:10–22) and also presaged the ultimate slaughter of the priesthood of Shiloh on the orders of Saul (1 Sam. 22:8–19); the other led to the demand by the elders of Israel for a king (1 Sam. 8:4) and so, despite Samuel's disapproval, to the ultimately disastrous reign of Saul. These family stories attest to the author's detestation of corruption in powerful families and to the unsatisfactory state of affairs in Israel prior to the institution of the monarchy.

Other stories in Samuel about the relations between fathers and their sons are more edifying; they depict a harmonious relationship which was evidently considered to be 'normal' by the authors and so as conducive to the good life. In 1 Sam. 9:1–10:16 Saul, the son of Kish, a wealthy Benjamite, contributes to the well-being of his family by obeying his father's request to go in search of some donkeys, returning home after being told by Samuel that they have been found. In 1 Sam.16:1–13 another family is depicted: that of the Bethlehemite Jesse which Samuel visits, having been commanded by Yahweh to select one of Jesse's sons and anoint him as king. It is implied in this and a subsequent incident (17:12–18) that Jesse and his eight sons live harmoniously together, and there is no suggestion that the seven sons who were not chosen were jealous of David's elevation (contrast the attitude of Joseph's brothers to him, Gen. 37). In 1 Sam. 22:3–5 David behaves as a caring son when in danger of his life by placing his parents in safety with the king of Moab. Later, after David had ascended the throne, he appears to have loved two of his sons in particular: Amnon, although he had raped his half-sister

Tamar and incurred David's anger (2 Sam. 13:21), and more famously Absalom (2 Sam. 13:39), who he continued to love even after he had rebelled against him, and showed a passionate affection when he was killed (2 Sam. 18:33–19:8).

A few other stories depict parental relationships with their children. In 1 Sam. 18:17–27 Saul behaves in a characteristically autocratic fashion when he first proposes to marry one of his daughters to David and then changes his mind and marries him to another daughter. In 2 Sam. 14:1–11 it is recounted how a woman of Tekoa tells a fictitious story in which she pleads to David to spare her son, who constitutes her only support now that her husband is dead. Athaliah's action in murdering the family of her deceased husband in order to seize the throne is regarded as an act of extreme wickedness (2 Kings 11:1).

The depiction of *marital relationships* in Samuel and Kings discloses a wide variety of situations. In a few cases the wife is the dominant partner. This is very much the case in the stories involving Ahab and Jezebel. Jezebel despises her husband as a weakling (1 Kings 21:5–7), arranges on her own initiative the judicial murder of Navoth, and is depicted in other passages as virtually ruling the country (e.g. 1 Kings 18:13, 19; 19:1–3). Other forceful wives include Abigail (1 Sam. 25), the woman of Shunem who took the initiative in sending for Elisha to save her dead child (2 Kings 4:18–37) and Bathsheba (1 Kings 1:11–2:37).

In 1 Sam. 1:1–2:11, 18–21 there is a story of family life which, although not without marital difficulties due to animosity between the two wives of one man, displays evidence of marital affection. It is stated that Elkanah loved Hannah and expressed his affection in giving her additional delicacies. In this respect the husband is presented as the dominant partner in the marriage. However, Hannah is another strongminded woman, and pays a private visit without her husband to the Shiloh temple and obtains what she particularly wanted to have: Yahweh's promise of a son, whom when he was weaned she dedicated to Yahweh to serve in the temple. Her husband Elkanah, who was a pious man and paid annual visits to the temple, was evidently acquiescent in all this, and was blessed by the priest Eli together with his wife (2:20). It would seem that the author of this story, with which he begins his book, intended it as a model of family life, and so of the 'good life' – if not an entirely ideal one – for the edification of his readers.

A charming, though pathetic, incident depicting love between husband and wife occurs in 2 Sam. 3:14–16, when Michal is taken, presumably against her will, from her husband Paltiel, who accompanied her back to David, 'weeping as he walked behind her all the way'. Michal's renewed relations with David are not described until the marriage came to an end. It is stated, however, in 1 Sam. 18:20 that she had loved him when she was first married to him, and that as a loyal wife she had enabled him to escape from the messengers sent by Saul to kill him (1 Sam. 19:11–17); but that later, when he had become king, she despised him and reviled him to his face for dancing in public clad only in a linen ephod when the Ark was brought to Jerusalem, and that he rejected her and she had no children (2 Sam. 6:16–23). The author makes no comment on David's behaviour in the matter.

The practice of polygamy seems to have been mainly restricted to kings according to the books of Samuel and Kings, although Elkanah's bigamy suggests that it was not altogether unknown and was not regarded as sinful. Royal polygamy, at least in the cases of David and Solomon, appears to have been taken for granted; probably some of these marriages took place for reasons of foreign policy (e.g. Solomon's marriage with the daughter of Pharaoh, 1 Kings 7:8). No adverse comment is made about David's many wives, though Solomon, who is reported as having 700 wives and 300 concubines (1 Kings 11:3) is condemned for allowing his foreign wives to lead him into idolatry (1 Kings 11:1–2, 4–8). Rape, as in the incident of Amnon and his half-sister Tamar (2 Sam. 13:1–22) was regarded as an abominable crime, although marriage between a brother and his half-sister appears to have been acceptable, at least for the children of kings (2 Sam 13:13). David took no action against Amnon, and it was left to Absalom to take vengeance for the crime against his sister (2 Sam. 13:23–29).

It is a characteristic of the books of Samuel that some

relationships of love or loyalty (between men, not women) *outside* the family play at least as important a role in the unfolding of events as do such relationships *within* families. This is not, however, a feature of the books of Kings – another illustration of the difference between these books which reflects the respective author's recognition of the exigencies of the portrayal of the widely varying circumstances of different periods in Israel's history.

The relationship between David and Jonathan is a major theme in 1 Samuel, which has been described as a portrait of ancient Israel's 'heroic age', when the close association between warriors could create intimate bonds of affection in which women had no part. As has been stated above, one of the most poignant features of David's life in later years was his extreme love for his son Absalom; but his love for Saul's son Jonathan is depicted as even greater. In fact David and Jonathan are not represented as having been companions in war: 1 Sam. 18:1–4 relates that the affection between the two young men began spontaneously at their first meeting at Saul's court after David's defeat of Goliath. It appears that then and afterwards the love and devotion was mainly on Jonathan's part. It continued in the face of Saul's growing hostility towards David (19:1–7; 20) and when David was a fugitive fleeing for his life, when the relationship was sealed by an oath and a covenant (23:16–18). In 2 Sam. 1:17–27 David, in his lament over the deaths of Saul and Jonathan in the battle of Gilboa, speaks of that love for Jonathan, describing it as 'wonderful, surpassing the love of women' (v. 26).

The love between David and Jonathan may well have been only an extreme example of relationships between warriors at that time, and have been a factor in the growing confidence of David's soldiers at the time of his military successes, so contributing to the 'good life' of the nation. David was evidently capable of inspiring the love of his subordinates, a fact to which Joab gave expression when he persuaded the grieving David to go out and congratulate his troops on their victory over the army of the rebellious Absalom, speaking of himself and others as 'those who love you' (2 Sam. 19:6). The account of David's retreat in the face of Absalom's rebellion in particular is full of references to men who showed great personal loyalty to David: Ittai the Gittite (presumably a Philistine) (2 Sam. 15:19–22; 18:2, 5); Hushai (2 Sam. 15:32–37; 16:16–17:14) and, after David had been forced to retreat beyond the Jordan, those inhabitants of Mahanaim who brought beds and food for David's exhausted troops (2 Sam. 17:27–29). In addition, it is recorded that 'the whole land (i.e. the Judahites) were weeping aloud' as David and his troops fled toward the wilderness (2 Sam. 15:23).

Another facet of close extra-familial relationships between males appears in 1 Samuel in two stories of loyal service of the young towards older men: those of the boy Samuel's service at the Shiloh temple as the protégé of Eli (1 Sam. 3:1) and of David's position as Saul's personal attendant whom Saul at first 'loved greatly' (2 Sam. 16:21–23).

Law and Justice

In the books of Exodus, Leviticus, Numbers, Deuteronomy and Joshua the law of Moses was the essential criterion of loyalty to Yahweh, and the behaviour of Israel's leaders was judged by their obedience or disobedience to it. It does not appear in the lawless period described in Judges, but it reappears in Kings as the basic requirement not only of kings (1 Kings 2:3; 11:11; 2 Kings 14:6; 18:6; 23.25) but also of the people as a whole (2 Kings 18:12; 21:8). It is therefore strange that it does not appear at all in the books of Samuel; this is a further indication of the difference between the two works.

From the information that they gave about the practice of justice in the long period covered by their works, it seems clear that the authors of Samuel and Kings intended their readers to see a gradual development in its administration. In particular, it is possible to observe a distinction between different stages in the history: pre-monarchical times, the early and the later monarchy.

In the first period the situation of the nation is portrayed as not significantly different from that of the lawless period of the judges. Samuel is in fact represented as the last of the judges (1 Sam. 7:15–17), and as with the earlier judges his rule was succeeded by a further time of lawlessness as his sons took over (1 Sam. 8:1–3). The account of the behaviour of Eli's sons (1 Sam. 2:12–17, 22) follows a similar course as regards the cultic aspect of the national life. This situation was clearly not favourable to the promotion of the good life.

It is clear that throughout the period of the monarchy the power of life and death resided in the king: in other words, the king was the supreme judge over his people and could, for example, order the execution of any person, often acting quite arbitrarily. No information is given in these books about the existence of a legal system or of courts of justice in which others were appointed as judges. From time to time, however, the people as a whole are depicted as exercising power: it was they who chose the first king (1 Sam. 8; 11:15), and they who countermanded Saul's decision, backed by the casting of lots, to condemn Jonathan to death (1 Sam. 14:37–45). Later the 'people of the land' took the initiative and acted as king-makers as certain crises arose in Judah, after the death of the previous king (2 Kings 21:24; 23:30).

In the books of Samuel (but not in Kings) decisions concerning guilt could be made on the basis of consultation of the will of Yahweh through the use of the mysterious Urim and Thummim (1 Sam. 14:41). The ephod is similarly used to discover the future (1 Sam. 23:9–12) and Yahweh's will in war (1 Sam. 30:7–8). David is sometimes mentioned as consulting Yahweh by unspecified means as in the book of Judges, when deciding to go into battle (1 Sam. 23:2, 4; 2 Sam. 2:1; 5:19, 23), a practice already employed by Saul (1 Sam. 14:37). The information in 2 Samuel about David's general administration of justice is contradictory: according to 2 Sam. 8:15 he administered justice and equity to all his people, but in 2 Sam. 15:2–6 Absalom secured support for his rebellion by complaining that justice was not obtainable because David had not appointed an official to hear judicial suits. Elsewhere David is credited with having established certain principles to regulate particular questions. According to 1 Sam. 30:23–25, before he ascended to the throne, he decreed that the spoils of battle should be shared by all his troops whether they had participated in the actual fighting or not, a regulation that the author declares to have continued 'to this day'. David's principle that the king's person as anointed by Yahweh's command was sacrosanct so that hands could not be laid on him with impunity seems to have been peculiar to him (1 Sam. 24:6; 26:9).

A number of instances are cited in 2 Samuel of David's judicial practice. In Nathan's parable (2 Sam. 12:1–6) he is made by a trick to reveal his reaction to the theft of a poor man's lamb by a rich man, swearing that the thief ought to be executed, but mitigating the punishment to fourfold restitution. In 2 Sam. 13:21, however, he refrained from punishing his son Amnon for the rape of his half-sister Tamar although he was angry. In another act of mercy (2 Sam. 14:1–11) he reprieved a poor widow's son who – it is alleged by the widow – had killed his brother in a fight. Incidentally, this passage appears to imply that the local community had the power to execute a murderer, or one accused to be one, for a crime committed locally.

The books of Kings contain only a handful of stories about the administration of justice under the kings who succeeded David. The case which is described in the greatest detail and which was to have drastic political consequences is that of the judicial murder of Naboth (1 Kings 21:1–14). It raises the question of the nature and limitations of royal power, and suggests that at any rate in the eyes of a prophet such as Elijah this was not, or ought not to be, absolute in the sense that a king (or in this case, a queen consort acting in her husband's name) could do exactly as he pleased to satisfy a mere whim: kings were morally responsible for their activities. This is another case that seems to assume that the elders and nobles (*ḥōrîm*) of a city had the authority to impose the death penalty – though in this case on an innocent person who had offended the sovereign and had been wrongly accused of blasphemy and treason. It also reflects the use of *lettres de cachet* overruling such local authority, and the employment of false witnesses.

Another story about the royal prerogative in judicial cases is one which eulogizes Solomon. This is the so-called 'judgement of Solomon' (1 Kings 3:16–28) in which the king is represented as showing extraordinary wisdom in discerning the rights and wrongs of a disputed case. It implies that the royal claim to administer jurisdiction in person and to give audience even to litigants of the lowest social class was – sometimes at least – justified. A further case of the proper exercise of royal justice occurs in 2 Kings 8:1–6, where a king of Israel (unnamed) orders the restoration of the property of a woman whose house and land had been wrongly taken from her during an enforced residence abroad at the time of a prolonged famine. In 2 Kings 14:5–6 there is recorded what appears to be a legal innovation (though an appeal is made to an earlier law of Moses which appears in Deut. 24:16) introduced by King Amaziah of Judah, who established the principle that the children of convicted criminals should not be put to death for crimes committed by their parents.

Finally the statement in 2 Kings 21:16 that Manasseh of Judah 'shed very much innocent blood' is a further indication that for this author, as in the case of Naboth, such criminal activity by a king was not to be condoned. In fact the books of Kings are filled with other summary executions; the authors perhaps supposed that victims were guilty.

So the picture of the people's expectation of fair treatment by the prevailing judicial authority during the period covered by the books of Samuel and Kings is a very mixed one. In the early chapters of 1 Samuel the situation was not unlike that presented in the book of Judges. After the coming of the monarchy the supreme judicial power was entirely in the hands of the king, who was not only the supreme judge but also the sole 'court of appeal' against decisions made locally by groups of leading citizens. The criminal actions of kings were, however, denounced in some cases by prophets. There is little evidence that Israelite citizens, whether of Judah or northern Israel, could be said to have legal rights; the one instance we have of a citizen's claiming ancestral rights (that of Naboth) ended in the overriding of those rights by royal authority. There is also no evidence of an established legal system or of a system of institutional legal procedure. The arbitrariness of the royal judicial power, although it was sometimes exercised justly, meant that the people had no personal security, and to that extent the good life was denied to them.

Wisdom

It is interesting to observe that the words 'wise' and 'wisdom' occur, in these books, only with reference to the reigns of David and Solomon. They are used there in a wide variety of ways, and in many instances the passages in which they occur have little or no relevance to the good life among the citizens of Israel generally. In the story of Amnon's rape of Tamar (2 Sam. 13:1–19) the 'wisdom' attributed to Amnon's friend Jonadab (v. 3) is no more than cunning, here employed as a device to assist Amnon's crime. A somewhat similar meaning is found in 1 Kings 2:6, where it consists of advice given by David to his son Solomon to commit political assassination; the 'wisdom' of the 'wise woman' in 2 Sam. 20:16 is of a similar nature. The 'wise woman' of Tekoa also is employed in a cunning trick. In 1 Kings 7:14, however, 'wisdom' is used of the skilled Tyrian bronze-worker Hiram.

Wisdom is attributed to David only in one passage, 2 Sam. 14:20, where the 'wise woman' of Tekoa flatters him by saying that he 'has wisdom like the wisdom of the angel of God to know all things that are on the earth'. This is a different kind of wisdom, perhaps more relevant to the lives of ordinary people; indeed, this is clearly a saying that originated among the people. In this context David's wisdom is the ability to know the motives of people, and to be aware of everything that is going on in his kingdom. All the remaining occurrences of 'wise' and 'wisdom' in these books refer to the wisdom of Solomon (some 20 occurrences). It is stated in 1 Kings 3:12, 5:21 and 26 that an especial wisdom was given by Yahweh to Solomon, who at the beginning of his reign had requested 'an understanding mind to govern your people, able to discern between good and evil' (3:9). An example of this wisdom is given later in the chapter, when Solomon as judge discovered which mother belonged to each of two babies, one of whom was alive and the other dead (vv. 16–28). This agrees with statements later in the history of Solomon, where his reign is described as having enabled Judah and Israel to flourish and to live the good life (1 Kings 4:20). The author also evidently takes pride on behalf of his people in Solomon's international reputation for wisdom (1 Kings 4:29–34; 10:4, 6–8, 24). But there is much else in the history of Solomon that betrays a lack of wisdom (though the term is not used), especially with regard to his failure in his old age to follow the good example of his father David, a failure to which the author attributes the subsequent division of the kingdom (11:4–13).

In the subsequent history of the kings wisdom is never specifically attributed to the ordinary people, although some examples are given of actions which might well have been so described, showing that perspicacity was not lacking in Israel. Such was, for example, the action of the whole people in saving the life of Jonathan (1 Sam. 14:45–46), of Nabal's wife Abigail (1 Sam. 25), and of Joab's use of the woman of Tekoa to persuade David (2 Sam. 14). A notable example of cleverness in debate is the deliberately false advice given to Absalom by Hushai, David's friend (2 Sam. 17), which defeated the advice of Ahithophel, who is described in 2 Sam. 16:23 as having been highly esteemed by both David and Absalom 'as if one consulted the oracle of God'. But in the later chapter of Kings such examples are hardly to be found.

The fate of the whole people depended on the behaviour and the policies of their kings; and the entire history of the monarchy, though the words 'wisdom' and 'folly' are not used, is represented by the biblical authors as punctuated by a long series of acts of non-wisdom which eventually destroyed the monarchy and with it the existence first of the northern kingdom and then of Judah. While the deportation of the greater part of the once united Israel is attributed by the authors to the action of God in response to Solomon's apostasy, politically it was the folly of the young king Rehoboam in rejecting the wise advice of the elder states-men to concede the demands of Jeroboam and the people ('all the assembly of Israel') for a less onerous rule than before, and accepting the disastrous advice given to him by his contemporaries, that was the initial incident in the process (1 Kings 12:1–11). The author, who gave great prominence to this incident and its immediate consequence, clearly regarded it as the act that set in train the successive and fatal disasters.

Pleasure and Enjoyment

Most of the references to luxurious living occur, not unexpectedly in passages concerning kings and the royal court. These are almost entirely confined to the reign of Solomon, where the author takes obvious delight in describing Solomon's immense wealth (1 Kings 10) and the extraordinary provisions for him and his household supplied by the people through his twelve regional officers (1 Kings 4:7–19, 21–28). There are occasional notes about pleasures at the courts of Saul and David: the young David entertained Saul with his harp-playing (1 Sam. 16:23), and in 2 Sam. 19:35 the old man Barzillai refers to professional singers at David's court, presuming this form of pleasure to be a matter of course there. It is probably significant that no allusions of this kind – apart from a few incidental references to 'the king's garden' near the royal palace in Jerusalem (2 Kings 21:18, 26; 25:4) – occur in Kings after the death of Solomon. Presumably the magnificent palace built for himself by Solomon (1 Kings 7:2–11) still stood in Jerusalem until the fall of Judah (2 Kings 25:9), though on several occasions the kings of Judah were forced to strip it of its treasures to pay tribute to foreign conquerors (1 Kings 14:26; 15:18; 2 Kings 14:14; 16:18; 18:15; 24:13). Hezekiah, however, still had 'treasures' to boast of when he showed them to the visiting Merodach-baladan (2 Kings 20:12–15). In northern Israel special mention is made of the 'Ivory House' built by Ahab (1 Kings 22:39). In the latter parts of Kings constant reference is made to the *impoverishment* of the kings of Judah caused by their need to find tribute to the neighbouring great powers, and nothing is said about their enjoyment of life.

Apart from what the reader is told about the pleasures

enjoyed by kings, a number of passages in these books refer to those enjoyed by their subjects, though these are confined to the reigns of David and Solomon. The later chapters of Kings describe the many privations that the people of Israel had to endure. But there is no reason to suppose that they were unable to find enjoyment, including no doubt the pleasures derived from family life, even though there is no mention of these in chapters mainly preoccupied with political developments. The window on the lives of the people provided by, Samuel and 1 Kings 1–11 suggests that this was so.

There was obviously a great difference between the rich and the poor as regards the opportunities for pleasure, even though it is stated that under Solomon the whole nation was prosperous and happy (1 Kings 4:20). Occasions for general rejoicing were provided especially by the giving of feasts, which were often connected with the offering of sacrifice but were also opportunities for the pure pleasure of eating and drinking together. The clearest example of a purely 'secular' feast given by a very wealthy man with apparently no religious motivation is that given by Nabal (1 Sam. 25:36). This is strikingly described as 'like the feast of a king' (the same expression is used at a feast given by Absalom in the Greek text of 2 Sam. 13:27). It was held in Nabal's house, and at it Nabal – and presumably also some of his guests – became 'very drunk'; but it is also stated that he was 'merry' (literally, 'his heart was happy [ṭôb] upon him').

At a lower social level the dinner party of Elkanah and his family at Shiloh (1 Sam. 1:4, 9) seems to have been enjoyed by all except Hannah, who was sad, though at a subsequent family meal she also became cheerful (v. 18). These meals probably took place in the precincts of the temple there; it is explicitly stated that Hannah was *not* drunk (v. 15), although Eli, perhaps reasonably, supposed that she was (v. 13). Other descriptions of feasts suggest that over-indulgence in wine was a regular occurrence on such occasions. The feast presided over by Samuel in the 'land of Zuph', where he was the resident 'man of God' (1 Sam. 9:11–24) was connected with a religious sacrifice and was attended by 30 guests and was clearly an enjoyable one, with the young man Saul, as the honoured guest, being given the best portion of meat. There was public merrymaking on the occasion of the successful bringing of the Ark to Jerusalem by David (2 Sam 6:12–19). This also was accompanied by sacrifices, and David 'danced before Yahweh' and distributed food to 'the whole multitude of Israel' (v. 19). Only Michal was displeased (vv. 20–23). According to 1 Kings 8:65–66 a seven-day feast was held with many sacrifices in which 'all Israel' and even people from Lebanon and the Brook of Egypt participated and are recorded as having been 'joyful and in good spirits' (*śĕmēḥîm wĕṭôbē lēb*). There is thus a clear indication that under those kings there was sometimes opportunity for the whole people to participate in the good things that were provided, either to consume or to take away.

God and the Good Life

The name Yahweh occurs more than 1,000 times in the 102 chapters of Samuel and Kings. The importance of the role played by Yahweh in these books can thus hardly be overestimated, though it is noteworthy that a large number of incidents are recorded in which there is no mention of God at all, or at most only peripheral references, for example in oaths such as 'as Yahweh lives'. On the other hand, occasional comments by the author at crucial points in the narrative (2 Sam. 11:27; 12:24; 17:14) attest to an authorial awareness that even when his actions were not obvious to the persons concerned Yahweh was in fact 'behind the scenes', guiding events.

It is taken for granted in these books that the fortunes of the nation were ultimately wholly in Yahweh's hands. Not only his actions by which he intervened directly in the course of events, but also his words, usually spoken through the medium of a succession of prophets or 'men of God' many of whom (notably Samuel, Nathan, Ahijah, Elijah, Elisha, Isaiah, Huldah) are named, are effective and decisive. These prophets are Yahweh's spokesmen, encouraging, promising, warning or condemning kings. Some kings were anointed by prophets or other servants of Yahweh (1 Sam. 10:1; 16:1–13; 1 Kings 1:39; 2 Kings 9:1–13), though it was 'the people of Judah' who anointed David king of Judah (2 Sam. 2:4), and the 'people of the land' who anointed Jehoahaz after Josiah's death (2 Kings 23:30). After the assassination of Athaliah it was the priest Jehoiada and the temple guards who 'put the crown on him (Joash), gave him the covenant, proclaimed him king and anointed him' (2 Kings 11:12). In some of these cases it is not stated that the anointing had been sanctioned by Yahweh, but it is natural to suppose that this was taken for granted. But it was equally Yahweh who, mainly through his servants, deposed kings and rejected their dynasties (e.g. Saul, 1 Sam. 13:14; also 1 Kings 13:34; 14:6–16; 21:20–24), and who brought to an end the kingdoms of both northern Israel (2 Kings 17:18) and Judah (2 Kings 20:17; 21:10–15; 22:16–17; 23:27; 24:20).

These events, held by the authors of Kings to have taken place under Yahweh's direction, were clearly determinative of the possibility of the Israelites, whether of the north or the south, enjoying the good life in their land. Of the condition of the exiled people after they had been deported from the land the authors are silent; perhaps for them exile was a kind of death. The conquests of Samaria and Jerusalem by foreign armies will have also caused great misery; this is made clear of the last days of Jerusalem (2 Kings 25:1–7). However, the authors repeatedly make it clear that these disasters were not occasioned by the behaviour of the kings alone: the whole people also sinned with them (e.g. 1 Kings 14:15–16, 22–24; 2 Kings 17:7–20).

It is taken for granted in Samuel and Kings that Yahweh has complete control over nature, withholding rainfall at will and causing famine – activities detrimental to the good life for the people. It is recorded in 2 Sam. 21:1 that he inflicted a three-year famine on the land because of an unavenged slaughter of the Gibeonites, not by David but by his predecessor Saul. In 2 Sam. 24:12–14 Yahweh proposes through Gad the 'seer' to punish Israel for a sin of David which he himself had provoked in a fit of unexplained anger (v. 1). He offered alternative punishments, one of which was a three-year famine; but David left the decision to God, who sent pestilence, causing the deaths of 70,000 people. In three other instances (1 Kings 17:1; 2 Kings 4:38; 8:1) Yahweh sent famines on the land for no apparent reason. His control over the rainfall was further demonstrated when he sent thunder and rain at the time of wheat harvest to devastate the crops, to punish the people for choosing a king (1 Sam. 12:16–18), and in 1 Kings 18 he put an end to the long drought by sending torrential rain, so demonstrating his power and the powerlessness of Baal. Thus in Samuel and Kings Yahweh is a wholly unpredictable God on whom the people are forced to depend in order to survive and to enjoy the good life as best they can. His unpredictability, which might also be described as irresponsibility, is further demonstrated by the sudden death of Uzzah who had, with the best of intentions, put out his hand to steady the Ark during its rough journey, an act which had the unique consequence of arousing David's anger against Yahweh (2 Sam. 6:6–9).

However, this same unpredictability could lead to the enjoyment of good fortune by ordinary Israelites in trouble. So, for example, Elijah acting on Yahweh's orders went to Zarephath and there miraculously provided a starving widow with food (1 Kings 17:8–24), and Elisha similarly provisioned the wife of one of the 'sons of the prophets' in a similar case (2 Kings 4:1–7). Elisha also answered the prayer of the Shunammite woman for a son, and subsequently restored that son to life when he had died of sunstroke (2 Kings 4:11–37). The granting of a son to Hannah in 1 Sam. 1 is another example of unexpected fulfilment of a desire for a son. On the other hand, individuals could be punished unexpectedly for their sins through Yahweh's prophets: Gehazi, Elisha's servant, was afflicted with leprosy for obtaining goods by deceit (2 Kings 5:19b–27). Another negative incident comparable with that of the death of Uzzah is the fatal attack by bears on 42 small boys who had mocked the 'man of God' Elisha, on his cursing them in the name of Yahweh (2 Kings 2:23–24). Incidents like this and the death of Uzzah presumably served to impress on the readers that Yahweh was a free and sovereign God whose unpredictability must be accepted and who was as much to be feared as loved.

What part did religious worship and piety play in the lives of ordinary Israelites in the period covered by Samuel and Kings, and to what extent did their piety influence their enjoyment of the good life? The authors present a very mixed picture. This is apparent already in the initial chapters of 1 Samuel. That book begins with a picture of a quietly pious family, with its annual visits to Shiloh, Hannah's prayer and the dedication of her son Samuel to serve in the temple; but in those very chapters the reader learns that something is very wrong with the administration of the Shiloh temple, whose priests, Eli's sons, are cheating the worshippers who come to offer their sacrifices (2:12–17) and sleeping with the women who served in the temple (2:22–25), and also learns of the doom pronounced by Yahweh on Eli's family (2:12–3:18).

On the positive side, there are many indications of the central importance of particular religious symbols during this period. One of these was the temple. The Shiloh temple was evidently an important place of pilgrimage, and, despite the defects of its priesthood, was a place where the life of a family could be enriched through the birth of a longed-for child in answer to prayer to Yahweh. Later the temple built by Solomon was a great centre of worship to which prayer to Yahweh could be made in times of distress (1 Kings 8); and it may be assumed that it retained that centrality until its destruction by the Babylonians (2 Kings 25), when the kingdom itself came to an end. When Jeroboam set up his golden calves and made Bethel and Dan alternative places of worship and established his newly created priesthood and national festivals (1 Kings 12:28–33) he did this because he feared that the population of his newly established kingdom in the north would still travel to Jerusalem to worship and sacrifice there (vv. 26–27). Another religious symbol of great importance for Israel was the Ark of the Covenant of Yahweh, which was carried into battle to ensure Yahweh's support and the people's victory over the Philistines (1 Sam. 4:1–9) and which after its return to the land after its 'exile' in Philistia (1 Sam. 6:10–7:2) was eventually carried to Jerusalem by David (2 Sam 6:1–15) by 'all the house of Israel' with great rejoicing. Another indication of the people's devotion to

Yahweh is the great prominence accorded to the series of prophets of Yahweh and other 'men of God' who appeared at intervals as Yahweh's agents. In this capacity they were regarded as instruments of healing; and their words and actions performed in Yahweh's name were accepted by the people as powerful and authoritative.

On the other hand, the authors report a strong inclination on the part of the people of Israel to abandon the worship of Yahweh and to turn to the worship of other gods, especially Baal (or 'the Baals'). This is first noted in 1 Sam. 7:3–4, when Samuel urged them to put away foreign gods and worship Yahweh alone, promising them that if they did so Yahweh would deliver them from the Philistine enemy. The struggle between the cults of Yahweh and Baal is most fully described with regard to northern Israel in 1 Kings, where it appears that this form of idolatry was not confined to the kings. Ahab and Jezebel in particular vigorously promoted the worship of Baal, and Elijah despairingly complained to Yahweh that he alone was left to champion Yahweh's cause (1 Kings 19:10, 14), though Yahweh assured him that he would leave 7,000 alive who had not worshipped Baal (v. 18). In the previous chapter (18) Elijah is represented as having performed a miracle which proved that Yahweh was the true God, but it is stated there that 'two opinions' divided the nation on this question. Later Jehu is said to have destroyed all Baal's worshippers (2 Kings 10:18–28).

It is clear, however, from later chapters of Kings that idolatrous worship continued in Israel, and it is affirmed that this was the cause of the fall of the nation of northern Israel (2 Kings 17). Indeed, 1 Kings 15:30 states that Jeroboam with his idolatrous practices 'caused' Israel to sin, and it is stated in later chapters that his successors on the throne continued to do so. In Judah also 'the people still sacrificed and made offerings on the (idolatrous) high places' (2 Kings 15:4), and in 2 Kings 21:10–15 unnamed prophets of Yahweh pronounced Yahweh's intention to destroy the whole people because King Manasseh had 'caused Judah to sin', but also 'because they have done what is evil in my sight and have provoked me to anger, since the day their ancestors came out of Egypt, even to this day'.

Summary

The books of Samuel and Kings present a picture in which there were opportunities for the people of Israel to enjoy the good life, but this was by no means always the case. The security of their lives was constantly threatened by powerful enemies who in the end deprived them even of the possession of the land itself. They were dependent on the arbitrary rule of their kings, whose folly or wickedness eventually led them to disaster. Their prosperity and an adequate supply of food depended on the independence of the nation, which was constantly threatened, and there were also great differences between the lives of the poor and the wealthy. We are told of exceptional cases of longevity, but there was little medical knowledge to heal the sick, although the prophets sometimes performed miraculous cures. On the other hand, many examples of loving relationships within families are recorded, and also of affection outside the family circle. There was no regular system of justice, and the fate of the innocent depended on the decisions of the kings, which were sometimes just or merciful and sometimes ruthlessly unjust. Despite these uncertainties it appears that opportunities for enjoyment were not entirely lacking. These books attest to a general belief that Yahweh was the all-powerful controller of the lives and destinies both of individuals and of the nation as a whole and the source of the good life, and there is ample evidence of genuine piety, though especially at certain times the worship of the Baals and other gods drew many Israelites away from his worship. But it was recognized that Yahweh was unpredictable and his actions mysterious, and that he was therefore as much to be feared as loved.

8

Chronicles

The books of Chronicles add very little to the topic of the good life. Apart from their early chapters (1 Chron. 1–9) which consist almost entirely of genealogies beginning with Adam, they are almost entirely devoted to retelling the history of the monarchy from David to the final destruction of Jerusalem which is also the subject that appears in Samuel and Kings. This is told in the form of extracts from these books. Chronicles, however, carries the story further than Kings, recounting the decree of Cyrus king of Persia (also found in a variant form in the first verses of the book of Ezra) in which he declared his intention to rebuild the Jerusalem temple and gave permission to the exiled Jews to return to Judah if they so wished.

But the history as recounted in Chronicles varies considerably from that of Kings, both adding a great deal to it and omitting much. In particular, these books add to the description of the reign of David by inserting a lengthy and detailed account of his preparations for the organization of the temple which Solomon was to build in Jerusalem (1 Chron. 22–29), and they also add or embellish numerous incidents in the reigns of the kings of Judah. These additions led the Greek (Septuagint) translators of Chronicles to give these books the title Paraleipomena, 'Things Omitted', that is by Samuel and Kings.

Chronicles' most substantial *omissions* from Kings are the entire blocks of material that relate the history of the northern kingdom of Israel after the division of the united monarchy of David and Solomon. From this point (from 2 Chron. 10 onwards) Chronicles becomes a history of the kingdom of Judah alone. Consequently the book lacks all the stories about the lives of ordinary people which are such a characteristic feature of Kings and which are the main sources of information about the topic of the good life; for those stories, many of which are told in connection with the activities of northern prophets, especially Elijah and Elisha, belong solely to the history of northern Israel. In fact it is noteworthy that Chronicles provides virtually no information even about the lives of ordinary citizens of the kingdom of Judah. Neither family life nor the activities of ordinary individuals is recorded in Chronicles. Almost all the individuals whose activities are mentioned are kings and prophets; and those prophets, many of whom do not appear in Kings, are mentioned only in connection with their delivery of divine messages to various kings. The only other individuals mentioned by name who do not appear also in Kings are military officers serving under David and his successors, royal wives, musicians, priests and Levites and other temple servants; and no anecdotes are told about these. The author of Chronicles was clearly not interested in such details; his purpose was quite different from that of the author of Kings. He was governed by a rigid theology which stressed the sovereignty of God and his distribution of rewards and punishments to the various kings and the nation in accordance with their faithfulness or otherwise to him. He was also much concerned with the right performance of the national cult in the temple in Jerusalem, on which the well-being of the nation was held to depend, rather than with other aspects of the good life enjoyed by individual citizens.

Place and Security

Chronicles inevitably follows Kings in recording how following the glorious times of David and Solomon the people of Judah as a consequence of their sinful behaviour and their abandonment of the true religion of Yahweh were eventually expelled from their land. This fate is summed up succinctly in 1 Chron. 9:1: 'And Judah was taken into exile in Babylon because of their unfaithfulness'. Chronicles omits the statements of 2 Kings 24:14 and 25:12 that some people – at least the very poor – remained behind. For the Chronicler there was no such remnant: the entire population of Judah was taken into exile in Babylon. The final statement about the reason for their fate is made in 2 Chron. 36:15–16:

> And Yahweh the God of their fathers had sent repeatedly to them by his messengers because he had compassion on his people and on his dwelling place; but they persisted in mocking God's messengers, mocking his words and despising his prophets until there was no remedy.

The indictment was a comprehensive one, including the king, the leading priests and the people (vv. 11–14). It is characteristic of Chronicles that it ends with the statement that these had all 'polluted the house of Yahweh' in Jerusalem. For this author the loss of the land was above all due to failure to maintain the holiness of the temple and its rites.

But the chief difference between Chronicles and Kings with regard to the security of the nation and its possession of its God-given place in the world is the positive and hopeful note on which Chronicles concludes. Whereas the books of Kings end with no more than a statement that the exiled Judaean king Jehoiachin was released by the Babylonian king Evil-merodach from a 37-years' imprisonment and thereafter treated kindly and honourably and given a status above that of other captive kings at the Babylonian court, Chronicles carries the story down to an even later date. It records that Cyrus king of Persia issued an edict stating that Yahweh the God of heaven, who had 'given him all the kingdoms of the earth', had commanded him to rebuild his temple in Jerusalem, and giving permission to any Jews who wished to do so to return to their former homes (2 Chron. 36:22–33). Thus the Jews were to have the opportunity to recover their homeland and their temple and to find a new security, despite the fact that they remained under foreign rule. Here, for the first readers of the book, there was a new hope for the Jewish people, both those who had already returned and those who had not yet done so, of a secure future under a benevolent imperial government.

The differences between the two accounts of Jewish history given by Kings and Chronicles with regard to place and security are obvious to the modern reader, but would not have disturbed the original readers of the two books. To such readers they would have appeared complementary rather than contradictory. Chronicles adduces reasons for the loss of the land which are not stressed in Kings, but these would simply be regarded as additional to those adduced in Kings. Chronicles recorded the deportation by Nebuchadnezzar of all the citizens of Jerusalem without exception, while Kings states that the poorest people were left behind to maintain the vineyards and till the land but this difference was clearly not regarded as significant. Neither writer, both of whom lived after these events took place, hints at the existence of a substantial Jewish community who continued to live and manage their affairs for many years until the return of the exiles. Both imply that during the period of the exile the land remained virtually uninhabited, at any rate by Jews.

Power

Although the author of Chronicles repeats much of the text of Samuel and Kings while making his own characteristic comments at intervals, the former differs to a considerable extent in his concept of the royal power. Many stories concerning the activities of the kings are abbreviated, while elsewhere incidents are recorded which are omitted from Kings. This is also true of that part of the book which deals with the reign of David which is covered by the books of Samuel. Chronicles omits the entire account in Samuel of the rise of the monarchy and the debates that took place concerning the people's decision to appoint the first king. The reign of Saul is also omitted: only his death on Mount Gilboa is recorded (1 Chron. 10). The gradual rise of David and his struggle for power are also omitted. Consequently David appears abruptly on the scene: the fall of Saul and the appointment of David are laconically recorded in 1 Chron. 10:14 with the words 'Therefore Yahweh put him to death and turned the kingdom over to David the son of Jesse'. David was anointed immediately as king over all Israel, no reference being made to his having first been anointed over Judah alone (1 Chron. 11:1–3 – although 1 Chron. 29:26, following 1 Kings 2:11, records that he reigned for seven years in Hebron before reigning in Jerusalem). David is thus presented as having supreme power over the entire nation from the moment of his first appearance in the book.

Political power in Chronicles is in the hands of the kings, whose activities occupy almost the whole of the text. However, there were limits to that power. These limits are amply demonstrated by the reports of the activities of numerous prophets, seers and other messengers from Yahweh, who, far more frequently than in Kings, addressed a succession of kings in Yahweh's name with words sometimes of encouragement but more often of warning, prophesying disaster for them and for the nation if they turned from God and disobeyed his commands. The kings did not always heed these prophets and in some cases they punished them (e.g. Hanani, whom Asa put in the stocks, 2 Chron. 16:10, and Zechariah, stoned to death on the orders of Joash, 2 Chron. 24:21–22). But their prophecies were duly fulfilled. It may thus be said that the fortunes of both king and nation were determined by the supreme power of Yahweh who spoke through his prophets. Finally it is stated that it was due to failure to heed the prophets that the kingdom of Judah was finally destroyed when Nebuchadnezzar, summoned by Yahweh, brought it to an end for the continuing apostasy of both kings and people (2 Chron. 36:14–17). The eventual renewal of the nation's fortunes also took place at the instigation of Yahweh, who stirred up the spirit of Cyrus king of Persia to release the exiles and to rebuild the Jerusalem temple in fulfilment of his word spoken through the prophet Jeremiah.

In Chronicles the varying fortunes of the nation are accounted for by Yahweh's assessment of the kings' obedience or apostasy. This principle is carried out so rigidly that in some cases a single king is represented as having brought both success and military defeat on the nation at different times during his reign, having changed his attitude towards God. The reigns of Asa and Manasseh are examples of this. King Asa at first secured freedom from foreign aggression for his people through his piety and religious reforms (2 Chron. 15:15); but later he disobeyed Yahweh and plunged them into foreign wars (2 Chron. 16:9). Manasseh on the other hand changed his stance in a contrary direction. At first an exceptionally wicked and impious king, he brought on himself and his people an Assyrian invasion at Yahweh's instigation and was himself taken captive (2 Chron. 33:11), but when he prayed and repented he went on to great achievements, having restored the pure worship of Yahweh (2 Chron. 33:12–20). Other kings who were consistently unfaithful consistently suffered defeat, while those who were consistently faithful were consistently delivered by Yahweh from their enemies (e.g. Hezekiah). The political and military power of the kings of Judah was thus totally dependent on the infinitely superior will and power of Yahweh.

Law and Justice

Throughout Chronicles, as in Samuel and Kings, the administration of justice rested ultimately in the hands of the kings. The books of Kings say nothing about the establishment of lower courts of justice, though it may be presumed that justice was in some fashion exercised locally by elders and other prominent citizens (cf. 1 Kings 21:8–14). But Chronicles supplies additional information about the development of an official judicial system. David already appointed Levites to act as judges (1 Chron. 23:4), though no more detailed information is given about their functions. There was, however, a further important development in the reign of Jehoshaphat. That king first sent a group of officials accompanied by priests and Levites to go into all the cities of Judah instructing the people in the law of Yahweh (2 Chron. 17:7–9). It is assumed that it was this body of laws, sometimes known as the law of Yahweh and sometimes as the law of Moses, which was the sole authoritative law intended to govern the behaviour of king and people alike both in its moral and ritual ordinances. Later Jehoshaphat appointed judges for all the cities of Judah, and, for Jerusalem, priests, Levites and other prominent citizens, to hear cases and give impartial judgement (2 Chron. 19:5–11).

It is to be presumed that this system continued until the destruction of the kingdom, and the first generation of readers of the book will probably have taken it to be the forerunner of the judicial systems of their own times.

Pleasure and Enjoyment

It is a notable characteristic of Chronicles that nothing whatever is said about the enjoyment of the good life by individuals or families. Whenever joy and celebration are mentioned, sometimes with feasting, it is always the whole population as a body, often together with priests, Levites, musicians etc., which expresses pleasure; and almost always the occasion has to do with cultic affairs and public worship. The only exceptions are the rejoicing at the appointment of David as king (1 Chron. 12:39–40) and at the enthronement of the boy king Joash after the expulsion and execution of the usurper Athaliah (2 Chron. 23:21). Otherwise the people rejoice at the bringing of the Ark to Jerusalem (1 Chron. 15:27–28), at the completion of the building of the temple (2 Chron. 7:10), on the restoration of the temple worship by Jehoiada (2 Chron. 24:21), at Hezekiah's temple reform (2 Chron. 29:36) and the celebration of Hezekiah's Passover (2 Chron. 30:21–23, 26). On those occasions the people act as a kind of chorus. Any private pleasure and joy in the good life remains unrecorded. The people silently acquiesce in the doings of the kings whether successful or disastrous and whether pious or impious. As the kingdom draws to its ignominious end there is no more mention of joy.

Summary

The books of Chronicles, although they repeat much of the text of 2 Samuel and Kings, are in fact very different in their aims. They were probably regarded from the first as supplements to the earlier works giving a fuller picture of certain aspects of the reigns of the kings, while abbreviating, summarizing and omitting much of the earlier narratives as already familiar to the readers. For the period after the division of the kingdoms they confine themselves entirely to the history of the kingdom of Judah, so omitting the descriptions of the lives and families of the northern kingdom that provide important information on the topic of the good life. There is in fact very little indeed in Chronicles that bears on the good life for individual citizens.

The author's purpose was evidently to present a different picture of Israel and Judah from that given in Samuel and Kings. It depicts the good life as having been possible for the nation only in periods when the reigning king was obedient to Yahweh; when he was not, disaster was the inevitable consequence. One of the most important aspects of the national good life was the faithful performance of God's cultic requirements; and it was chiefly at such times that the joy of the people is recorded. The people performed no independent actions of protest against the policies of the kings but followed their examples implicitly whether they were fortunate or disastrous. Only the prophets as God's messengers dared to denounce policies when they were opposed to the will of God. There was, however, a system of justice inaugurated by Jehoshaphat.

The final part of Chronicles differs from that of Kings in that while on the one hand the deportation and exile involved the whole population without exception, presumably depriving them of a good life, the restoration of the nation by the decision of King Cyrus is recorded. Thus while Kings ends in despondency or at least in uncertainty about the good life in the future, Chronicles ends with the concrete promise of the good life for the people.

9
Ezra and Nehemiah

These books resemble Chronicles in several respects. They contain little or no information about the lives of individuals: their subject is the varying fortunes of a whole community: here that of the return to Judah of the exiles – or those who desired to return – with the permission of certain Persian overlords. The rebuilding of their national life was made possible by the work of a new kind of leader. As in Chronicles it is the kings whose actions had determined the fortunes of the people, so in these books it is two non-royal leaders, Ezra the priest and scribe and Nehemiah the layman, who do so. It is their actions that are related here, partly recorded by them in their personal memoirs.

Place and Security

These aspects of the good life occupy an important place in these two books. The exilic community had experienced a complete *displacement*: they had travelled under their leaders from their places of exile in the Persian empire to their former homeland – or the homeland of their fathers – to settle there and rebuild Jerusalem and its temple. There was therefore rejoicing in their return to the land whose possession had been promised long ago to their ancestor Abraham, a promise that had been fulfilled until by their unfaithfulness they had lost it (cf. the prayer of Ezra, Neh. 9: 6–37). But their joy was by no means unalloyed. Ezra's prayer discloses a poignant awareness of their lack of independence and their continued subordinate and precarious position within a foreign empire:

> Here we are slaves to this day – slaves here in the land that you gave our fathers to enjoy its fruits and its good things. Its rich yield goes to the kings whom you have set over us because of our sins; they have power

also over our bodies and over our livestock at their
pleasure, and we are in sore distress. (Neh. 9:36–37)

But in addition, the living of the good life was beset by
troubles of various kinds caused both by external enemies
and by internal dissensions. These troubles were not the
fault of the kings of Persia, who are constantly depicted as
full of good will towards their Jewish subjects and as
showing great generosity to them. The book of Ezra begins
with a statement by King Cyrus similar to that with which
the books of Chronicles conclude (Ezra 1:1). He gave
permission to the Jewish exiles to return to Judah, claiming
that he had been commanded by Yahweh to rebuild his
temple in Jerusalem; and he ordered those Persian citizens
who were their neighbours to provide them with money,
goods and livestock for their journey (Ezra 1:1–4). Later,
when the building of the temple had been halted by
direction of the local officials, King Darius overruled them
and gave permission for the work to proceed (Ezra 6). Later
still, Ezra was commissioned by King Artaxerxes to travel to
Judah together with a further contingent of willing exiles
and given a generous allowance of money and full powers,
especially to provide for the temple services (Ezra 7); and the
royal official Nehemiah similarly obtained leave of absence
from Artaxerxes to visit Judah in order to deal with
destruction wrought by the enemies of the Jews there and to
rebuild the walls of Jerusalem to provide the city with
protection from further harm (Neh. 1–2).

Nevertheless these two books reflect an atmosphere of
tension and uncertainty among the returned exiles lasting
through the reigns of several Persian kings and only ending
with the completion of the work of Nehemiah at the conclusion of that book. Although there was rejoicing at the
laying of the foundations of the new temple shortly after the
first Return (Ezra 3:10–13) and again later after its completion (Ezra 6:16–22), the builders and their leaders,
especially their governor Zerubbabel, were harrassed by
opponents who declared that they had no right to build
(Ezra 4–5) and who caused a long delay lasting many years
until the reign of Darius (Ezra 4:24). There was evidently a

genuine feeling that even after the Return the good life had
not become possible. The laying of the foundations of the
temple was an emotional moment for the people: while
some shouted for joy because they at last had a temple
again, those who remembered the more splendid former
temple wept loudly, so that the joy and the weeping became
mixed together (Ezra 3:11–13). For the latter at least the
good life remained an unfulfilled dream.

Evidently the security of that community of Jews who
had returned from exile and were living in Jerusalem was by
no means ensured. The next crisis was an internal one. Ezra,
when he arrived in the city armed with legislative and
administrative powers granted to him by Artaxerxes to see
that adequate provision was made for the worship of his
God in the temple and also to set up magistrates and judges
in the province who would enforce obedience to the laws of
both God and the king, found that the integrity of the
community had been endangered by the marriages of some
of its members with women of the 'peoples of the land' –
that is, Canaanites and adherents of other neighbouring
peoples (Ezra 9). What had begun as a community of Jews
worshipping Yahweh was in danger not only of losing its
ethnic purity but also its faithfulness to God, since these
foreign wives were worshippers of pagan gods. Ezra dealt
with the situation by ruthless treatment of the offenders,
who were forced not only to confess their faults but also to
divorce their foreign wives (Ezra 10). The author makes no
comment on the disruption of social life and the misery of
the divorced wives and their families which must have
ensued. For him the good life was defined as the life that was
lived by all Jews in faithfulness to the will of Yahweh; and
this was clearly to be the lesson which he intended to be
learned by his first readers and by succeeding generations.

It is evident that the external security of the Jerusalem
community continued to be threatened for some time.
Nehemiah's mission, which entailed his being given guber-
natorial authority by the king, was occasioned by his
learning that the Jews in the province of Judah had been
attacked by enemies, and that the fortifications of Jerusalem
had been destroyed and its gates burnt (Neh. 1:1–3). (No

details of this incident are given.) His main purpose, to which King Artaxerxes assented, was to secure the safety of the city by rebuilding the walls. For this he was granted diplomatic status and an armed escort (Neh. 2:7–8).

Nehemiah's attempt to rebuild the walls of the city with the help of many willing volunteers, however, met with serious opposition from the leaders of the neighbouring provinces, who did not wish the 'people of Israel' to prosper (Neh. 2:10), and who did everything they could to hinder the building work (Neh. 4:7–8). Their opposition was such a menace to the Jews' physical security (Neh. 4:10–14) that Nehemiah was obliged to arm half of his team of workers to enable the other half to proceed with the work (Neh. 4:16–21). He also had to contend with plots against his life (Neh. 6:1–13). But he overcame all these difficulties and completed the work in only 52 days (6:15), although it was still necessary to secure the gates of the city against attack at night (7:3–4). Once the walls were repaired and the gates replaced he was then able to repeople the city which up to then had been sparsely populated (7:4; 11:1–2) and proceed to necessary reforms and the reorganization of the temple and the city. The book closes on a confident note: the good life had been restored, and Nehemiah was able to thank God and to pray 'Remember me, O my God; and do not wipe out my good deeds that I have done' (13:14; cf. 13:22, 31).

Power

It is clear from the books of Ezra and Nehemiah that there was an awareness among the returned exiles living at that time in Judah and Jerusalem that supreme earthly power lay with the kings of Persia, and that they were in a real sense only their 'slaves': that they had no control over the products of the soil or over their livestock which were the only source of their wealth, on which they had pay taxes to their foreign rulers, or even over their own persons (Neh. 9:36–37). They could not aspire to ownership of the very land in which they had now been permitted to live. This situation was one that was destined to continue, and of which the first readers of these books were themselves aware in their own time. But in another sense they knew that ultimate power belonged to their God, who had given those kings 'all the kingdoms of the earth' and had also commanded Cyrus to rebuild his temple in Jerusalem (Ezra 1:2–3).

The prayer of Ezra expresses thankfulness to this God for his mercy to his people despite the sins which had caused him to expel them from the land that he had chosen for them, in at last granting them a respite from their misery. Ezra (Ezra 9:8–9) puts this in positive, though modest, terms:

> But now for a brief moment favour has been shown by Yahweh our God, who has left us a remnant, and given us a foothold in his holy place, that he may lighten our eyes and grant us a little respite in our slavery. For we are slaves; yet our God has not forsaken us in our slavery, but has extended to us his steadfast love before the kings of Persia, to give us new life to set up the house of our God, to repair its ruins, and to give us a wall in Judah and Jerusalem.

Before the exile the people of Judah had been ruled by their kings, successors in a dynasty that Yahweh had ordained. Now in exile they again had their leaders, whom also Yahweh had approved through influencing the hearts of the Persian kings. For the author of Ezra and Nehemiah, Sheshbazzar, Zerubbabel, Ezra and Nehemiah were the leaders who under God achieved the three things that were necessary for the rehabilitation of a disillusioned people: the rebuilding of the temple, the inauguration of the Law, and the rebuilding of the walls of Jerusalem. Although their power was challenged from within the community as well as from without, they had been accepted as rulers by the people, had given commands and had been obeyed. The attitude of the Persian kings was benevolent and they are not represented as interfering in Jewish affairs. Judah and Jerusalem were left free to live their own lives, despite the feeling that they were mere slaves. The author clearly intended to represent, first Sheshbazzar, who had been the leader of the first return, and then Ezra and Nehemiah as men of power. His thought ran along the following lines: God ruled the world including the kings of Persia; the Persian kings in turn held power over the lives of the Jews; but political power was put into the hands of Ezra and Nehemiah by God, and by the Persian kings acting under God's direction.

Sustenance and Wealth

The wealth in which the author of Ezra and Nehemiah seems to have been mainly interested as contributing to the good life for the Jewish people consisted of donations made first for the construction and then for the equipment and regular worship of the temple in Jerusalem. Successive Persian kings contributed largely to this cause (Ezra 1:4–11; 7:15–20; Neh. 2:8). The authors depict a community gathered round the temple and concerned with its affairs that could reasonably be called a temple state.

The two books do, however, provide some information about economic conditions among the returned exiles, some of which is allusive rather than descriptive. There were clearly considerable differences of wealth. According to Ezra 2:68–69 some – though not all! – of the 'heads of families' who had arrived with the first group of returned exiles were able immediately on arrival at the site of the former temple to make extraordinary large donations, presumably out of wealth acquired in exile, of 61,000 darics of gold and 5,000 minas of silver for the building fund. Yet when Nehemiah arrived to find the city in dire straits there was clearly no money available (or offered) to repair the walls or provide the city with new gates. But when he had carried out his programme of reforms and set the province on a new footing there were sufficient if not abundant stocks of agricultural products from the countryside or purchased from foreign traders (Neh. 13:12–18). Nehemiah must himself have been a man of great personal wealth, since as governor he entertained on a grand scale, though he did not tax the people to provide for this but paid for it out of his private resources (Neh. 5:14–18).

There are no specific references to the poor in Ezra and Nehemiah. But Neh. 5:1–13 shows that there were serious inequalities of wealth within the community. Verse 3 refers to a famine which caused widespread shortages of food for some, while others seized the opportunity to make greater profits. The common people (*hā'ām*), both men and their wives, raised a great outcry about their plight and against the profiteers. The famine had caused inflated prices of corn, and these people had been forced to mortgage their farms and their houses in order to buy enough to keep themselves alive or simply to pay the taxes imposed by the Persian authorities, and in some cases even to sell their children as slaves. Their case was brought to the notice of Nehemiah, who appears to have been unaware of what was happening; but in his memoirs he claims to have taken firm steps to remedy the situation, forbidding the charging of interest which when unpaid led to expropriation and forced slavery, and forcing those who had seized property to return it. In his memoirs Nehemiah claims that his orders were duly enforced. But that such practices had previously been carried on with impunity shows that the newly restored community was far from free from injustice by Jew against fellow-Jew, and that the good life was by no means enjoyed by all.

Family

Although no information is given in these books about the details of family life, genealogical descent was of paramount importance to the members of the Jewish community who had returned from exile or who were descended from those who had. They regarded themselves as a 'holy seed' which must not become 'mixed with the peoples of the lands' (Ezra 9:2) – a concern reminiscent of that of the patriarchs in Genesis – and in order to be accepted as a member of the 'people of Israel' it was essential that every person should be able to prove his descent. Genealogical records had been kept for this purpose, presumably dating back through many past generations (Ezra 2:62). Some individual genealogies are recorded: for example, at Ezra 7:1–5, in which Ezra himself is first mentioned, the author proves the purity of his own descent by citing a list of his ancestors through 16 generations beginning with Moses' brother Aaron and including David's priest Zadok, the progenitor of the 'sons of Zadok' who elsewhere, especially in Ezekiel, constituted the sole genuine priesthood of Israel during the post-exilic period.

Because of the importance of preserving purity of descent, lists are given of the names of families who had returned from exile in successive groups (Ezra 2:1–58; 8:1–14; Neh. 7:5–65; 12:1–26). The 'heads of families' (Ezra 1:5 and frequently) were responsible, with the priests and levites, for such initiatives. All had to prove their ancestry. It seems that lay persons who could not do so were accepted within the community although not granted full enjoyment of its rights and privileges, but priests were prevented from actively working as priests until a competent religious authority decided on their position by means of sacred divination (Ezra 2:59–63). Only those whose ancestry was definitely non-Jewish were expelled. This exclusiveness based on purity of descent is well illustrated in Ezra 4:1–4, where some groups of people, presumably co-residents in Judah, who identified themselves as of foreign origin, descendants of forced deportees from the Assyrian empire, approached Zerubbabel and the heads of houses and asked to be allowed to assist in the rebuilding of the temple. Their plea that they also worshipped the Jewish God and had offered sacrifice to him (presumably on the site of the ruined temple) ever since their arrival did not impress the Jews, who not only rebuffed them but repudiated their motives, referring to them as 'the *enemies* of Judah and Benjamin'. The Jewish religion as depicted in Ezra and Nehemiah was thus entirely opposed to proselytism and rejected any form of Yahwism other than their own because their practitioners did not belong to the 'holy seed' of the chosen people. The good life, which for the author was available to those who had the privilege of worshipping at the Jerusalem temple, was denied to all outsiders.

This principle naturally applied also to those who, though they were themselves accredited Jews, either married foreign (i.e., pagan) wives or permitted their children to do so. This question of 'mixed marriages' was a serious one and occupies an important place in the books of both Ezra and Nehemiah. Ezra on his arrival was appalled to learn that 'the people of Israel' (i.e., the laity) and the priests and levites had 'not separated themselves from the peoples of the lands with their abominations' and had involved themselves in such marriages (Ezra 9:1–2). Nehemiah faced a similar situation to that of Ezra and exacted promises from the members of the community that they would not henceforward permit such marriages (Neh. 10:30; but again in Neh. 13:23–27 it appears that the problem still remained at the very end of Nehemiah's career.

Law and Justice

Like all the peoples under Persian rule the community of returned Jewish exiles living in Jerusalem and the surrounding province was subject to the rule of the kings of Persia. According to the books of Ezra and Nehemiah this rule took the form of the king's personal decree. (Contrast the somewhat different situation described in the book of Esther, which refers to 'the laws of the Medes and Persians which cannot be altered' [Esth. 1:19] about which the king consulted his legal experts [Esth. 1:13–19].) In Ezra and Nehemiah every decision is attributed to the king, who issued commands (dāt) and decrees (tĕ'ēm), the first found in both the Hebrew and the Aramaic portions of Ezra, the second an Aramaic word. The Jewish community in Jerusalem indeed owed its very existence to a decision by Cyrus to allow the exiles to return to Jerusalem to rebuild the temple; it was Artaxerxes who, on listening to the objections of the 'peoples of the lands' and their hired officials, decreed that the building work should cease (Ezra 4:24), and Darius who on the discovery of the earlier decree of Cyrus ordered that it should be resumed (Ezra 6:12). It was again Artaxerxes who commissioned Ezra and gave him special powers concerning the temple services and the general supervision of the province (Ezra 7), and who gave

Nehemiah his commission to rebuild the city walls (Neh. 2:1–8) and who appointed him governor (Neh. 5:14).

But the law with which the two books are mainly concerned is the law of Moses, sometimes called 'the book of the law of Moses' (Ezra 6:18; Neh. 8:18), the law of Yahweh (Ezra 7:10), or simply 'the law' (Ezra 10:3; Neh. 10:35; 12:44). This was the law which, especially under the guidance of Ezra and Nehemiah, governed the affairs of the Jerusalem community. Thus Ezra, who had 'set his heart to study the law of Yahweh and to do it, and to teach his statutes and ordinances to Israel' (Ezra 7:10), was an expert, a 'scribe skilled in the law of Moses' (7:6), and was recognized by King Artaxerxes himself as 'Ezra the priest and scribe, a scribe versed in questions concerning the commandments and statutes of Yahweh which are laid on Israel' (7:11). His commission from the king was a double one: to enforce 'the law of your God and the law of the king' (7:26) disobedience to which was to be punished by death, confiscation of goods or banishment (7:26). The Persian kings left the conduct of the daily affairs of the community in the hands of Ezra and Nehemiah the governor and did not interfere in this, though the imperial taxes had to be paid.

The aspects of the law of Moses specifically attested in these books as having been applied and enforced do not concern civil justice or moral or criminal behaviour. They are of two kinds only: the organization of worship in the temple and of the livelihood of the priests; and the avoidance of 'contamination' with foreigners. With regard to the first of these, Zerubbabel and Jeshua on their arrival, even before the rebuilding of the temple had begun, set the altar on its foundations and organized the sacrificial system and that of the religious feasts (Ezra 3:1–7); and when the temple was completed and had been dedicated the people organized the divisions of priests and levites who were to officiate in it (Ezra 6:18). Later Ezra taught the people the law by means of public readings (Neh. 8). It was found there that mixed marriages were forbidden, and that Ammonites and Moabites were to be excluded from the 'assembly of God' (Neh. 13:1); and it was as a result of hearing the law that the people decided to separate themselves entirely from all who were of mixed descent (Neh. 13:3). Finally Nehemiah and others obligated themselves to ensure the regular bringing of the first-fruits of the products of the land to the priests and regularity in the payment of tithes (Neh. 10:35–37; cf. 12:44). All these things were believed to be the essential conditions under which the good life could be lived.

In the book of Nehemiah there are a number of passages from Nehemiah's memoirs recording his other activities in his capacity of governor. But they do not come within the category of laws; no new laws were promulgated, and these incidents are mainly administrative decisions made *ad hoc*. They include a note of the governor's abstention from imposing exactions on the people in order to supply food for his household (5:14–19); his reaction to the slander that had been put about that he was intending to rebel and make himself king (6:5–9); his orders to ensure the security of the city by closing and barring the gates at night (7:1–3); the holding of a census (7:5–73); the repopulation of the city through the casting of lots (11:1); the expulsion of the Ammonite Tobias from the room in the temple that he had been permitted to use during Nehemiah's absence from Jerusalem (13:4–9); orders about keeping the sabbath and the sanctions against foreign traders (13:15–21); and the expulsion of a priest who had married the daughter of the Samaritan Sanballat (13:28–29).

One of Nehemiah's actions testifies to a concern for equity, and should perhaps be reckoned as legislation: this is his action putting an end to exploitation of the rich by the poor (5:1–13), which was presumably intended to be binding for the future. Taken together with 5:14–18 this incident was intended by the author to indicate the just character of Nehemiah's rule, justifying his admittedly complacent prayer in 5:19: 'Remember for my good, O my God, all that I have done for this people.'

Wisdom

Although he employs the word 'wisdom' only once, there can be no doubt that the author of Ezra and Nehemiah conveys the impression that it was due to the abilities as well as the piety of their leaders that the Jewish exiles whom the kings of Persia permitted to return to Judah were transformed into a well-ordered and responsible community. But their wisdom was no mere human wisdom: it was the wisdom that comes from God, a fact that was understood even by Artaxerxes in the decree in which he commissioned Ezra to 'appoint magistrates and judges to judge all the people in the province Beyond the River who know the laws of your God' and also 'to teach those who do not know them' 'according to the divine wisdom that you possess' (*kĕhokmat 'ĕlāhāk dî-bîdāk*) (Ezra 7:25).

Ezra 7, which may be regarded as a paradigm for both books, emphasizes Ezra's personal qualifications, all of which come under the heading of the Old Testament concept of God-given wisdom. He was a scribe and a scholar who was learned in the law (v. 11), and he was also a teacher of his people (v. 10) as well as a man to whom the king was able to give virtually unlimited powers within the province of Beyond the River. But it is perhaps especially in the activities of Nehemiah that we learn of a man who, while no less pious (e.g. Neh. 1:11), displayed his wisdom both in his powers of persuasion in obtaining the king's permission to send him on his mission (Neh. 2:1–8) and in his period of administration as governor of the Jerusalem community, when he successfully overcame the various and difficult problems that he had to face, confident that God would give him success (e.g. Neh. 1:11; 2:20; 4:9, 20).

Joy

As Ezra and Nehemiah contain no information about the private lives of individuals, the emotions of individuals and families go unrecorded. The instances of joy and rejoicing that are recorded are, as in Chronicles, exclusively corporate: the whole community rejoice together on specific solemn occasions, all of which are connected with the welfare of the city as a whole, and particularly with the temple and its worship, the keeping of religious feasts and the public reading of the law of Moses. The people unanimously rejoice when the foundations of the temple are laid (Ezra 3:11–13) and at its dedication (Ezra 6:22), at the dedication of the walls of the city (Neh. 12:43), on hearing the public reading of the law (Neh. 8:10–12) and at the newly revived celebration of the Feast of Booths (Neh. 8:17).

The allusions to sadness are rather more varied, and include some more personal references. When the foundations of the temple were laid it is recorded that the shouts of joy were mingled with the weeping of those who were old enough to remember the former temple (Ezra 3:12–13); Ezra wept and mourned on learning of the mixed marriages (Ezra 9:3; 10:1–6), and the people wept bitterly when they realized the seriousness of their sin (Ezra 10:1). Nehemiah in Persia wept on learning of the desolate state of Jerusalem (Neh. 1:4), and his sorrow was noticed by the king (Neh. 2:1–3). On hearing the reading of the law the people wept (Neh. 8:9), though they were told to rejoice (Neh. 8:10–12).

It might seem to be the view of the author that the good life for the Jewish community in Jerusalem was a matter of conformity by the people to the will of God as expressed in the correct worship in the temple, in religious and ethnic purity and in obedience to their leaders whom God had appointed to build up the security of the city whose centre was the temple. On the other hand, all those who opposed this strict way of life – the 'adversaries' of Ezra 4:1–3, those who had contaminated the purity of God's community, Nehemiah's opponents etc. – were to be excluded from participation in that good life.

God and the Good Life

Ezra's two lengthy prayers (Ezra 9:6–15; Neh. 9:6–37) stand out from the rest of these books, yet they are of the first importance in that they reveal a doctrine of God that is far richer and more comprehensive than may otherwise seem to be implied by the other chapters. Here Ezra expounds a theology according to which God's concern for the good life of his people was not just a matter of their maintaining

ethnic purity, correct worship and strict obedience to the
law. The two prayers resemble one another in important
respects. They both confess the sins and acknowledge the
guilt of the Israelite people in the past and of the Jerusalem
community in the present. They both confess that God dealt
justly with them in the past in expelling them from their land
and in not destroying them completely as they deserved,
but also stress that he has not restored the good life that
they had previously enjoyed. But the two prayers differ
considerably in other ways. Whereas Ezra 9:6–15 concentrates on one issue – the mixed marriages that Ezra has just
discovered and which appalled him because God had strictly
forbidden that practice – and leaves it to God to pardon
them once again if he wills to do so, his prayer in Neh. 9:6–
37 is oriented towards a hope for the future, conditional on
obedience to the law that has just been read in public and
which the whole people now solemnly undertake to obey
(Neh. 9:38; 10:28–31).

The prayer in Neh. 9:6–37 expounds a broader theology
in which, although the particular question of the mixed
marriages remains a crucial one, God's dealings with his
people are presented in detail in a way which transcends a
limited concern with the minutiae of temple, worship and
the law which might otherwise seem to be the sole concern
of these books. Ezra here begins with a confession of
Yahweh as the creator of heaven and earth who gives life
not only to his own people but to all his creatures. He refers
to the giving of the law on Mount Sinai (vv. 13–14), but,
drawing not only on the laws of the Pentateuch but also on
its narratives, sets that event in a historical context. The call
of Abraham and the covenant in which God promised the
land of Canaan to his descendants, the exodus from Egypt
and the miracle of the crossing of the Sea, God's guidance of
the people through the wilderness, the fulfilment of the
promise in the conquest of the land, the prophetic warnings
against rebellion and the persistent disobedience of the
people, and their final expulsion from the land are all
described; and the prayer ends with an acknowledgement of
God's mercy in the present, coupled with an implied plea for
an extension of that mercy towards a people whom God still

allows to be enslaved by a foreign conqueror. The reader is thus presented with both a reminder of the breadth and continuity of the gift of the good life by an all-powerful God in the past and an explanation of the unsatisfactory situation of the present in which the good life is by no means completely enjoyed, and with a hope of an alleviation of that situation in the future.

Summary

The books of Ezra and Nehemiah describe the life of the community of Jews who had returned to live in Jerusalem and the immediately surrounding countryside under the rule of the Persian kings. These were aware that their attempts to live the good life were subject to severe limitations – that because of the past sins which had caused expulsion of the people from the land of the promise they were no longer its owners, and that their very existence as a community was due to the mercy of God, who had granted them the good will of the kings of Persia. However, they were fortunate in having their own excellent leaders, who succeeded in building up the community and securing its physical safety, with the result that with the completion of the work of Nehemiah important *elements* of the good life had been made possible. These, however, were available only to Jews of pure descent who observed the law of Moses. Life was centred on the law and on the correct worship offered in the newly restored temple of Yahweh. Nehemiah was concerned to see that individual injustices were corrected, but inequalities of wealth within the community remained. No details are given of the private lives of members of the community; but they all found their principal source of joy in participation in their worship together.

10
Esther

The book of Esther recounts events at the court of the
Persian king Ahasuerus at the time when Persia dominated
large parts of the ancient Near East. The Jewish people at
that time were scattered throughout the empire, and many
were living in Persia itself. Among these were Mordecai and
his young and beautiful cousin Esther whom he had adopted
as his own daughter (2:5–7). The author makes it clear that
he is writing some time after the events that he describes
(1:1). Whenever the book was written, its portrayal of Jews
living under Persian rule will have held great interest for
Jewish readers at any time afterwards, since foreign rule was
to be their lot for several more centuries, and many of them
had experienced the conditions of living in strange lands.

Place and Security

The place where the story is set is Susa, the capital of the
empire, where Ahasuerus has his palace. But the Jewish population both of the capital and of the other provinces of the
empire enjoy no security: they depend utterly on the whim
of the emperor, whose power is absolute. Moreover
Ahasuerus is a weak-minded and capricious monarch, easily
persuaded to change his mind even on matters which
involve the very lives of his subjects. Having been induced
by the wicked Haman, his vizier, whom the Jew Mordecai
has offended, to issue a decree condemning all the Jews to
death, he is then induced at the request of Esther, his queen,
to revoke the decree and instead to permit the Jews to
destroy their enemies. The book thus ends with the triumph
of the Jews, with Mordecai appointed to succeed the disgraced and executed Haman as vizier of the kingdom. It
shows how it is possible for a Jew to achieve high rank as a
foreigner living in a great empire (cf. Joseph, Gen. 37–50,
and Daniel, Daniel 1–6); but it also reflects the dangers faced

by the Jewish people when it has to deal with a hostile ruler and a hostile local population.

Power, Wisdom and Courage

The interplay of power, wisdom and courage are the major topics of the book. It demonstrates how even absolute political power can be turned to the advantage of those who are ostensibly entirely without power. It is admittedly by strokes of good fortune that the Jewess Esther rises from obscurity to become queen of Persia, first through the deposition of the former queen Vashti (1:5–20) and secondly through the unexpected chance of her infatuating the king by her beauty (2:2–17). But from that moment she makes skilful use of her newly acquired power to frustrate the king's insane design against her fellow-Jews.

The chapters that follow are a fascinating account of the interplay of intrigues in the course of which Ahasuerus, despite his apparent supreme power, is revealed as no more than a puppet, outwitted by Esther and Mordecai. Haman, who has foolishly boasted of his wealth and power, is the loser; Mordecai is raised from obscurity to the status of 'the man whom the king wishes to honour' (6:11) and then to the position of vizier 'next to the king' (10:3); Esther continues to the end of the story to enjoy her position of power.

Esther, advised by her cousin, first shows her wisdom in concealing her Jewishness from the king (2:10, 20); and then, after making sure of his favour (8:4), displays her courage, making – at great risk to herself – and obtaining her request that he should annul and reverse his earlier decree against the Jews (8:7–8). Meanwhile Haman has unwisely and arrogantly boasted of his wealth, power and intimacy with the king (5:10–12), but is then brought to disgrace and death by means of Esther's cunning invitation to him to dine in private with her and the king (5:2–8; 7:1–10). Mordecai's advancement is due not to his wisdom but to his loyalty in having earlier warned the king of a conspiracy to assassinate him; but he also acts with wisdom in persuading Esther to make a dangerous request to him (4:13–14). So

Esther, enjoying herself the 'good life' of luxury which she has obtained by chance good fortune, turned this to good account by saving the lives of her fellow-countrymen.

Law and Justice

Two of the aspects of the good life which appear in many Old Testament books – health, old age, and family life – are not features of the book of Esther, except in so far as the family relationship between Esther and her cousin and Esther's concern for the welfare and solidarity of the Jewish people can be counted as 'family life'. But there are clear allusions to law and justice, or at least to what passed as such in Persia. In depicting the absolute rule of the Persian monarch the author has not concealed his distaste and contempt. In fact Ahasuerus is fundamentally a comic character – a man who cannot enforce obedience even within his own family and has actually to make a decree enforceable throughout the empire that all wives must obey their husbands (1:13–22). Nevertheless, he is able to divorce and depose his disobedient queen Vashti at will (1:19), and it is clear that Esther's position also depends entirely on his good will (4:11; 5:2; 8:4). In the political sphere Ahasuerus, though the author may have made him a cari-cature of a capricious monarch, is represented as suspicious, cruel and dangerous. His decrees, though he pretends to consult his obsequious legal experts (1:13–19), have the force of law which, it is claimed, cannot be altered (1:19), but in fact he simply assumes the power to annul them whenever it suits him (8:8–14). They are enforceable throughout the empire. Despite his legal experts whom he summons to 'advise' him, there is no mention in the book of the existence of lawcourts or any other legal institutions. The king's will is supreme. This is not conducive to the good life for his Jewish subjects, or, it may be presumed, for the Persian people themselves. However, thanks to Esther's courage and wisdom the book concludes with a joyous celebration by the Jews of their deliverance from death and the command that they should for ever afterwards celebrate the feast of Purim in commemoration of it (9:26–32).

Joy

In its happy conclusion Esther is a joyous book. The Jews celebrate their escape from the terrible fate that had been prepared for them. But the book is also a lesson that the good life cannot be taken for granted. Danger and insecurity are notes that are sounded up to the very end. What the Jews celebrate is a deliverance from peril at a particular moment in history, not a guarantee that they will never again be free from trouble. Even Esther herself, living though she did in unparalleled luxury, was denied the enjoyment of the good life up until her final triumph, having been constantly tormented by doubts and the sense of danger. The book was intended to encourage its Jewish readers to believe that there were opportunities for them to prosper and live a peaceful existence under foreign rule, but it also taught them that the good life would continue to be precarious and dependent on the good will of their rulers.

God

The book of Esther is almost unique among the books of the Old Testament in that it contains no reference to God. The Jews do not pray to him in their distress or thank him for their deliverance (we may contrast especially the book of Ruth). Although it may be supposed that the Jews living within the empire would be worshippers of Yahweh in contrast to the pagan Persians, the author did not seize the opportunity to present their situation in religious terms; references to Persian religion are equally absent from the book. As for the motivations of the characters, they all act according to what they perceive to be to their advantage without any declared awareness of a higher spiritual authority. The Jews are presented as a large ethnic community, not as a body of people united by a common religious faith. They have enemies (9:1, 5, 16, 22) of whom Haman is the chief (3:10; 7:6), but there is no suggestion that they were hated for their religion. The tone of the book may be said to be nationalistic rather than confessional. When they

are told of the decree against them the Jews fast and weep
(4:3), and when they learn of its annulment they rejoice and
celebrate with feasting (9:17–23); but it is not stated that
either their fasting or their rejoicing has the character of
religious observance. Even the feast of Purim established in
commemoration of their deliverance is not given a religious
character.

It is not easy to discern either the reason for this surprising omission or how the book would have been received
by its first readers. But it is not difficult to imagine that it
would have had great popular appeal to readers dispersed
throughout a foreign empire, whose situation was not entirely dissimilar from that depicted in the book. Moreover,
the annual feast of Purim with which the book is closely
associated was evidently from the first a popular, rather
secular celebration. The motif of the Jews' slaughter of their
enemies at the close of the book is a frequent one in the Old
Testament (compare, e.g., Deuteronomy, Joshua and Judges),
and would not necessarily have shocked the readers'
sensibilities.

There is one sentence which the first readers of the book
may have interpreted as a reference to God. In 4:14 Mordecai,
urging Esther to pluck up her courage and intercede with the
king on behalf of her fellow-Jews, warns her: 'If you keep
silence at such a time as this, relief and deliverance will
appear *from another place*, but you and your father's family
will perish.' If this interpretation was given to these words
by its first readers, it might have been possible for them to
interpret other passages such as the references to the Jews'
fasting and rejoicing in a religious sense; but it remains
difficult to understand why the allusion to God's saving
action should be couched in such obscure language.

A few other features of the book may reflect Jewish
customs, though these also are not specifically connected
with their religious beliefs or practices. They include
Mordecai's care and nurture of Esther his young cousin
(2:7); the loyalty of both Mordecai and Esther – the former's
towards the king (6:1–3), the latter's towards her fellow-
Jews; mourning customs and fasting (4:3, 16); Esther's self-
sacrifice; the Jews' abstention from taking plunder (9:10, 15,

16; cf. Gen. 14:21–24); and the giving of gifts to the poor
during a feast. It may be assumed that 8:17 refers to
proselytism, which was not necessarily insincere.

Summary

The book of Esther ends on a triumphalist note. It tells how
on one occasion those Jews who were scattered throughout
the Persian empire came to enjoy the good life, triumphing
over their enemies through the action of particular individuals who had attained positions of power at the Persian
court, and commemorated their triumph by instituting a new
joyous annual festival. But that is not the whole story. The
author also presents a very different picture of the perilous
circumstances suffered by Jews under the rule of their
foreign masters. They had no security even of life itself but
were subject to hostile and murderous attacks. Only by a
fortuitous combination of courage and wisdom shown by
persons raised up 'for such a time' (4:14) were they enabled
to survive and flourish. They were powerless against the
arbitrary whims of monarchs who regarded neither law nor
justice.

There is no doubt that it was the intention of the author
to give hope to others who lived their lives under comparable circumstances. He showed them that it was possible
for Jews to prosper and even attain to positions of influence
in a foreign empire. But was it also his intention to warn his
readers of the precarious circumstances and dangers of their
situation? The triumphant end of the book makes it difficult
for us to be certain of this. But we may well suppose that
this story of a pogrom planned and only narrowly averted,
even though it is presented in highly coloured detail, will
have struck a familiar note to Jewish readers powerless under
foreign rule, and will have reminded them that the good life
which they themselves might be enjoying in their present
circumstances was a precarious one which could only be
assured if and when relief came 'from another place', that is,
from a power beyond themselves.

11
Job

The book of Job begins (1:1–5) and ends (42:10–17) with a narrative about a man who epitomized the good life. He was a great landowner, and so possessed an apparently inviolable *security*. He was the possessor of unimaginable *wealth* and possessed a great household of slaves, and this gave him great *power*: he was 'the greatest of all the people of the east'. He was blessed with a large and apparently successful *family*. But it is also significant that before describing this ideal state of affairs the author of the narrative begins, in his very first sentence, by stating that this man, Job, was also an exceptionally righteous man and that he 'feared God' and 'shunned wrongdoing'. In 1:5 the author gives an example of the genuineness of his piety. He does not explicitly state that Job's enjoyment of a good life was the *consequence* of his goodness and piety; but he implies that this was so. He implies also that he deserved his good fortune.

In the latter part of the Prologue (1:6–2:10) in which, quite contrary to the reader's expectation, Job is stripped of his wealth, his social prestige and even his health through the action of the Satan but with God's approval, the genuineness of his piety is confirmed. By means of a severe testing it is demonstrated that his devotion is independent of his enjoyment of God's gifts. The Satan, who has sneeringly asked 'Does Job serve God for nothing?' is proved wrong. These incidents were no doubt intended to raise questions in the readers' minds about the predictability of God and the relationship between human deserts and their actual consequences, but they do not alter the writer's view that the good life is a gift from God, for this is reinforced in the final section of the book (42:10–17), when God *restored* Job's fortunes. There Job receives from God 'twice as much as he had before' (v. 10): a restored family life, a new family of children and greater wealth. In addition he receives new gifts – an exceptionally long life enabling him to see his descendants to four generations – and he finally dies in peace, 'old and full of years'.

Although some aspects of the good life are missing from this picture – there is no explicit reference to health, law and justice, wisdom or pleasure – (the feasting, 1:4–5, is enjoyed by Job's children, not by Job himself), the reader would assume that for the author it represents not perhaps the norm, in view of Job's enormous wealth, but the ideal of the good life. This is suggested also by the structure of the book, in which these passages form the framework to the whole. The epilogue constitutes a 'happy ending'. Whatever may be the meaning of the central part of the book, the work is structured on the simple lines of the familiar folktale, in which the hero, after an initial setback and severe trials, finally triumphs and achieves an even greater wealth and happiness than he had had before.

This conclusion appears to be reinforced by some other parts of the book, especially by chapter 29, where the now impoverished and humiliated Job nostalgically (v. 2) describes his former state in greater detail. There he first refers to the fact that *God* had been his intimate companion and had blessed and watched over him and he had enjoyed *wealth* and prosperity (vv. 2–6). He then remembers his former position of *power* and authority in his city, when he was its acknowledged leader whose words were listened to in silence and with awe (vv. 7–10, 21–25). He particularly stresses his function as dispenser of *justice* (vv. 11–17), when he 'sat as chief' (ro'š) and was 'like a king' (v. 25) – a feature of the good life not specifically mentioned in the Prologue. He also refers indirectly to his *enjoyment* of his position and admits that he had assumed that he would never be deprived of it (vv. 18–20). In chapter 31 he defends his record for justice (vv. 13–15, 21) despite his wealth (vv. 24–25).

Job evidently believes that he has lost everything that makes life worth living, and desires to die (chapter 3). However it is clear that Job has in fact *not* been wholly deprived of all essential elements of the good life. He has *friends*, who have travelled long distances to comfort him (2:11–13); and he still has a house, a wife, a *family* and servants (19:16–19), even though he complains that in his

present state he has lost their respect and has become
repulsive to them. He has not lost the *security* of his home:
he has not suffered the fate of those who have been driven
from their homes and from society (18:14–15, 18, 24:4–8;
10; 30:5-8). Nor has he lost his life and descended to Sheol
from where there is no return (7:10; 16:22).

Which of the features of the good life, then, has Job
actually lost? He has admittedly suffered the loss of his vast
estates (1:13–19) which are described in 1:11 as 'all that he
possesses'; but that does not mean that he became destitute.
Nowhere does he speak of himself as materially deprived or
hungry. He complains principally of losing his health and his
position of power and social prestige. Even with regard to
these, however, the reader needs to make allowance for
poetical hyperbole; and the ancient reader of poetry as well
as the modern one would have recognized his mode of
expression for the over-dramatization that it obviously is. It
is also recorded (1:19) that Job has lost his sons, but he
makes no complaint about this, and one can only conclude
from 42:13–15 which records that he was provided with a
new family that that loss was not a main consideration for
the author.

In fact, it becomes clear that the good life as presented in
the book, especially in Job's speeches, is somewhat *different*
from that of the other books that we have considered, where
it consisted mainly of material things such as wealth,
security and family. But it is the loss of his former personal
relationship with God that is Job's chief lament. This takes
precedence over everything else, even over the loss of health
and social position. However, the exact nature of his
complaint against God is difficult to identify. His complaint
is expressed either in very vague terms or in extravagant
metaphors which are intended to reflect the intensity of his
fears and his bewilderment. God has torn him in his wrath
and gnashed his teeth at him (16:9), slashed open his kidneys
(16:13), closed his net round him (19:6), walled up his path
(19:8), taken the crown from his head (19:9), attacked him
with his troops (19:12). These are simply dramatic ways of
saying that God, who had been his friend (29:4) has now
suddenly become his enemy (13:24; 33:10). It was not the

sudden loss of his wealth that had driven him to this conclusion. The impression given to the reader who perceives the
metaphorical character of so many of Job's complaints is that
the root of the matter is largely psychological: for Job, the
good life had consisted not in his wealth but in his former
relationship with God, and it is that that he feels has been
taken from him and has driven him to such despair. The
restoration of his material prosperity at the end of the book is
not primarily to be seen as that it is such things that in
themselves constitute the good life, but rather as an indication
that Job has at last recognized his error in attributing his
sufferings to God's hostility because he has failed to comprehend God's mysterious activity as ruler of the cosmos
(42:3).

Wisdom

Human *wisdom* is much discussed in the book of Job, where
the words 'wise' and 'wisdom' occur more frequently than in
any other Old Testament book except Proverbs and
Ecclesiastes. But here, in contrast to Proverbs, wisdom is
not put forward as the way to attain the good life. Job's
interlocutors (including Elihu) all claim in some sense to be
wise, and scorn Job's own equal claim to wisdom. But the
wisdom under discussion has little to do with the practical
wisdom of Proverbs. These discussions are conducted on a
broader basis: they are concerned with the nature of God,
especially on the right way to understand how God behaves
towards his human creatures. There is a consensus that all
wisdom comes from God; but it is a closely guarded secret,
not made available to human beings. The friends claim,
however, that there is a kind of wisdom that has come down
through the generations (Eliphaz, 15:7–11, 18); but this is
still not the wisdom that guarantees success in life: Job's
wealth and power (1:3) are not said to be due to his wisdom.
The divine wisdom – the wisdom that God manifested in
creating the world – cannot be acquired by human beings
(28:1–27), and if there is any human wisdom it consists in
the fear of God and the renunciation of evil (v. 28).

Summary

The book of Job, and especially the prose narrative and Job's account of his life in chapters 29 and 31, presents Job as a great landowner, possessing security, wealth, power, and a large family, and emphasizes his goodness. He declares that he dispensed justice in the community in which he sat as a chief. Even after disaster struck he still possesses friends, a wife, a house, family and servants. His primary loss is his relationship with God, who now appears to him as an enemy rather than a friend. For Job the good life consisted not in his wealth but in his friendship with God. Wisdom, frequently mentioned in the book, is not the practical wisdom found in Proverbs, but is the wisdom that God alone possesses. The good life as presented in the book of Job, therefore, is somewhat different from that in the other books of the Old Testament.

12
Psalms

Of all the books of the Old Testament it is probably the Psalter that opens the largest window on how the ancient Israelites viewed the good life and the extent to which they believed that they had attained it or that it was within their grasp. This is partly due to the prodigious variety of its contents. Between them the many psalmists give expression to an immense range of emotions, fears and hopes, joys and sorrows. It is this quality that has caused the Psalms to be constantly used through the ages and up to the present time as a vehicle whereby believers, both Jewish and Christian, are still able to give expression to their faith in its many aspects both individually and corporately.

A further aspect of the value of the Psalter for our present purpose is that the majority of the Psalms are the prayers of individual worshippers. Many of the books that we have considered so far, though they are extremely valuable in their portrayal of the good life in Israel, have an impersonal quality – they are mainly narratives which describe the events of the past from the standpoint of third persons, that is, their authors, who are not themselves involved in those events. The laws given through Moses have the same impersonal quality. The majority of the Psalms are the prayers of individuals in which the worshippers express their own thoughts: they are personal testimonies of persons who are actually themselves experiencing what they describe. There is an actuality about the Psalms which is unique.

Place and Security

In the Psalter the place *par excellence* to which the psalmists direct their thoughts is the temple on Mount Zion. No less than 52 of the 150 psalms refer to this temple. Various phrases are employed to refer to it such as 'his (Yahweh's) holy hill', 'the house of Yahweh', 'his holy temple'; but it is most frequently known by the name 'Zion'. This word occurs 38 times in the book; and there are in addition numerous references to sacrifices and ceremonies performed in the temple or its precincts. Often the psalmist appears to be living near, or in reach of, the temple; in other psalms the same strong attachment to the temple is attested by persons who are living far away from it, sometimes in forced exile, but who express their longing to visit it and to participate in its worship, or who see it as Yahweh's dwelling-place from which they hope that Yahweh will emerge to bring about the restoration of the defeated nation. A few psalms refer to the fact that it has been destroyed, but long for it to be rebuilt (Pss. 69:36; 74:3–7; 79:1–7). Others express the wish to travel there so that they may live there all their lives (Pss. 23:6, 27:44; cf. 84:4). A characteristic expression used of it is 'I love the house in which you dwell' (Ps. 26:8). References in comparable terms to the land in the Psalter are relatively few (Pss. 37:3, 22, 29, 34; 85:1, 9, 12; 101:6; 106:24; 135:12; 136:21).

For these psalmists the Zion temple was essential for the good life. It was for this reason that such praise and even adoration are lavished on it (Pss. 9:11; 11:4; 46:4; 76:2). It was the centre from which Yahweh was believed to exercise his invincible power over the world, give strength and power to his people, and commission Israel's kings (Ps. 110:2). From there he ensured the security and peaceful existence of Jerusalem, the city in which the temple lay (Ps. 122) and which was the source of national blessing and prosperity. Individuals in distress also addressed their petitions to Yahweh as the one who dwelt in the temple, and it was believed that it was from there that he answered their prayers (Pss. 18:6; 20:2; 28:2) and banished their fears.

A closely related belief was that the king, as Yahweh's vicegerent, was able to ensure the good life for the nation: military success providing national security, just rule, and the fertility of the crops which was the source of prosperity and well-being for all (Pss. 18, especially v. 50; 20:6, 9; 21:1–7; 61:6–7; 72). The situation described in Ps. 89, however, is one in which this has not occurred. It is one of military defeat; and the writer accuses Yahweh of breaking the covenant that he had made with David to establish his dynasty for ever, and to give the nation lasting victory over its enemies. But now the king (of Judah) has been humiliated and deprived of his throne, and the psalmist fears that God's wrath has fallen on the nation (v. 46). This psalm, no less than those that speak of the blessings conferred on the people by their possession of a legitimate king protected by a divine promise, provides further evidence of that belief which is now seemingly called into question.

The numerous individual psalms of complaint in which the psalmist speaks to himself in the first person singular are evidence of personal insecurity. The great majority of them complain of personal enemies who in various ways delight in making personal attacks, oral or physical, on the psalmist, who in some cases has fallen ill as a consequence or even believes that he is at death's door. These 'enemies' are never identified, and these psalms therefore shed no light on the nature of the social and personal antagonisms in question. But it is noteworthy that in most cases the psalmist ends on a note of confidence that Yahweh will at last come to his rescue. A few such psalms, however, appear to accuse Yahweh of being responsible for the psalmist's plight (e.g. Ps. 89). The author of Ps. 51 on the other hand confesses that his troubles are due to his sin. Ps. 120 is a cry of distress from an individual Israelite obliged for some reason to live far from his country. It is possible that a considerable number of the Psalms were composed by persons in similar situations.

These psalms of lamentation in which the psalmist speaks for the whole people of Israel ('we') provide clearer information about Israel's concern for its secure possession of its land than do the purely individual lamentations. Although they remain on the national level, it is legitimate to conclude that the disastrous situations of which they speak would have severely affected the ordinary citizens and made the living of the good life precarious if not impossible. These psalms are far less numerous than the individual lamentations and number about a dozen. The nature and historical causes of the disasters that have afflicted the nation are not always as clearly reflected as in the books of Samuel and

Kings, but generally it appears that they are the consequence of invasions by foreign enemies and/or foreign rule. They all appeal to God to exert himself and demonstrate his power by saving them from their enemies and/or restoring the independent life of the nation.

In Pss. 10 and 12 the identity of the enemies is left vague. These resemble some of the individual lamentations in that they speak in general terms of 'the wicked'; and it is probable that these are fellow-Israelites rather than foreign armies. They are said to prey especially on the poor, revealing a society in which there are no effective leaders to redress the wrongs of individuals. Ps. 14 also refers to persons who 'devour my people', and appeals to Yahweh to 'deliver Israel' and restore the fortunes of his people (v. 7). But Pss. 44:9–26; 60:1–3, 10–12; 80 and 83 speak of Israel's defeat by foreign enemies whose intention is to destroy the very existence of the nation; and Pss. 74 and 79 lament the destruction of the temple and the city of Jerusalem. Ps. 85 attributes the present situation to Yahweh's anger (vv. 4–5). It refers to an earlier time when Yahweh had shown favour to his land and pardoned the people's sin (vv. 1–3) and now implores him to do so again (vv. 4–7). The present situation to which the psalm refers appears to be one in which the land no longer produces a sufficiency of crops and there is a lack of social harmony (vv. 8–13). Finally one psalm (137) comes from a specific historical situation: it is sung by a group of Judaean exiles in Babylonia after the fall of Jerusalem. It testifies to their passionate love of their distant homeland and their consequent state of desolation.

These psalms reflecting personal or national misery and insecurity are, however, matched by a mass of psalms of praise and thanksgiving, again both personal and corporate, which express a radiant confidence in God's care for his people. These contrasting moods illustrate the very broad scope of the Psalter, reflecting many different individual and personal situations. Ps. 147, which ends with a triumphant boast that Yahweh 'has not dealt thus with any other nation' (v. 20) is representative of a situation of well-being.

A key term in the Psalter is the verb 'to trust' (*bāṭaḥ*). This term, with Yahweh/God as its object, occurs in no less than

26 psalms. It is used in a variety of contexts, ranging from that of the individual who is experiencing suffering but still manages to trust Yahweh to bring him help (e.g. Ps. 13:5) to that of the psalmist who concludes his psalm of praise on behalf of the nation with the triumphant statement that 'Our heart is glad in him because we trust in his holy name' (Ps. 33:21). Another psalmist oppressed by his enemies gives expression to the meaning for him of his confidence in a significant statement of his faith: 'In God I trust; I am not afraid; what can flesh do to me?' (56:4). A similar confession, though the verb to trust does not occur in it, is that of the psalmist of Ps. 73, who exclaims, 'Whom have I in heaven but you? There is nothing on earth that I desire other than you' (v. 25).

A comparatively small number of psalms refer specifically to the *land*. The immense importance of the privilege of living in the land in which God has placed his people is a major theme of Ps. 37, which refers to this no less than six times in a kind of refrain (vv. 3, 9, 11, 22, 29, 34), each time in similar though not identical phrases. Verse 3 states that those who trust in Yahweh 'will live in the land and enjoy security.' Five verses speak of *inheriting* the land: this will be the good fortune of those who 'wait for Yahweh' (v. 9), of the meek (v. 11), of those whom Yahweh blesses (v. 22) and of the righteous (v. 29). According to v. 34 such good fortune will be for those who 'keep his way', that is, who obey his commandments. Similar ideas are found in Pss. 25:13, 101:6 and 112:2. That the land was a gift of God is affirmed in Pss. 44:2, 80:8–11, 85:1, 105:11, 135:12 and 136:21. It is Yahweh who gives fertility to the land (Pss. 72:16; 85:12).

Power

Only three possessors of power find mention in the Psalter: Yahweh (simply 'God' in some psalms), the human king, whose power is derived from God, and the 'enemies' (or the 'wicked') who attempt to destroy Israel and attack the individual psalmist.

It is affirmed throughout the Psalter that Yahweh alone is the true God and that he has supreme power over the whole universe. The psalms which make this affirmation are too many to enumerate here; some of his chief attributes may be mentioned. Most striking is the series of psalms (93, 95–99) which celebrate his kingship; Ps. 47 is another. It is frequently stated that it is he who created the world (e.g. Pss. 24; 33; 63) and who controls the phenomena of the weather permitting the existence of human life (e.g. Ps. 29), and giving fertility to the crops (e.g. Ps. 65). Yahweh gives victory to his people (e.g. Pss. 20; 21), though he can withhold this when he is angry, and he also cares for his individual worshippers: the author of Ps. 30 praises him for saving him from death and Ps. 116 for his mercy towards those who are afflicted; several psalms (e.g. 91) speak of his protection of those who take refuge in him. Some psalms make it clear that Yahweh has appointed the human king, and that the king's power is entirely derived from him. Ps. 2 speaks of the king as Yahweh's 'son' whom he has begotten, and recalls his promise that the king will be victorious over the nations. According to Ps. 110 God has given the king the place at his right hand, and through him has given his people the heritage of the nations. Ps. 21 affirms that he has given the king a long life and eternal blessings since the king puts his trust in him. Ps. 72 is a prayer to God that he will make the king a just ruler, governing peacefully and having dominion 'from sea to sea and from the River to the ends of the earth'. Ps. 44, however, laments that God has withdrawn his support and unexpectedly used his power to allow his people to be humiliated by its enemies.

The Psalms stress the uniqueness and the power of Yahweh, contrasting him with the useless gods of the other nations who, it is implied, are the subject of similar claims by their worshippers. This dismissal of the other gods (possibly including false gods worshipped by some Israelites) is expressed particularly in three psalms: 96; 97; 115. In two of these psalms those gods are described as *'ĕlîlîm*. This term is frequently rendered by 'idols'; but its more probable meaning is 'worthless' or 'powerless'. Ps. 96:5 quite simply claims that 'All the gods of the nations, are *'ĕlîlîm'*; it then interprets the real meaning of power in the next line: 'But it is Yahweh who made the heavens'. Ps. 97:7 speaks of the futility of those who worship such gods, specifying the form which this worship takes by adding the word *pesel*, 'idols': that is, this worship is directed towards wooden or other images of the gods in question. The psalmist asserts that 'All worshippers of a *pesel* will come to grief (*yēbōšû*) — those who take pride in *'ĕlîlîm*. In Ps. 115, in answer to the nations' taunting question 'Where is their God?' (v. 2), the psalmist replies, 'Our God is in the heavens; he does whatever pleases him' (v. 3), and then adds, 'Their idols (*'ăṣabbîm*) are silver and gold, the work of human hands' (v. 4). Yahweh's superiority over all other gods is expressed in various ways in other psalms. In Ps 86:8 he is praised as incomparable: 'There is none like you among the gods.' This psalmist also maintains that he is the creator not only of Israel but of all the nations: 'All the nations that you have made will come and bow down to you' (v. 9). Elsewhere in the Psalter Yahweh is simply described as 'a great God and a great king above all gods' (Ps. 95:3; cf. 135:5); as 'exalted far above all gods' (Ps. 97:9) and as 'God of gods' and 'Lord of lords' (Ps. 136:2, 3).

Finally, Ps. 82 deserves especial notice. This psalm has since been understood in different ways; but it may be assumed that the early readers of the Psalter would have interpreted it as presenting God (that is, Yahweh) as pre-siding over a divine assembly (*'ădat-'ēl*) and as exercising supreme power over the assembled gods (*bĕqereb 'ĕlōhîm*, v. 1). He accuses the gods of acting unjustly towards the disadvantaged and of acquitting the wicked (vv. 2–4). In vv. 6–7 he announces his sentence, which may be seen as announcing the 'twilight of the gods'. Although the gods are all 'sons of the Most High', they will nevertheless die as human beings die. This psalm, like the psalms just con-sidered, regards the gods as real; far from being useless as some other psalms describe them, they have possessed real power, but have exercised it unjustly. Now their power has come to an end. The final verse appeals to God to rise up and judge the earth, for it is he alone who rules over the nations.

Many of the Psalms, written in times of acute persecution whether of individuals or of the nation, attribute, with good reason, real power to *human enemies*. Yet these psalmists never doubt Yahweh's power to overcome these enemies. An individual, though surrounded by enemies who boast that his God is unable to help him, is nevertheless confident that Yahweh will protect him and destroy them (Ps. 3); another, protesting that he is innocent and has done nothing to provoke his troubles, is sure that he can rely on Yahweh's help, appeals to him to rise up in anger against his attackers, and ends by thanking him for doing so (Ps. 7). Others, speaking on behalf of the people of Jerusalem, pray to Yahweh for help even though the city and temple have been destroyed by foreign armies (Pss. 74; 79). Even in Babylon the dejected exiles, with their thoughts filled with memories of Jerusalem and the temple worship with its 'songs of Zion', are still able to address Yahweh as the one who has the power to 'remember the day of Jerusalem's fall' and so to avenge it by destroying those who were responsible for this destruction (Ps. 137).

It may thus be said that in every circumstance, individual or national, the psalmists are sustained by their confidence that the ultimate power resides not in their cruel enemies, nor in the heathen gods, but in Yahweh and, in monarchical times, in their king, whom Yahweh has appointed and to whom he gives his support.

Wealth, Prosperity, Sustenance

It is a striking fact that the psalmists, whatever their circumstances and despite their great variety of mood and outlook, are united in their indifference — sometimes even their hostility — to the possession of wealth. (It is interesting to observe that the same is true of the book of Proverbs.) Of the few psalms that refer to this topic, only Ps. 112 speaks of wealth as one of the rewards given to the righteous (v. 3). The same psalm (vv. 5, 9) speaks of generosity to the needy as a meritorious activity of the righteous. The author of Ps. 119 appears to acknowledge that it might be good to be rich, but maintains that wealth is less desirable than the keeping of the laws of Yahweh (v. 14). He does not state whether he regards the two as compatible. Elsewhere in the Psalter wealth is associated either with the wicked or with folly. Ps. 73:12 states that the wicked can be known by the fact that they live in comfort and get steadily richer. Wealth is a principal topic of Ps. 49, which describes the wicked as trusting in their wealth and boasting of it (v. 7), but also points out their folly in doing so: like all human beings they are mortal, and are doomed to leave their wealth behind them when they die (vv. 17–20). However, this psalmist recognizes the actual existence of a wealthy class: it is addressed to 'the rich and the poor together' (*'āšîr wĕ'ebyôn*, v. 2). The term 'rich' (*'āšîr*) is always used in a pejorative sense in Proverbs, and this appears also to be the attitude of the Psalms in general. No psalmist claims to be rich, let alone boasts of this. In the Psalter there is little talk of amassing wealth (Ps 112:3 is an exception). Prosperity of that kind is typical of the wicked and the persecutor.

At least 45 psalms contain words (*'ebyôn, dal, 'ānî*) supposedly meaning 'poor'. In four places (40:17; 70:5; 86:1; 109:22) the psalmist complains, using a clearly fixed formula, 'I am poor and needy' (*'ănî 'ānî wĕ'ebyôn*). These terms, however, have somewhat wider meanings than that of economic poverty, and it is not always easy to know when they are being used in a literal sense – though actual poverty could be the consequence of persecution. Such persecution is almost invariably the subject of the psalmist's complaint. It cannot therefore be ruled out that these terms would be better rendered by a translation such as 'oppressed'. In Ps. 109:16, 22, however, the reference is to persons being pursued by creditors, and 'poor' is the meaning intended. In most cases there is either an expression of confidence that Yahweh will come to the rescue or an appeal that he will do so. There are certainly some verses which allude to economic poverty. In Ps. 112:9, as already noted, it is said of the righteous that they are very generous to the poor.

Yet, the Psalms speak of a much more modest prosperity. The most that the psalmist aspires to on behalf of those who fear and obey God is that they will 'eat the labour of their hands' – that is, that they will produce sufficient food for themselves and their families (Ps. 128:2–3). The Psalter abounds in references to agricultural and pastoral concerns: to a sufficient supply of water from springs and rain to nourish the crops; grain, fruit, vines, green grass, full barns, abundant harvests – in other words the produce of the land, all these things being provided by the benevolent God. It is he who saves his people, especially the poor, from the ravages of famine (e.g. Pss. 37:19; 33:18–19) and satisfies them with adequate sustenance (Pss. 37:25; 107:9, 36; 132:15; 146:7). This concern is expressed not only in literal terms but also in metaphorical ones. Yahweh is the people's shepherd and they are his flock (Pss. 23; 80:1; 79:13; 95:7). His faithful are compared to well-watered trees (Pss. 1:3; 92:12–14). Their God is the fountain, or spring, of life (36:10). Their king is said to be like the rain that falls on the grass (72:6). Ps. 23, a psalm of confidence, deploys the imagery of the divine shepherd in some detail: he is the shepherd who cares for his flock, leading it to green pastures and refreshing streams from which the sheep can drink, protecting them from marauders and giving them the nourishment that they need. All these things speak of the modest aspirations of an agricultural and pastoral people.

Health, Longevity and Death

Whatever their mood, the psalmists frequently take note of the fact of human mortality as decreed by God. Ps. 49:16–20 comforts those who envy and resent the material good fortune enjoyed by the rich, reminding them that they will be unable to carry their wealth with them beyond the grave. Ps. 90:3–4 deplores human mortality in the light of God's eternity. On the other hand, Ps. 103:13–14 praises God for graciously 'remembering' that human beings are mere dust and so showing kindness to those who fear him, and Ps. 115:17 similarly praises him for his benevolence to them before they pass out of this world and join those who can no longer praise him. Ps. 144:3–4 expresses amazement that he should regard such ephemeral creatures as we. There is a general assumption that human beings will not enjoy a positive existence after death, although at least two passages (Ps. 49:15; 73:23–28) may well have been understood in that sense by the early readers of the Psalter.

Despite this inevitable limitation, the few psalms that speak of longevity and old age envisage the possibility of human beings living long lives. According to Ps. 90, however, this was not something to which one could look forward with pleasure. Having regretted human mortality (vv. 3–6), the psalmist makes the remarkable statement that the normal lifespan is 70 years, and that a robust person may live even to 80 (v. 10). It has been suggested that this is regarded by him as an aspiration (or perhaps an alarming possibility) rather than a statement of fact based on actual knowledge, but it shows that such longevity could at least be envisaged. However, to this psalmist it would be nothing but toil and trouble. Two other passages speak of old age. The psalmist of Ps. 71, which is an appeal to Yahweh to protect him against his attackers, pleads with him not to abandon him when he approaches old age (vv. 9, 18), whereas Ps. 92, a hymn of praise, speaks of the righteous who flourish like palm trees in the temple courts, confident that even in old age they will produce fruit and be full of sap.

A large number of psalms are lamentations in which the psalmist speaks of his fear of imminent and premature death. In the majority of cases it is the wicked, or the enemies, who seem to the psalmist to be on the point of bringing about his death, and he appeals to God to save him. Occasionally, however, he believes that his attacker is God himself, who is punishing him for his sins (e.g. Ps. 38). It is only these psalms that speak of sickness and disease, always caused by such attacks. Some of these psalms list parts of the body that are suffering: eyes, mouth, bones, loins etc. – or the whole body which is failing in strength. Other psalms, in a different mood, express complete confidence that God protects them from every evil. The author of Ps. 3, also a lament psalm, expresses the certainty that even when he is asleep Yahweh will sustain him and enable him to rise again unscathed from sleep (v. 5), and the psalmist of Ps. 4:8 is sure that thanks to Yahweh he will sleep in peace (bĕšālôm) and in safety (*lābeṭaḥ*). It is remarkable that whatever their situation the prevailing feature of all these psalms is *trust* in God (*beṭaḥ*), who can be relied on to keep the psalmist in safety or bring him to safety.

Family

We learn comparatively little from the Psalter about family life in Israel. That, no doubt, is precisely because other concerns predominate in the collection. The two most prominent types of psalm are the individual lament and the hymn of praise. The latter type is corporate in character, concerned not with individual families but with the fate of the nation as a whole. In the individual laments the psalmist concentrates almost wholly on his personal fate. A single verse, however (Ps. 103:13), clearly reflects a loving family relationship which may be taken as a normal one because it assumes it to be such and goes on to postulate another by analogy:

> As a father loves (*raḥēm*) his children,
> so Yahweh loves those who fear him.

The following verse gives the reason for Yahweh's tenderness: 'For ... he remembers that we are dust'. The implication is that earthly fathers also bear in mind their children's weakness and fragility in their treatment of them.

Two psalms (127 and 128) depict family concerns in somewhat more detail. Ps. 127:3–5 states that sons (and perhaps also daughters – the 'fruit of the womb') are an inheritance (*naḥălâ*) and a reward (*śākār*) from Yahweh. They are 'like arrows in the hand of a warrior' – perhaps an allusion to the father's virility – and a large family gives a man a social position which enables him to impress his adversaries when he speaks with them in the gate of the city. Ps. 128, closely related to the previous psalm, affirms that a man will enjoy a good life whose sons contribute to the productivity of his farm; he will be happy at home when he sees them assembled round his table. Tribute is also paid in this psalm to his wife, a 'fruitful vine'. The psalm ends with a blessing: this man will live to see his grandchildren.

The importance for the good life of fathering a family of sons is very strongly reflected in many Old Testament books. It is also reflected in the Psalter, though the references are few. Children were, it appears, chiefly valued, apart from their usefulness on the farm, for their potential begetting of children in turn so that the family life would be continued. In the case of the king this is related to Yahweh's promise to David of an eternal dynasty (Pss. 18:50; 89:4, 35–37); but it is evident that the possession of sons to perpetuate the family line was of equal importance for fathers of other families (Pss. 37:26; 69:36; 102:28; 115:14; 127; 128). Family life itself is, however, hardly described at all in the Psalms apart from the above mentioned reference to fatherly love (Ps. 103:13). References are mainly confined to hopes for the childrens' inheritance of the land or, more generally, to the topic of God's blessing (Pss. 25:13; 37:26; 112:2) or the wish, accompanied by a prayer for full barns and prolific herds, that the children should be sturdy like healthy plants or pillars supporting the house (Ps. 144:12). References to wives and daughters are even fewer. Of the two references to Israelite wives, Ps. 128:3 simply refers to the wife's capacity for bearing children and Ps. 113:9 to Yahweh's ability to provide a barren woman with children. The latter verse reflects a widespread human desire and is reminiscent of Hannah's situation in 1 Sam. 1. Ps. 144:12 is the only reference in the Psalter to Israelite daughters. Ps. 45 is a marriage song for a (presumably) foreign princess on her marriage to an Israelite king; she is urged to forget her own family (v. 10) and is promised many children (v. 16).

The comparative lack of references in the Psalter to family life in a book that almost more than any other in the Old Testament describes a great variety of emotional states illustrates the necessarily fragmentary nature of the evidence for the good life in Israel. There is no reason to suppose that their families were less important to these psalmists than to other Israelites. It is simply that their uppermost concerns when they composed their songs were of a different nature.

Each Old Testament book displays a different facet of Israelite life, and it is important to compare one with another and also attempt to form a composite picture. As far as family life is concerned, the books of Samuel and Kings present a considerably fuller account than does the Psalter.

Law and Justice

Human laws and human justice are only an intermittent topic in the Psalter. The justice most frequently mentioned is that of God, who is supreme judge over Israel, the nations and the whole world, and has laid down the principles of justice which are incumbent on all. He is frequently appealed to by individuals or by the nation as a whole, those who are being attacked by unnamed personal adversaries or by foreign enemies, and it is confidently asserted that he has helped them or will help them. This help does not always, however, take the form of legal action through the human courts; rather it is often by the sword, by giving victory to Israel's armies, or by mysteriously striking the lives of the enemies (e.g. Ps. 110:5–6).

But there are some psalms which, in setting out the conditions on which the would-be worshipper is to be allowed to ascend Yahweh's 'holy hill' and worship at his temple, enunciate principles of conduct towards others which we may take to be the principles on whose basis the human courts would, or should, operate. The most outstanding examples of this are Pss. 15 and 24. These psalms first set out in general terms those actions that exclude persons from the temple but are not necessarily subject to criminal prosecution, and then actions that are: the taking of bribes to secure the condemnation of the innocent and lending to fellow-citizens at interest (Ps. 15:5) and bearing false testimony in court (Ps. 24:4). From these strictures and from the evidence of other psalms it is clear that such practices were commonplace when these psalms were composed. In Pss. 27:12 and 35:11 the psalmists complain that their enemies are giving false testimony against them, while in Ps. 35:23 the psalmist appeals to Yahweh to intervene when he is brought before the judges, in order to secure for him a fair trial. Ps. 37 expresses confidence that Yahweh, who 'loves justice' (v. 28), will not abandon the righteous person whose death has been demanded by his enemies, and will 'not let him be falsely condemned when he is brought to trial' (bĕhiššāpĕṭô, v.33).

Many psalmists speak of God's 'judgements' or laws, which they claim to have obeyed. Ps. 99:4, addresses God as 'lover of justice' and says to him 'You have established equity' (mĕšārîm). They also speak of the human king as God's representative and divinely appointed supreme judge (e.g. Pss. 72:1–4; 122:5). It is he whose duty is to defend the poor and to judge his people in righteousness. The psalmists clearly regarded the proper administration of justice as an essential part of the good life, though they frequently lament the lack of this and desperately appeal to God to put things right and ensure that it should be universally available to the people of Israel.

Wisdom

The words 'wise' (ḥākām), 'wisdom' (ḥokmâ) and the verb 'to be wise' (ḥākam) occur only in a handful of passages in the Psalter. As elsewhere in the Old Testament this group of words has more than one meaning, though these meanings are related. In Ps. 107:27 ḥokmâ simply means 'skill'. However, it is here apparent that this human 'wisdom' is ineffective, and that human beings must rely for their safety on Yahweh's help. This passage refers to sailors caught in a storm, whose skill proved to be useless but who were saved by the intervention of Yahweh who stilled the storm and guided them safely to harbour. Here wisdom is a human quality by means of which one can normally expect to live one's life in safety, but which is in fact insufficient. The 'wise men' of Egypt claimed to possess another specialized kind of wisdom employed in the service of the Pharaoh (Ps. 105:22), but Moses and Aaron, Yahweh's chosen servants, were endowed with greater powers than they. Somewhat similarly the author of Ps. 119 speaks of Yahweh's commandment as making him wiser than his enemies (v. 98). In Ps. 104 it is the wisdom of Yahweh himself that is singled out for special praise (v. 24). This psalm praises him as the creator and maintainer of the world and its inhabitants. It is there stated (v. 24) that it was by his wisdom that he made the world. The ephemeral character of mere human wisdom is stressed in Ps. 49:10, where the reader is reminded that even those who are or claim to be wise must nevertheless die like other mortals.

Human wisdom, then, in the Psalter is either God-given or it is inadequate for successful and prosperous living. The remaining passages that speak of it directly claim that the wisdom that God gives is in various ways an important contributor to the good life. Ps. 107, a psalm that recounts the wonderful benefits conferred by Yahweh on various groups of people in peril, ends with the words

> Let those who are wise give heed to these things,
> and consider Yahweh's steadfast love (v. 43).

This is a teacher's recommendation to those who are already counted among Yahweh's 'wise' to deepen their wisdom still more by contemplating his infinite power and care for his people. Two other psalms similarly pray to Yahweh to *teach* them (more) wisdom. In the penitential Ps. 51 the psalmist, confessing his sins, prays 'Teach me wisdom' so that he may be purified and begin a new life (vv. 6–10). The psalmist of Ps. 90, reflecting on human frailty and God's anger, asks that he may be taught prudence in ordering his life so that he may attain a wise heart, and so hopes for a better future (vv. 12–17). For the author of Ps. 37 the righteous, among whom he evidently counts himself, and whose speech is full of wisdom, will be preserved by Yahweh from disaster: 'their steps do not slip' (vv. 30–31). Finally the author of Ps. 111, praising God for his great deeds on behalf of his people, sums up the value of wisdom in the phrase 'It is the fear of Yahweh that is the beginning (or essence) of wisdom' (v. 10).

The value of wisdom for the attainment of a good life for the individual is recognized in several other psalms, even though the word itself may be lacking. Wisdom is often understood as equivalent to fearing Yahweh or living a blameless life. For example, according to Ps. 37 the person who trusts in Yahweh, commits his life to him and 'does good' will live securely in the land and be granted whatever he wishes (vv. 3–4). Ps. 90 is a kind of meditation akin to wisdom thought; the psalmist reflects on human mortality, but still hopes for happiness while life lasts. Several psalms stress the importance of *teaching* wisdom to others. The author of Ps. 73, a teaching psalm, reflects on his lack of hope which was transformed by what he learned in the temple, namely that the wicked will be destroyed and that he will at last find satisfaction in God's presence. The psalmist of Ps. 119 frequently requests that Yahweh will teach him so that he understands his will; he takes delight in God's law, and anticipates that he will so be saved from persecution. Ps. 49 is the work of a teacher of wisdom (vv. 3–4). Despite some sombre reflections on human mortality he also draws from his meditation the conviction that he has nothing to fear from his persecutors (v. 5) and that God will rescue him from death (v. 15).

Pleasure and Enjoyment

At least 60 psalms mention joy, and another 20 happiness ('asĕrê, 'Happy is/are ... !'). Some psalms mention the expression of joy in song, with accompaniment by the harp or other musical instruments, or, rarely, dance. But the Psalter contains very few clear indications of the ways in which people enjoyed themselves. This is hardly surprising: almost all of the Psalms are prayers, and such references would be out of place.

In some Old Testament books eating and drinking and the giving of feasts are mentioned as a normal way of expressing happiness; but these activities play no part in the Psalter. Ps. 41:9 speaks of a meal shared with friends; Ps. 22:26 of an expectation that the poor will praise Yahweh for satisfying their hunger; Ps. 128:2 promises that those who fear Yahweh will be happy because the produce of their land will be adequate for the family; but that is all. There are very few references to drinking, and the word *mišteh*, 'feast' or 'dinner party', does not occur at all. Ps. 69:12 refers, however, to the songs sung by drunkards in the gate of the city. The numerous references to joy and happiness are almost all related in some way to God, who is praised especially for help against enemies personal or national, but occasionally for himself. A large proportion of psalms express joy in participation in temple worship when God's presence was especially experienced. In Ps. 119 and some other psalms the psalmist expresses his joy simply in contemplating Yahweh's laws. Only Ps. 113:9 speaks of a mother's joy in her children.

God

We cannot know to what extent the Psalter is representative of the religious attitudes of the people of Israel as a whole. We may assume that many of the psalms were sung on occasions of public worship, while others are the prayers of individuals. We may also surmise that the Psalter as a book came to express the devotion of a later generation of Israelites. But whether the intensity of religious devotion expressed in these psalms was characteristic of the mass of the people is beyond our knowledge. The picture that it presents, which may or may not be true to all the facts, is of a nation which, despite moments of joyful victory, was frequently at the mercy of foreign enemies and social malefactors who made the attainment of the good life precarious, but nevertheless survived and even achieved happiness through an indomitable trust in God. Such devotion, and the spiritual satisfaction that it brought, is memorably summed up in the words of Ps. 73:25–26:

> Whom have I in heaven but you?
> And there is nothing on earth that I desire other than you.
> My flesh and my heart may fail,
> but God is the strength of my heart and my portion for ever.

Summary

Because the Psalms reveal a great variety of human emotions and express the thoughts of individuals, they offer a rich picture of the way the Israelites viewed the good life. Filled with a confidence that is centred on Mount Zion and the temple and looking to the king, who, as Yahweh's vicegerent, was deemed able to provide national prosperity, many of the psalmists nevertheless complain of enemies who threaten this security, and seek Yahweh's help. Alongside these laments, however, are the many psalms of thanksgiving and confidence based on trust in God. To the psalmists, power resides uniquely in Yahweh. Both the king and the enemies who attempt to destroy Israel and attack the individual psalmists are powerful; but the psalmists trust in God and never doubt his power to overcome the enemies. The psalmists are indifferent to wealth, at most seeking only a modest sufficiency. Frequently they refer to themselves as 'poor' and oppressed. They accept their mortality, and often voice their fear of premature death, although they are confident of Yahweh's protection. The family is rarely mentioned in the Psalter, although similar attitudes to those expressed elsewhere in the Bible are found. Equally, human law and justice are seldom mentioned, the main references to justice being that of God who is the supreme judge. The words for 'wise' and 'wisdom' occur only in a small number of psalms, but in these the wisdom which comes from God contributes to the good life, while merely human wisdom is inadequate for successful living. A few psalms reflect on life after the manner of the teachers of wisdom. A large number of psalms mention joy and happiness, usually in relation to the worship of Yahweh. Finally, as a collection of prayers and praises the Psalter is naturally dominated by a sense of devotion to God.

13
Proverbs

Like the Psalter, Proverbs provides a good deal of information about the good life, but from the point of view of an observer rather than of a participant in life's experiences. Its principal purpose is to instruct the readers about the attainment of a good life. It is almost wholly concerned with individuals rather than with the nation, although it has much to say about the immediate community in which they live and their role in it. Although it does not refer specifically to Israel, it is clearly addressed to an Israelite readership.

Place and Security

In contrast to the books that have been considered so far, Proverbs contains very few references to the land. What is meant by the term 'the land' is not defined, though it may be presumed that the references are to Palestine, the territory elsewhere defined as the land that God has given to his people. Apart from 31:23, which refers to 'the elders of the land' who sit 'in the city gates', the most significant references to the land as the place where the good life can be enjoyed in safety occur in a few verses that contrast the fates of the 'righteous' (ṣaddîqîm) or 'upright' (yĕšārîm) and the 'wicked' respectively. It is characteristic of this book that people are uncompromisingly divided into these two groups. It is implied, then, that to live in the land is conditional upon acceptable moral behaviour. What is meant by saying that the wicked will 'not reside' in the land or will be 'cut off' from it is not stated. The notion is not, however, peculiar to Proverbs but is found elsewhere, in the Psalms, especially Ps. 37, and Deuteronomy.

The need for security was, however, never far from the thoughts of the authors of Proverbs. But it is expressed most frequently in terms of the *house* (*bayit*) in which a person lives. The settled life is, in fact, taken for granted. The word *bayit* can mean either the physical structure in which one lives or the people who live in it: that is, one's family or household. In Proverbs it is used in both senses, but the two are to a large extent interchangeable: the fall of the one can be the fall of the other. In a number of proverbs the contrast between the fates of the righteous and the wicked is expressed in this way. In 12:7, for example, it is stated that the house of the righteous will stand though the wicked will be overthrown; similarly 3:33; 21:12. The fall of the house of the wicked is also asserted in 15:26 and 17:13. In contrast, 15:6 speaks of the abundant treasure that will be found in the house of the righteous. For the authors of these proverbs it was the righteous alone who would enjoy the security which makes the good life possible.

The fullest expression of this is found in 31:10–31. This passage, which constitutes the climax of the book of Proverbs, describes the character and activities of a capable, virtually omnicompetent wife (*'ēšet ḥayil*) who is clearly intended as a model of the ways in which an individual, in this case a wife and mother, can achieve a secure life for herself and her dependents. She is presented as the sole source of the family's security; her husband plays a very minor role. But thanks to his wife he has an honoured place among the dignitaries of the town (v. 23). He trusts her and her achievements (v. 11) and is loud in her praise (v. 28). The author of the passage was evidently concerned to enhance the status of women, perhaps in order to counter an impression gained from reading the rest of the book in which, especially in chapters 1–9, much prominence is given to the activities of another sort of woman, who is destructive of good morals and of the well-being of society in general, while elsewhere in the book women are only rarely mentioned. However, reading between the lines the reader would have applied many of the details in the description to men: the qualities of this capable and successful wife and mother are in the main also those to which men may aspire and which are generally commended in the book.

The security of the wife and her family depicted in this passage is principally security from the fear of poverty. Her enterprises are so successful that she can 'laugh about the future' (v. 25). She herself is called happy, or fortunate ($\check{s}r$) by her children, and her husband praises her (v. 28). The sources of this sense of security are listed. She gives prosperity to her family because of her enterprise, diligence, hard work and management of her household, and also because she is generous to the poor. More generally, she is praised for her wisdom and her instruction of others, presumably her children and her servants (v. 26). Finally all is attributed to her fear of Yahweh (v. 30).

In the rest of the book the individual's desire for security and so potentially for the 'good life' is frequently expressed in proverbs that draw a contrast between the respective fates of two kinds of person: the righteous, upright, wise on the one hand and the wicked, foolish on the other. In Prov. 1–9 the contrast is mainly between the pupil who heeds the instruction of the teacher of wisdom or of a personified Wisdom herself and the person who does not. These proverbs are often expressed in very general terms with no definition of what is entailed by being righteous, wicked, wise or foolish.

The security of the righteous or wise person is frequently expressed, especially in chapters 10–16, in one or other of a number of recurring terms. For example, the noun *beṭaḥ*, 'safety, security', occurs several times; it may qualify a verb such as *šākan*, 'dwell' (e.g. 1:33) or 'walk' (i.e. the journey of life: 3:23; 10:9). Alternatively, it is asserted that the righteous will never be moved or removed. Other terms referring specifically to safety include: to be established, to be delivered (from trouble), to stand, to escape, to preserve one's life, simply 'to live', to be guarded or preserved, to take refuge in Yahweh as a 'strong tower' etc. The fate of the wicked or the fool is expressed in corresponding terms such as 'fall', 'perish', etc. These terms clearly denote some kind of disaster, or even premature death, though the form taken by such disaster is not specified.

Power

The existence of monarchy is taken for granted in Proverbs (30:27), but does not appear to have been central in the minds of the authors. Of the 900 verses in the book only some 30 make mention of kings. Rather, the impression given to the reader of the society of which the authors speak is of a mainly acephalous community much concerned with agricultural pursuits, in which anti-social elements existed but which were to some extent kept from disintegration by the responsible initiative of the 'righteous' and the 'wise'. The authority of the king, though ultimately paramount, seems to have been rather remote in the eyes of the authors of the book.

Kings are represented as ruling under the aegis of wisdom (8:15), and their thoughts are held to be unsearchable (25:3). They are to be feared and obeyed as is Yahweh himself. Their decisions are divinely inspired and their judgements are unerring (16:10). Many of the royal proverbs are concerned with the king's judicial powers and his ability to discern between the righteous and the wicked (e.g. 14:35; 16:12–13; 20:8; 25:2), but the reader is warned to fear the king's anger, which may suggest some arbitrariness on his part (16:14; 19:12; 20:2). In fact, the authors were well aware that there were evil kings as well as good ones: 29:4b speaks of kings who ruin the country by heavy taxation and 25:5 refers to kings who may be deceived by wicked advisers. By implication, the statement that if a king judges the poor with equity his throne will be established (29:14) suggests that there were kings who did not give justice to the poor. Proverbs 16:12a is ambiguous: it probably means that the just king abhors evil-doing by his subjects (cf. v. 13: 'Righteous lips are the delight of a king, and he loves him who speaks what is right'), although it may mean that kings who do evil commit an abomination.

The functions of other classes of person who are reckoned as possessing political power (*mōšēl*, 'ruler', *nādîb*, 17:26; 25:7, *śar*, 19:10, *hāgîd*, 28:16 and *qāṣîn*, 25:15) are not defined. *Mōšēl* is probably another term for 'king'; but the occurrence of the other titles may suggest that there was some delegation of power from the king to subordinate officials. Power was evidently also *de facto* exercised by the wealthy over others, especially the poor (those who were totally destitute), as it is indicated by the line 'The rich person *rules over* the poor' (22:7a). It may indeed be said that especially in the short proverbs of chapters 10–29 there is a 'bias towards the poor'; the rich are resented not merely because they are wealthy, but because they misuse the power that wealth gives them. Of all the nine references to the rich (*'āšîr*) in these chapters there is not one that expresses approval of them, even though the attainment of wealth through diligence is spoken of with approval. Prov. 18:23, for example, speaks of the rough way in which the rich address the poor, who in turn are obliged to speak to them obsequiously, while 28:6 attributes integrity to the poor (or to some of them) but dishonesty to the rich. The power exercised by the rich is also mentioned in connection with their manipulation of justice (see below). The attitude of the authors of these proverbs towards this extreme disparity is summed up in two proverbs which remind the readers of the *equality* between the two classes in the sight of their creator; here it is significant that whereas 22:2 speaks of the rich and the poor, 29:13, which is otherwise verbally identical with it, speaks rather of the poor and the *oppressor*.

The words *qāhāl* (5:14; 26:26) and *'ēdâ*, with which it appears together in 5:14, appear to denote a general assembly of the people (perhaps only of a limited locality) which exercised some kind of power to discipline, or at least to disgrace, offenders against morality or to expose persons who attempted to disrupt the harmony of the community by malicious and lying speech. However, there is no explanation given in these proverbs of the precise functional status of the assembly: whether its authority was only a moral one, able to express the community's disapproval or ostracism of such offenders, or whether it possessed more formal judicial powers. These two terms occur in other Old Testament books in various contexts including a cultic one, but without any suggestion of formal powers. (See below on *justice*.)

Wealth and Sustenance

Although the wealthy as a class are disapproved of in Proverbs because of the misuse of the power that their wealth confers on them and of their treatment of the poor, wealth in itself is not despised, and indeed those who become rich through their application to hard work and through honest means are praised and encouraged. The way in which many proverbs speak of 'the rich' and 'the poor' indicates that their authors regarded themselves as belonging to neither of these classes. Frequent references to agricultural pursuits suggest that the cultivation of small family-owned farms was the principal occupation of those to whom these proverbs are addressed.

Many proverbs indicate that wealth was by no means a rarity in the society reflected in the book. In 3:9–10, in a passage containing the advice of a father to his son, the pupil is advised to honour Yahweh by setting aside for him a portion of his produce so that his barns and his wine vats will be filled to overflowing. Such surplus produce is referred to in 11:26, where wealthy farmers are urged not to keep it for themselves in times of shortage but to sell it to their less successful neighbours. Other incidental details confirm the existence of private luxury. The seductress of 7:6–27 offers the inducements of a good dinner and luxurious surroundings to her intended lover, and assures him of the absence of her husband, who has gone on a long journey taking a bag of silver with him, presumably profits from his farm or from commercial transactions. In 1:13 it is alleged that the ruffians against whom the father warns his son are out to find 'all kinds of costly things' in the houses which they propose to rob, and so to fill their own houses with the looted objects.

Besides the seductress's invitation to the young man in chapter 7 there are three other passages referring to dinner-parties that imply the existence of a considerable degree of wealth. Two of these are metaphorical in character. In 9:1–5 the account of the personified Wisdom's sending her maids out into the streets to invite the 'simple' to a meal celebrating the building of her house is doubtless based on a familiar social custom, and the same is true to some extent of the invitation by the woman Folly in v. 17 of the same chapter. The passage in 23:1–3 is to be taken quite literally. It is advice to a young man about proper etiquette when invited to dinner by a (or the) 'ruler'. Further, the occurrence of a word (*mat'ammôtâw*, 23:3, 6) apparently meaning 'delicacies' and of another such in 18:8 (= 26:22), *mitlaḥămîm*, used in a metaphorical sense, points to a refinement of taste normally characteristic of people of means, for whom gastronomy was an important part of the good life. Finally, the poem with which the book concludes (31:10–31) depicts the life of an obviously wealthy family living happily and in mutual harmony, showing that wealth, when obtained by honourable means, does not necessarily corrupt.

Many proverbs set out the circumstances in which wealth may be honourably obtained. Chief of these is diligence or hard work. The work in question is often the tilling of the land (12:11; 28:19), and this is probably the meaning also in other proverbs. Prov. 27:23–27 describes in some detail how responsible and diligent farming will yield at least a sufficiency of food for the family. The passages in 12:27, 13:4, 14:23 and 21:5 teach a similar lesson. Several of these proverbs contrast these benefits with the poverty that will befall the lazy; the folly of laziness is a constant theme in others, while 24:30–36 is an extended moral tale with the same intention. Other proverbs speak of the blessing of Yahweh (10:22), of generosity towards the poor (11:24, 25; 14:21; 19:17; 22:9; 28:27), of righteousness (15:6) and of wisdom (8:21) as guaranteeing the acquisition of wealth.

But there is also an awareness that wealth cannot be attained by certain types of person, or that such persons are destined to lose it and be condemned to poverty: the wicked (11:4), sinners (13:21), adulterers (5:10); but also those who are too eager to possess it (28:20, 22), those who are greedy for it (28:25) and those who are confident that they will never lose it (11:28). The author of the only *prayer* in the book rejects wealth because it can lead him away from faith in God (30:9b). Two proverbs rate other assets more highly than wealth: wisdom (16:16) and a good reputation (22:1), while 23:4–5 and 27:24 point out that it cannot be relied on to stay permanently with its possessors but is essentially ephemeral.

Significant in view of the general fear of poverty expressed in the book is a series of proverbs that hold *relative* poverty to be preferable to wealth. Verses 16–17 of chapter 15 aver that the subsist on a meagre diet in the fear of Yahweh and to be blessed with love for others is preferable to wealth, which brings only troubles and hatred: 16:8 similarly associates having 'a little' with righteousness and wealth with injustice, and 17:1 and 28:6 express a similar view. However, 30:7–9 regards both poverty and wealth as conducive to sin. This author sees the good life as possible only for these who avoid both extremes.

In general the references in the book to wealth and poverty suggest that the fact of economic inequality was taken for granted. Theft from the rich is condemned as an illegitimate way to acquire wealth (1:8–19), but some sympathy is shown to those who steal out of desperate hunger (6:30; 30:9). Kindness is to be shown even to personal enemies who have fallen into poverty and lack food (25:21–22). An inordinate attachment to luxuries or wine is regarded as a sure way to poverty (21:17; 23:20–21).

What, then, is the impression conveyed by the book of Proverbs about wealth as a concomitant to the good life? There are admittedly some differences of opinion about this; there are some tensions, but no real contradictions. There is a general agreement that *extremes* of both wealth and poverty are to be deprecated: both tend to corrupt. The proverbs that speak of the possession of 'a little' as preferable to disharmony and other social evils are representative of the book in general. A middle way is advocated, and the moderate increase of economic prosperity through constant hard work and other honest means is regarded as desirable and deserves, and receives, the blessing of God.

Health and Longevity

Life and death are important topics in the book of Proverbs. For these authors it is clear that 'life' stands for all that is good for human beings. 'Life' is reserved for the good and the wise. It is stated that whoever finds wisdom finds life and obtains Yahweh's favour (8:35) and that the wise will obtain life and so avoid Sheol (15:24). Life is also given to those who obey the instructions of the human teachers (3:2; 10:11; 13:14) and who 'keep the commandment' (19:16). It is the reward of the righteous (10:16, 17; 11:4, 19; 12;18) and of those who fear Yahweh (10:27). It will also be obtained by those who have a tranquil mind (14:30). The expressions 'fountain of life' (10:11; 13:14; 14:27; 16:22) and 'tree of life' (3:18; 11:30; 13:12; 15:4) are used to convey the same notion. The term 'death' is also frequently employed, often in the same verses, to denote the fate suffered by those who lack these qualities or who are motivated by malice.

It is not clear, however, how far these references to life and death in Proverbs are intended to be understood in a literal sense. It is therefore uncertain to what extent they have a bearing on notions of health and longevity. 'Life' in Proverbs as elsewhere in the Old Testament has a range of meanings. These include a full and successful life and also a long life (but never a life beyond the grave). A similar uncertainty appertains to the references to death. If they are to be taken literally they must, since death is the eventual fate of all human beings, presumably denote an unexpected, premature or in some way unpleasant kind of death; or they may be seen as speaking of a 'living death' — that is, the opposite of 'life' in its figurative sense of a fortunate and successful life. The variety, and often the vagueness, of the expressions used to denote the fate of the wicked, however (e.g. 'come to ruin', 10:8; 'go astray', 10:17; 'are no more', 10:25; 'fall', 11:5; 11:28; 'perish', 21:28, etc.) is too great to permit a clear interpretation.

In a few proverbs, however, there are specific references to longevity, which is declared to be the consequence of obeying the commands of the teacher ('length of days and years of life and abundant welfare [šālôm] will they give you', 3:2), a gift of wisdom (3:16; 9:11), or the reward of those who fear Yahweh (10:27) or who hate ill-gotten gain (28:16). In 10:27 the contrast between the fates of God-fearers and the wicked is emphasized, affirming that the lives of the latter will be *short*, while 16:31 speaks of grey hairs as a crown and a sign of a righteous life. These proverbs, in which longevity and the positive *quality* of life are associated, are perhaps to be seen as clues to the meaning of life generally in the book.

Another group of proverbs that refer somewhat more specifically to bodily health or disease associate these with moral or religious behaviour. In 4:22 'life' is paralleled with 'healing of the flesh' as the consequence of heeding the teacher's instructions. On the other hand, those who continually ignore reproof (29:1) or who are consistently malicious (6:15) will suffer physical damage beyond repair. While fearing Yahweh and turning from evil will bring healing (or health) for the flesh and refreshment for the bones (i.e. the body, 3:8), 'rottenness of the bones' will be the lot of the shameful wife (12:4) and the jealous person (14:30). Only in 15:30, where good news refreshes the heart of the person who received it, is bodily health attributed to a non-moral cause. Nowhere in the book of Proverbs are health, sickness and longevity attributed to what we should call 'natural causes', nor is there any suggestion of medical skill that can give relief to the sick: only God can give life and only God can heal. Allusions to specific diseases (a decayed tooth, 25:19; paralysis of the legs, 26:7) throw no further light on the question of the concept of health in Proverbs.

Family and Friends

Despite the extreme brevity of most of the sayings the book of Proverbs gives a vivid impression of family life and of the relationships between its members. The *father* fills the role of educator of his sons (4:1, 3–4; 15:5; 23:22). Fathers are expected to exercise a strict discipline over their sons, including the application of corporal punishment (13:24; 19:18; 22;15; 23:13; 14; 29;17); but it is taken for granted that although fathers may need to reprove their sons they also love them (3:12). A son who turns out obedient to his father and so becomes 'wise' is a source of delight to him (10:1; 15:20, 23:24, 25; 29:3); but it is recognised that there

are some sons who are stupid and foolish and are a grief and
a trouble to their fathers (17:21, 25). Sons owe respect to
their fathers, and those who curse or mock their fathers and
are disobedient to their mothers will come to a bad end
(30:11, 17).

Sons

Frequently in the book sons are addressed by their fathers in
their character of pupils, with the formula 'my son' (some 15
times in chapters 1–9; 19:27; 23:15; 19, 26; 24:13, 21; 27:11).
Other proverbs specify what was expected of a son in
addition to obedience to his father's teaching. A son was
expected to perform active work for the family's welfare:
thus 10:5 refers specifically to the bringing in of the harvest,
stating that the son who sleeps during the harvest season
instead of helping his father brings shame on the family.
Diligence is in fact a major topic in Proverbs, and the lazy
person is both mocked and warned that he is on the way to
disaster. Other proverbs speak more generally of sons who
shame the family (e.g. 19:26), and 17:2 goes as far as to say
that such a son may be deprived of his inheritance in favour
of an intelligent and diligent family slave. On the other
hand, those sons who follow the example of the righteous
are pronounced 'happy' (20:7). *Grandparents* also have an
honoured place in the family: grandchildren are a 'crown' or
source of pride to their elderly grandparents (17:6) who may
be expected to leave them an inheritance (13:22).

Mothers

Mothers occupy a surprisingly prominent place in Proverbs.
The references to mothers, however, are almost always
paralleled in the same verse by corresponding references to
the fathers, so that both parents are portrayed as a single
unit. (There are two exceptions to this; 29.15, where a
mother is disgraced by the behaviour of an undisciplined
child, and 31:1–9, where the mother of King Lemuel gives

instructions to her son.) In 1:8 and 6:20 the mother shares
the education of her son with the father. Chapter 4, verse 3
refers to a son especially loved by his mother, while 23:25
speaks of a mother's joy in having a wise son. The number
of references to unsatisfactory or even criminal children is
remarkable; here especially the unfortunate parents are
considered together. Chapter 10, verse 1 refers to their grief
over a foolish son; 30:17 to a disobedient one; 15:20 and
23:22 to a son who despises his parents; 19:26 to sons who
maltreat their parents; 28:24 to sons who rob them and
20:20 and 30:11 to sons who curse their parents. It is striking
that there are no references in the book to *daughters*. The
word itself (*bānôt*) occurs twice, but in one case the reference
is figurative (30:15), and in the other (31:29), where it occurs
in the context of the encomium on the capable woman
(31:10–31) it is used to denote women in general including
the married woman who is mistress of her household. The
omission of specific references does not imply that
daughters were regarded as of no account: the mother
who educates her son (30:1–9) or who shares their education
with her husband (1:8; 6:20) or who is the 'crown' of her
husband (12:4), and whose intelligence is stated to be a
divine gift for him (19:14), may be presumed to have derived
these qualities from her own education by her parents. The
'household' (*bayit*) of the capable woman who benefits from
her care (as do also her female servants) presumably includes
her daughters. In fact the reference to her 'sons' (v. 28)
probably has the inclusive sense of 'children'. This may also
be true of some other passages in the book.

Husbands and wives

The proverbs dealing with the relations between man and
wife view marriage mainly from the man's point of view.
Marriage is generally highly regarded – 18:22 simply states
plainly and without reservation that 'Whoever finds a wife
finds a good thing', and adds that he will enjoy the favour of
Yahweh. In a passage warning men against adultery with
another woman, 5:18–20 describes the marital relationship

ecstatically in terms reminiscent of the raptures of the couple
in the Song of Songs (e.g. Song 2:7, 9, 17; 3:5; 8;14). The
husband in 31:10–31 is full of praise for his wife, who in
addition to her various capabilities also fears Yahweh (v. 30),
while 11:16 praises the wife who has charm ('ēšet-ḥēn), but
also contrasts her with one who brings shame on the family
(the meaning of the second line is uncertain). Chapter 11,
verse 22 rather crudely warns against marrying a woman
whose good looks belie the fact that she is lacking in
discretion. It is clear that while these proverbs praise the
married state in general they are aware of the existence of
unhappy marriages. While husbands were evidently not
infrequently tempted to be unfaithful, the chief fault in wives
appears to have been a scolding tongue. No less than five
proverbs (19:13; 21:9, 19; 25:24; 27:15) describe marriage to
such a woman as intolerable.

Although it is realistic about human failings within
families – e.g. unfaithful husbands, errant and violent sons,
nagging or otherwise unsuitable wives – the book of Proverbs
is very positive about the family, which was clearly regarded
as one of the most important elements in the enjoyment of
the good life. Monogamy appears to be taken for granted,
so the harmony of the family is not disturbed by quarrels
between wives as in some other Old Testament books, and
there is no mention of divorce – unless this is implied in
30:23b, which speaks of a maidservant supplanting or
succeeding her mistress. There is evidence of both paternal
and marital love and of harmonious family relations, which
include proud grandparents as well as parents and children.
The moral and spiritual education of children was a major
parental concern.

The fullest picture of a happy and prosperous family is
provided by 31:10–31. Here as elsewhere in Proverbs its
well-being is the result of hard work and enterprise, and as
manager of the household the wife is concerned with every
aspect of family life both material and educational. This
passage is remarkable for the fact that all these advantages
are due to the activities of the wife, while the husband's are
confined to 'sitting among the elders of the land' as a
prominent citizen, and publicly praising his wife. It is possible

that there is a certain irony in these verses, but perhaps not: he is concerned with public affairs, while her concerns are domestic (though on an unusually large scale). It is because he has chosen a wife who is 'more precious than jewels' that he is able to live in dignity and free from worry. As other proverbs state, she is his 'crown'.

Friends and neighbours

In Proverbs the relationships that make for the good life are not confined to the family. Proverbs is the only Old Testament book in which great importance is attached to other social relationships. The situation that seems to be presupposed in much of the book is that of a small community in which there is mutual acquaintance between the citizens; and the individual proverbs evince a strong feeling about the importance of social harmony within that community. Many of the proverbs condemn those who through malice or stupidity jeopardize that harmony, and praise those whose wisdom or integrity seeks to preserve or restore it. Among these social comments are sayings that refer specifically to neighbours – that is, fellow residents or citizens. Others mention the closer relationship of friendship. It is not always easy to distinguish proverbs that refer to neighbours from those that speak of friends, because in some cases a single word (e.g. *rēa'*) can denote either. But the context decides the case in the majority of instances.

In general the references to *neighbours* are expressed negatively: the prudent citizen is warned not to quarrel with his neighbour or harm him (3:29, 30; 11:9). In 3:29 he is similarly warned: 'Do not plan harm against your neighbour who lives peaceably with you', an activity attributed to the godless in 11:9. Other proverbs issue warnings against deferring a promise of help to a neighbour (3:28), making unwise pledges to him (6:1–3; 17:18), sleeping with a neighbour's wife (6:29), despising or flattering him (14:21; 29:5), leading him astray (16:29), visiting him in his house with excessive frequency (25:17), telling lies and then pretending to be joking (26:18–20), interfering in a quarrel (26:17) and giving false testimony against a neighbour (24:28; 25:18).

Some of the proverbs about *friendship* reflect particularly close relationships, using the word *'ōhēb*, 'one who loves'. In these and other proverbs there are insights into the nature of true friendship. A friend loves at all times (17:17); a true friend is closer than a brother (18:24); love covers all offences, whereas hatred stirs up strife (10:12). Friends should never be forsaken (27:10). Some proverbs recognize that friendship may be endangered by faults on one side, but forgiveness will preserve the relationship (17:9). Chapter 27, verses 5–6 probe the nature of true friendship even more deeply: the true friend rebukes his partner when there is cause to do so, but this is the distinguishing mark of friendship; it is only enemies who falsely pretend that all is well.

Law and Justice

There are no clear references in Proverbs to a system of law whether divine or human. The word *tôrâ*, which elsewhere in the Old Testament often denotes the law of Yahweh but also frequently means instruction or teaching, occurs 13 times in the book; in most instances (1:8; 3:1; 4:2; 6:20; 7:2; 28:7; 31:26) it denotes instruction given to young men by parents or teachers, or, in 13:14, by the 'wise'. In the other instances (6:23; 28:4, 9; 29:18) its source is not indicated but readers may well have interpreted it in the same way, although it is certainly possible that it came later to be understood as meaning the law of Moses or of Yahweh. No specific law is mentioned.

On the level of human justice also no specific laws are mentioned, though some proverbs probably imply their existence. There is, however, nothing to indicate their provenance. As a judge or administer of justice only the king is mentioned (e.g. 20:8) as having power and insight to judge between the innocent and the guilty. There is however in the book a general recognition that the life of the community ought to be governed by certain principles of justice. This is made clear in the general preface to the book

(1:2–6) in which the aim of the work is defined as the inculcation of wisdom. Prominent among the principles of wisdom listed there is the acquisition of ṣedeq, mišpāṭ and mêšārîm (1:3). These terms overlap in meaning to some extent, but not entirely. Mišpāṭ, often rendered in English by 'justice', is also frequently used in the Old Testament of legal judgements; ṣedeq most frequently denotes the principle of moral rightness; mêšārîm, which occurs less frequently, is often rendered by 'equity'. These three terms, which also occur together in 2:9 where it is stated that they proceed from Yahweh, combine to assert the importance of the equitable administration of justice in the life of the community.

That some kind of tribunal exists for the administration of justice is assumed, but its nature is not clearly defined. It appears to have been concerned with serious crimes, but also with 'civil' disputes between individual citizens – though in the latter case it is not always possible to distinguish between quarrels that could be settled informally and cases that came before the court, since the same term (rîb) is applied to both. That justice was sometimes done is clear from a number of proverbs (e.g. 21:15; 29:4); but many others refer to instances of the miscarriage of justice. Particularly frequent are allusions to lying witnesses (e.g. 12:17; 14:5, 25; 19:5, 9) The attitudes of the writers of the proverbs towards bribery are ambiguous. In 17:8 it is claimed that it works like a charm (cf. 21:14, where it is stated that gifts and bribery avert anger). A jealous and wronged husband cannot be bought off with gifts (6:35). There were cases of unjust punishment (17:26), and 18:17 refers to doubtful cases where there is conflicting testimony. In such cases decisions might be made by the casting of lots (18:18).

Far more frequent than these references to human justice are proverbs that speak of the fate of those who commit crimes or indulge in anti-social activities that are not punishable by legal sanctions. In such cases the authors are confident that retribution will come either by the direct action of Yahweh who controls human destinies or through the operation of a principle of natural retribution. Social disgrace is also mentioned (18:3; 19:26), as is private retaliation against the adulterer by the aggrieved husban. (6:32–35). Sexual offences are condemned, though it is not clear that the penalties fell within the jurisdiction of the law (see, e.g., the rather unclear passage 5:7–14).

Wisdom

The facts that the words 'wise', 'to be wise' and 'wisdom' occur more than one hundred times in Proverbs and that there is no chapter in the book that does not contain at least one occurrence is a clear indication of the paramount importance for its authors of wisdom as an essential prerequisite for the attainment of the good life. Parts of the book specifically claim to be the work of wise persons. Three main sections, those beginning in 1:1, 10:1 and 25:1, are attributed to Solomon, who was universally regarded as supremely wise, and two other sections are attributed in their superscriptions (22:17; 24:23) to anonymous 'wise men'. The persons named as authors of the two remaining sections of the book, Agur the son of Jakeh (30:1) and the mother of King Lemuel (31:1) are otherwise unknown, but they also were presumably accounted by the editors of the book to have been no less wise than the other, named, authors.

The general preface (1:2–6) states that the purpose of the proverbs that follow is to enable the reader to acquire a knowledge of wisdom, which is associated with instruction or education (v. 2), and proceeds to define some aspects of this. Wisdom can be learned by the 'simple' and by the young (v. 4); but even those who are already wise can profit by further instruction in it (v. 5). Such instruction will among other things inculcate the virtues of justice and equity (v. 3). For the authors or editors of the book this acquisition of wisdom is not an option to be taken up or discarded at whim; it is essential to the good life. This is emphasized in later chapters where it is asserted that wisdom is the most precious of all things, more precious even than jewels, gold or silver (3:15; 8:11, 19; 16:16). In 4:4, 7 the father or teacher claims to be following his own father's teaching in urging his pupil to 'Get wisdom!' whatever else he acquires.

What, then, is this wisdom that is so earnestly advocated in this book? It is not given a philosopher's definition, and the character and deeds of the 'wise person' and the advantages and benefits that his wisdom brings to himself and others can only be learned from a detailed perusal of the proverbs themselves, complemented and confirmed by passages in which wisdom is personified and speaks about 'herself'. Wisdom and the wise are frequently contrasted in many lines or passages with wisdom's opposite, folly, and the fools whose fate is precisely the opposite of the wise, hindering any possibility of the good life for themselves and for others who are affected or persuaded by them.

The number of proverbs in the book that describe the wise man (or speak more generally of the nature of wisdom) is so great that it is not possible here to do more then select some that illustrate the main characteristics of wisdom.

1. The wise do not boast of their wisdom. It is only fools who do so (3:7; 26:5, 12, 16; 28:11). The wise man, on the contrary, is humble (11:2). He realizes that he has more to learn, and is ready to take instruction and advice (1:5; 10:8; 12:15; 13:10; 18:15; 21:11). He is diligent and hardworking (cf. 6:6–11), and does not over-indulge in food or drink (20:1; 23:20–21). He avoids wrong-doing (14:16) and keeps his temper (29:11). Above all, he is one who recognizes that true wisdom consists in fearing Yahweh – that is, in acknowledging him and doing his will (1:7; 9:10; 15:33).

2. Secondly, the wise man has a definite aim in life; unlike the fool who loses his way, he 'finds the right way' and pursues it. He seeks the company of those whom he knows to be wise in order to learn from them and follow their example (13:20; 15:31). He is the person who above all tries to promote harmony in his community. While he avoids becoming embroiled in other people's disputes and refuses to go to law with a fool because to do so would only subject him to abuse and get him nowhere (29:9). He restrains his anger (29:11) and acts as a peacemaker, seeking to deflect the fury of quarrelsome neighbours (29:8).

3. A third service that the wise man performs for his fellow-citizens is carried out principally through the power of his *words*. Throughout the book of Proverbs a very strong emphasis is placed on the power of speech and its effects on others for good or evil. The mouth of the righteous brings forth wisdom (10:31), and the teaching of the wise is described as a fountain of life – that is, it makes the good life possible for others, who through heeding it will avoid the snares of death (13:14). Chapter 12, verse 18 similarly states that the tongue of the wise brings healing while rash words can be as sharp as a sword. The wise man's words help others to acquire knowledge (15:2, 7), and when his rebukes are heeded they are of great value to the listener (25:12). Their effectiveness is due to the fact that they proceed from a wise mind (16:23).
4. Every aspect of the good life is promised to the wise. First, security: those who 'walk by wisdom' will be safe (28:26), whereas those who trust in their own abilities are fools. This confirms the saying of 2:6 that it is Yahweh who is the source of human wisdom. Wealth (21:20; 14;14), honour (3:35) and power (21:22) are also among the rewards of the wise, although the reader is also warned that a good reputation is preferable to wealth (22:1) and that those who are in a hurry to acquire wealth are at fault and will be punished (28:20). According to 10:23 to have understanding is a delight in itself; and 3:13–18 offers a list of the rewards of wisdom: it is more valuable than any treasure; it gives long life, wealth, honour, enjoyment and peace; for those who possess it it is a 'tree of life' and a source of unalloyed happiness.

This teaching about the nature, qualities and gifts of wisdom is reinforced in a number of passages by means of the device of presenting wisdom to the reader under the figure of a desirable woman. The principle passages in question are 1:20–33 and 8:1–36; in these the personified Wisdom herself speaks. In some other passages such as 3:13–18 and 4:6–9 also Wisdom is described in female terms. In chapter 8 she is represented as calling out to passers by in the streets of the city to associate with her, for 'whoever finds me finds life and obtains favour from Yahweh' (v. 35). She claims to possess and to offer to her audience gifts that are elsewhere stated to be those of the wise man: she is herself a teacher, and the instruction that she gives is more valuable than jewels (v. 11); she speaks what is true and righteous (vv. 6–9); she loves those who love her (v. 17); she offers riches, honour (v. 18) and wealth (v. 21). But she claims much more than these things: in vv. 15–16 she asserts that she – that is, wisdom – is not just a personal quality of certain individuals but is a cosmic power by which the world is governed. Moreover, in this chapter Wisdom asserts more clearly than anywhere else her intimate relationship to Yahweh himself who created her before he created the world (vv. 22–30) and set her to delight in the human race (v. 31). She thus confirms the teaching of the rest of the book by asserting that to 'find' her – that is, to become wise – is essential to the good life: 'whoever finds me finds life', and those who fail to do so or who hate her injure themselves and 'love death' (vv. 32–36).

In Proverbs, wisdom is closely associated with *education* and the function of the teacher; in this the book is entirely unique among Old Testament literature. In fact, as the Preface (1:2–6) states, the purpose of the entire book is to teach wisdom. These few verses are astonishingly replete with educational and intellectual terms: da'at, 'knowledge', mûsār, 'instruction', bînâ, 'understanding', haśkēl, 'insight', 'ormâ, 'intelligence', mĕzimmâ, 'shrewdness', leqaḥ, 'learning', nābôn, 'a person of understanding', taḥbūlôt, 'skill', hābîn, 'to understand'. This educational process is particularly addressed to the young and inexperienced, but is also applicable to those who have already acquired wisdom: it is a never-ending process.

That this teaching is however addressed primarily to the young is shown by the frequent occurrence of the phrase 'my son' introducing an admonition expressed in the imperative. In chapters 1–7, where there are a number of extended passages in which this kind of advice is given, the teacher describes himself as a father (1:8; 4:1; 6:20). But the formula 'my son' is not confined to these chapters. It occurs sporadically elsewhere in the book (19:27; 23:15, 19; 24:13,

21; 27:11). In other passages it is the father who is addressed
as the one responsible for his son's education: he is
admonished to exercise a severe discipline over his son,
particularly involving corporal punishment, in order to drive
out folly from him 'while there is hope' (19:18) and so ensure
that he does not misbehave in later life and suffer the
consequences of his misconduct (13:24; 19:18; 22:6, 15;
23:13–14; 29:17). The content of the teaching given has
been described above. One feature of it, emphasized
especially in the father's instruction in chapters 1–7, could
be called self-interest: the attentive pupil will live a long and
successful life. But both in these and the succeeding chapters
a more profound note is sounded: wisdom comes from
Yahweh himself, and the marks of those who possess it are
moral behaviour and the 'fear of Yahweh'.

Joy and Pleasure

The book of Proverbs takes its pleasures seriously. There are
very few explicit references to material pleasures. Wealth is
highly praised, but even wealth is profitless if not accompanied by righteousness (11:4) and is ephemeral (23:4–5).
There are very few references to feasting, and these do not
on the whole represent it as necessarily pleasurable (e.g.
23:6–8, 29–35). Only 9:1–6, where Wisdom is represented
(metaphorically) as giving a large party, represents such
entertainment as pleasurable. The full barns and bursting
wine-vats of 3:9–10 that are the reward of those who pay
their dues to Yahweh are no doubt a source of pleasure to
their owner. A group of proverbs refer to honey, which is
described as sweet and good (24:13). Wild honey,
discovered by chance, is a source of delight, but the writers
warn against eating too much of it (25:16, cf. v. 27) and
declare that a sated appetite spurns honey (27:7). Another
source of pleasure is the hearing of good news (25:25). The
specific source of pleasure that is most consistently referred
to is the possession of a good wife (e.g. 18:22; 31:10–31 and
especially 5:15–19).
  Pleasure, enjoyment and happiness in Proverbs are almost

always the reward or consequence of virtue or piety. They are the result of righteousness and goodness, of obedience to the teacher's instruction, of embracing or following wisdom, of just behaviour, kindness and generosity. But the nature of this reward is scarcely ever defined: the reader is not told of what it consists or what form it takes. It is expressed in a fairly small number of general terms: to rejoice (*śāmaḥ*), joy (*śimḥâ*), bless (*bērēk*), blessing (*bĕrākâ*), favour or delight (*rāṣôn*) and the exclamation 'Happy is/are ... !' (*'ašĕrê*).

Of the eight proverbs which use the term *'ašĕrê* (the meaning of one, 28:14, 'Happy is the one who is never without fear' (NRSV), is obscure) three associate happiness with wisdom: it comes to those who find wisdom (3:13), listen to it (8:34) or keep its ways (8:32). Happiness is also given to those who trust in Yahweh (16:20), are kind to the poor (14:21), imitate their righteous parents (20:7) and keep the 'law' (29:18). The verb *śāmaḥ* (to rejoice) is also used of the righteous, especially of the joy of parents when they have a wise son (10:1; 15:20; 23:15, 24, 25; 27:11; 29:3). But it can also be used of more mundane pleasures (27:9a). The adjective *śāmēaḥ* simply means 'cheerful' but the cause of this is not defined (15:13; 17:22), though the wicked obtain pleasure from doing evil (2:14). The noun *rāṣôn* is usually used of Yahweh's pleasure in the honest and the pious (11:1, 20; 12:2, 22; 14:9; 15:8; 18:22), but also of his reaction to those who find wisdom (8:35). *Bĕrākâ* is used similarly of those whom Yahweh deems worthy of his blessing.

God

Proverbs is unusual among the Old Testament books in that not one but two persons appear to be portrayed as wholly responsible for the attainment of the good life. Indeed, the book contains more references to wisdom than to Yahweh, and there are passages (e.g. chapter 4) in which wisdom is presented as the key to success and happiness and Yahweh is not mentioned at all. However, the book when read as a whole makes it plain that the wisdom that the reader is exhorted to acquire is entirely subordinate to God. In 3:19 it is stated that it was through wisdom that Yahweh founded the earth; and 8:22–31, in which the personified Wisdom herself speaks, elaborates this statement: Yahweh *created* wisdom at the beginning of his creative work (v. 22). In this chapter wisdom is seen as having been from the outset a link between Yahweh and his created world, rejoicing before him but also rejoicing in the human race (vv. 30, 32). To find wisdom is to find life: but it is also the way to Yahweh's favour (v. 35). The human teacher in 2:6 tells his pupil that it is Yahweh who will give him wisdom; and the repeated formula of 1:7 and 9:10 which frames chapters 1–9 defines wisdom in terms of the fear of Yahweh – another way of saying that, despite the extravagant terms in which the importance of wisdom is vaunted in some passages, it is in the faithful service of Yahweh that human beings find their true calling. In fact, 21:30 speaks of a potential conflict between wisdom and Yahweh in the sense that human 'wisdom' that does not recognize Yahweh as its source is not wisdom at all and is bound to fail.

Yahweh is praised in Proverbs both for his omnipotence and his benevolence. He is the creator of the world and everything in it; he sees, knows and tests the human heart; he controls human conduct and rewards the good and the righteous. In 3:19–20 it is asserted that he is the creator of heaven and earth, referring to his benevolent provision of water, in the form of rain and springs, which are necessary for animal and human life. In 8:22–31 there is a hymn which speaks in greater detail of his creation of the soil, the mountains, the sky and the sea. His creation of human beings is no less stressed, while 20:12 points out that it is he who gave them the ability to see and hear. In other proverbs this aspect of his creative work is mentioned in connection with his moral purpose and especially of his concern for the poor. Even the wicked, who are destined for disaster, are his creatures (16:4). It is emphasized that the rich and the poor (22:2) – or even the poor and their oppressors (29:13) – are equally his creatures. Those who oppress or mock the poor insult their Maker (14:31; 17:5), while those who are generous to the needy honour him (14:31). (In these verses God is referred to as their 'Maker' rather than by his name, probably to make the point that each person was created as an individual with a personal responsibility for his conduct.)

Several proverbs emphasize the fact that not only human actions but even their secret thoughts are constantly under Yahweh's scrutiny. His eyes are in every place (15:3), he sees into human hearts (5:21; 15:11) and he weighs or tests the human heart or spirit (16:2; 17:3; 21:2). He controls human actions and destinies and determines events (16:33; 20:24), often frustrating whatever human plans may have been made (16:9; 19:21; 21:31). Only if human plans have been previously submitted to him will they succeed (16:3).

Proverbs is emphatic about the benefits that Yahweh confers on those of whose conduct he approves. These benefits cover most of the range of what we have defined as the good life. Chapter 19, verse 23, referring to the 'fear of Yahweh', affirms that it leads to 'life', explaining this in terms of security and freedom from harm, while 22:4 further states that the reward for humility and the fear of Yahweh is riches and honour and life. In 18:10 and 29:25 there are two more proverbs that promise security, respectively to the righteous and those who trust in Yahweh. Wealth is promised also to those who trust in Yahweh (28:25) and to those who have received Yahweh's blessing (10:22), while 29:26 gives the assurance that it is from Yahweh that one will get justice, which may not be obtainable from rulers, although accord-ing to 21:1 even the hearts of kings are under Yahweh's control. In 6:16-19 it is affirmed that he will hear the prayer of the righteous. The wicked, on the other hand, are destined for punishment. In 6:16-19 there is a list of seven things that are particularly abominable to him; they comprise both actual crimes and other examples of anti-social behaviour — lies, deceit, murder, false testimony, disruption of family harmony — that are destructive of the good life and are identified in many other proverbs as incurring divine punishment. It is thus apparent that the good life in the book of Proverbs is offered to the person whose entire life is entirely controlled by Yahweh, who is its sole source.

Summary

Proverbs provides much information about the good life from the perspective of an observer. In contrast to many other books, there are few references to the land, but the need for security is never far from the thoughts of the authors. The monarchy is taken for granted, but the king is only one of those who possess power. Disapproval of the rich is expressed because they abuse their power, but inequality is taken for granted. Hard work is frequently urged on the young as a means to obtain wealth and avoid poverty. In Proverbs 'life' stands for all that is good for human beings, and is commonly used figuratively, as is 'death' also, yet long life is a positive good. Family life is frequently mentioned in Proverbs, where the teaching is often given by a father to his son. Monogamy is taken as normal, and mothers have an important place within the family. Although there is no reference in the book to daughters, this does not mean that girls received no education, and the book ends with a rich account of a happy family, whose prosperity depends on the wife. Great importance is attached to all social relationships within the community, with many references to friends and neighbours. Justice is important, and there are many references to lying witnesses and the fate that will befall those who commit wrong. Wisdom is of supreme importance to the authors, and the wise are frequently contrasted with fools. The authors enjoy pleasures, which are seen as the reward of virtue and wisdom. Uniquely in the Old Testament, Proverbs contains more references to wisdom than to God, but wisdom is subordinated to him. God is creator both of the world and of human beings, the maintainer of goodness and justice, and the source of the good life.

14
Ecclesiastes

Many of the elements of the good life are discussed in this book: security, power, wealth, longevity, the family, justice, wisdom, enjoyment and pleasure. Qoheleth (the Hebrew form of the word translated Ecclesiastes) recognized that these are the things that are most sought after; but he warned his readers that none of them could provide total satisfaction, either because they are not available to all or because they are in themselves of limited value. This unsatisfactory state of affairs he most frequently characterized by the word *hebel* ('vanity'), which occurs more than 30 times in this short book — roughly half the total number of occurrences in the whole of the Old Testament. The frequency of his use of this term could give the impression that he believed that there is nothing in human life that can be called 'good'. In fact the word *tôb*, 'good' occurs even more frequently in the book — about 50 times; and in many of the passages in which it occurs it is used of something that helps to make life worthwhile. So in 2:26 and 7:26 it refers to those who please God — that is, who are 'good' in his eyes. Qoheleth also speaks very positively of opportunities for enjoyment, eating and drinking and finding pleasure in one's activities (2:24; 3:12, 13, 22; 5:16; 8:15). In 9:9 he recommends the reader to enjoy the companionship of his wife, and in 9:10 to do whatever he does with vigour and enthusiasm. He asserts that it is good to be alive (9:4) and to see the sun (11:7), and, using the phrase 'Better (*tôb*) is ... than ... !', he advises his readers to chose a course of action which will be most advantageous to them: so. a quiet life is better than overwork (4:6); wisdom is better than brute strength and weapons of war (9:16, 18). Such pieces of advice, all involving the use of *tôb*, make it clear that, despite his occasional declaration that he hates life (e.g. 2:17), life for him was by no means entirely lacking in positive qualities. He was, however, a realist, recognizing what is bad in life. The word *ra'*, 'bad, evil', occurs 17 times and *rā'â* (with the same meaning) 14 times in the book. They refer especially to 'what is done under the sun' and to the evil that is in men's hearts (e.g. 9:3; 8:11, 12).

Place and Security

Like the authors of the other 'wisdom books' Proverbs and Job, Qoheleth makes no reference to Israel or its land. When he uses the word *'ereṣ*, which in Hebrew can mean either a particular country or the world, it frequently has the latter sense — e.g., 'God is in heaven and you on earth' (5:2); 'the earth remains for ever' (1:4). Only in two passages (5:9; 10:16, 17) does he use it to denote a particular political state, and these are not allusions to the land of Israel but general comments on the advantages and disadvantages of the monarchical system in general. Moreover, in contrast with Job and Proverbs which refer constantly to landed property and agricultural labour, Qoheleth only rarely mentions a connection with the soil (3:2; 11:4, 6); he is more preoccupied with business interests and the making (and losing) of money thereby (5:13–15; 7:12; 10:19; 11:1–2).

Although the readership envisaged by Qoheleth was a Jewish (Israelite) one, the book has a much wider reference: it is concerned with humanity (*'ādām*) in general. This word occurs some 50 times. In most cases (e.g. in the phrase *běnê hā'ādām*, literally 'the sons of men') it denotes the whole human race; in others an individual member of it. The contexts in which it is used describe aspects of the human situation in general: e.g. whether people gain any profit from their labour (1:3; 2:22); the similarity between human beings and animals (3:18, 19); human inability to dispute with God (6:10); whether in view of their mortality the lives of human beings can be called good (6:12); the evil in human hearts (8:11); human inability to foresee the future (9:12), etc. it is *universal* problems with which Qoheleth is concerned.

Qoheleth's concern, however, is with the place and the security of human beings in a special and unusual sense: he asserts that they lack security because their very place *in this world* is ephemeral. He asks, 'Who knows what is good for human beings who live out the few days of their unsatisfactory life (*hayyê heblô*) which they pass like a shadow?' (6:12). This insubstantial existence is due above all to the fact of human *mortality*, a theme that Qoheleth introduces into his reflections again and again. He teaches that the realization that we must all die ought always to be present in a person's thoughts and should even determine the way in which he lives his life. Thus 'It is better to go to the house of mourning than to go to the house of feasting, for that [i.e. death] is the end of everyone, and the living should take this to heart' (7:2). Qoheleth emphasizes the extreme brevity of a person's life in comparison with the eternity that follows his death, and seems to suggest that it is Sheol, the place of the dead, which is his true home: Sheol is 'where you are going' (9:10) and even those who live to be old should remember that in death 'the days of darkness will be many' (11:8). This does not mean that Qoheleth recommended a life filled with gloomy thoughts: on the contrary, the very fact that in Sheol 'there is no activity and no making of plans, no knowledge and no wisdom' (9:10) should inspire a person to put all his energy and enthusiasm into his activities while life lasts. Indeed, the awareness of one's mortality ought to increase rather than diminish the enjoyment of life especially while one is young (11:9–12:1). Nevertheless it was Qoheleth's purpose to remind his readers that life is transitory and that this world is not their permanent 'place'. There is no real security because even the time of our death is unknown to us and it could happen at any time: 'man does not know his "time"' (9:12) and has no control over the day of his death (8:8).

Another cause of the feeling of insecurity according to Qoheleth is that whatever a person may have achieved in life may come to nothing after his death. 'It sometimes happens that a person who has toiled by wisdom, knowledge and skill must leave it all to one who has not toiled for it' (2:21; cf. 6:2); 'As he came naked from his mother's womb, so he must return, naked as he came; he can take away nothing from his toil' (5:15). But the worst fear is that after death one will be completely forgotten as if one had never

existed, so making one's life and achievements meaningless
(1:11; 9:6).

Yet another cause of the feeling of insecurity is human
ignorance. Human beings have been set in a world that they
do not and cannot understand, and consequently feel help-
less. Moreover, this ignorance is deliberately intended by
their Creator, who has made it an ineluctible feature of
human nature. To illustrate this situation Qoheleth frequently uses the word *māṣā'* 'to find, find out, discover'
accompanied by the negative particle 'not'. It is by God's
decision that human beings 'cannot find out what God has
done from beginning to end' (3:11), nor can they find out
what will be their own individual futures (7:14). Even what
will happen to them after their death is uncertain (3:21).
However hard they may try to find out what God is doing
in the world they can never succeed (8:17). Qoheleth emphasizes that there are no exceptions to this barrier that God
has placed against attempts to understand: any claim by self-
styled 'wise men' to know what God is doing is false.
Qoheleth himself, who had the reputation of being a wise
man (12:9), recalls that although he had set out with the firm
intention of employing his intellectual resources to solve
these fundamental problems, he had discovered that they
were beyond his powers. Reality (literally, 'that which is'), he
confesses, 'is far off and deep, deep: who can find it out?'
(7:23–24).

Power

Qoheleth refers frequently to those who exercise power
over others. But the readers whom he addresses are clearly
not among the powerful; rather, if not themselves victims of
arbitrary power, they are on the receiving end of it; they are
subjects rather than rulers, and for them the existence of
such power is not represented by Qoheleth as conducive to
their enjoyment of the good life. He is clearly on the side of
the powerless, even though among his readers there may be
some who have personal fortunes. He shows no interest in
the lives and concerns of the ruling class, and makes no

reference to military power or displays of national pride. Power, however, like everything else, is ephemeral: he points out that even that of Solomon was ultimately futile and transient (2:11, 18–19).

Qoheleth had no illusions about human nature and its innate love of power. In 8:9–11, referring to the fact that those who oppress others are not speedily punished, he remarks that this encourages the following of their example; he attributes this to the inherent evil of the human heart (cf. also 9:3). That such practices were common in his time is indicated by the number of his references to them. He refers to powerful oppressors whose victims obtain no redress from their sufferings (4:1) and to the iniquity of a hierarchical system of power which permits the persecution of the poor (5:8–9), and deplores a judicial system that often acquits the guilty and punishes the innocent (3:16; 7;15).

Qoheleth's advice on behaviour towards those in authority (he mentions the king in 8:2–5 and 10:20, the 'ruler', *môšēl*, in 10:4 and *šallîṭ* in 10:5) is to be totally obedient. They have absolute power (8:3, 4) and moreover there is a system of informers (10:20). One must 'keep the king's command' (8:2) and also choose the appropriate time to approach him (8:5). If one does unfortunately offend the ruler the best thing to do is to keep calm (10:4). In 4:13–16, however, he points out that there may be sudden changes of regime, while in 10:5–6 he suggests that rulers are prone to misjudgements over the appointments of their officials. In general it is clear that Qoheleth's experience led him to the conclusion that power is most frequently the power to harm others rather than to promote the well-being of those who are obliged to submit themselves to it.

Wealth and Sustenance

For Qoheleth, personal wealth, like everything else in life, is a gift from God and is to be enjoyed (5:19); but it is not given to everybody, and God does not always give to its recipients the power to enjoy it (6:1–3). However, Qoheleth advises his readers to make the most of prosperity while they possess it and also to accept bad fortune if it comes their way because it also is sent by God. He warns them that God has seen to it that they will be unable to discover the reason for God's actions (7:14).

Qoheleth himself evidently did not consider himself or his readers to belong to the opulent class: this is shown by the fact that in 10:20 he advises them not to speak ill either of the king or of the rich because what they say may be reported to the authorities. On the other hand, he distinguished himself and his readers from the poor: this can be seen from his references to the poor as a distinct class (4:13; 6:8; 9:13–16). In 5:12, however, he points out that the labouring man – though not the completely destitute – has one advantage over the rich in that he is free from the worries that trouble the rich and so sleeps sound.

Qoheleth devoted a considerable part of his book to the topic of wealth. His main concerns were to point out the ephemeral nature of wealth and its precariousness, and also the folly of making its acquisition the most important goal in life. Chapters 1 and 2, where he speaks in the persona of the ancient and famous king Solomon, are a kind of parable designed to show the futility of both wealth and the search for wisdom. Solomon is here presented as the possessor of greater wealth than any person in history. He used his wealth to life a live of unparalleled luxury, acquiring houses, vineyards, gardens and orchards, slaves, herds and flocks, silver and gold, male and female singers and concubines in great numbers (2:4–8), making him greater than all his predecessors (2:9). Yet at the end of it 'Solomon' concluded that it was all *hebel*, 'vanity', fundamentally unsatisfactory and profitless (2:11). Moreover, he reflected that his possessions would not survive him but would pass into the hands of others who had not created it (2:18–21). He drew the further conclusion that these frustrations were not peculiar to him but applied equally to all human beings. With this 'Solomonic' monologue (1:12–2:23) Qoheleth set the tone for the rest of the book in which he questioned the value of both wealth and luxurious living and the human quest for wisdom. The reader was clearly intended to reflect that if even the great and wealthy Solomon had found no satisfaction in his wealth, this was bound *a fortiori* to be true of the experiences of ordinary mortals.

In 5:10–20, a section entirely devoted to the topic of wealth, Qoheleth expounds in greater detail the views put forward in the first chapters. Here he appears to refer to specific cases known to him. Verse 10 speaks of those for whom the *desire* for wealth is paramount, so that even when it has been fulfilled it breeds an insatiable desire for more. Verse 11 appears to refer to the swarms of hangers-on who by one means or another contrive to get hold of a rich man's money so that in the end he gets no benefit from it. Verse 12, as has already been noted, comments on the situation of the super-rich, whose continual worries about their business enterprises deprive them of sleep while the poor labourer has no such worries. Verses 13–14 refer to actual cases where these worries prove to be justified, and wealthy persons unexpectedly lose all their money and are left with nothing with which to provide for their children, and vv. 15–17 to the fact that death finally deprives the rich of their accumulated wealth. The conclusion (vv. 18–20) is that one should recognize that happiness comes from accepting what God gives, whether it is much or little. Clearly, in contrast with views reflected elsewhere in the Old Testament, the society in which Qoheleth lived was one in which individuals could easily make personal fortunes and equally easily lose them. His concern was to show by these varied examples that the achievement of happiness through contentment with one's lot is more important than the urge to make money.

Other references to wealth in the book are mainly in the same vein. In 3:22 Qoheleth states that happiness is to be obtained from the enjoyment of one's work, which has been allotted by God, and in 6:1–3 points out that wealth is not always accompanied by the ability to enjoy it. In 10:5–7 he notes the unpredictability of a society in which roles may be reversed so that the rich are reduced to a humble status. In 11:1–2, however, he gives practical advice of a specific kind: addressing, presumably, those with money to invest, and recommending dividing one's commercial enterprises into several parts to guard against total failure in a world where final disaster is a real possibility and unpredictable.

In view of these uncertainties Qoheleth has further positive advice. No less than five times he expresses his prescription for happiness in virtually the same terms: that of eating and drinking. In 2:24 he states that 'There is nothing better for a person than to eat and drink and find enjoyment in his work'. The same prescription, in similar words, is found in 3:13, 5:18, 8:15 and 9:7. It is not certain whether these references to eating and drinking are intended to be understood literally. Probably this is so, although they may also have a wider meaning. It would seem that Qoheleth is here recommending the living of a normal though modest life as distinct from the luxurious life-style of the rich.

Several of these verses occur at the end of a pericope: 2:24–26 conclude the Solomonic chapters; 3:12–13 follow a section on the 'times' that God has set for human lives, which they are incapable of discerning; 5:18–20 conclude the discussion on wealth; 8:15 forms the conclusion to a section on the iniquities of human injustice; 9:7–10 follow sombre reflections on mortality. The fact that Qoheleth depicted the enjoyment of normal, happy life in terms of bodily sustenance (eating and drinking) probably has its significance in that it appears to express an approval of modest, unostentatious wealth. In 2:24–26 indeed he makes this point explicitly: the person who eats, drinks and enjoys life (v. 24) is the one of whom God approves; and he is contrasted in v. 26 with the person of whom God does *not* approve, who amasses wealth but only to see it pass into the hands of others. In 9:7–10 Qoheleth also depicts a life of modest affluence as the pleasant lot of the person who pleases God. And above all, in 5:18–20 he depicts the life of the one who because God approves of him is given wealth together with the means to enjoy it, in contrast to those depicted in the previous verses as frustrated in their attempts to hang on to these things.

Mortality and the Human Life-span

In order to understand Qoheleth's views about the human life-span it is necessary first to consider his teaching about the value of life itself. He admitted that there were those for whom life appeared to have no positive value: for those who were desperately unhappy or whose life is a burden to them death or non-existence would be preferable to life. Even Solomon, who possessed everything that could have been expected to make life enjoyable, is represented as saying 'I hated life'. This was because his experience had taught him that his wisdom ultimately gave him no advantage over fools, and that after his death he would be forgotten (2:17–18 – though ironically Solomon was *not* in fact forgotten by Qoheleth, nor presumably by his readers, but was recognized as one of the great men of antiquity!). Qoheleth also gives other specific instances of persons whose lives are so marked by wretchedness that it would have been better if they had not been born or had been stillborn and so had remained ignorant of how wicked the world could be: such were the victims of constant brutal oppression (4:1–3) and those who, even though they lived a long life and were blessed with a numerous family, were temperamentally incapable of enjoying life (6:1–3). Qoheleth was nothing if not a realist, and he acknowledged that there are exceptional cases.

But for himself Qoheleth believed that life could and should be enjoyed, and so he taught his readers. He quoted with approval the proverb 'Life is sweet, and it is pleasant for the eyes to see the sun' (11:7), adding 'Even those who live many years should rejoice in them all' (11:8); and asserted that despite the evil and the madness that prevails in the world 'Whoever is counted among the living has hope', clinching this statement with yet another proverb: 'A living dog is better than a dead lion' (9:3–4). He advised both the old (11:8) and young (11:9) to enjoy their lives, even though or because the time would come when they would no longer be capable of doing so (12:1).

Qoheleth's call to make the most of life was made with a clear recognition of the limits of human existence. Human beings are mortal, subject to the inevitability of death; their lives are so brief as to be little more than a moment in the perspective of God's eternity. Moreover, no-one can predict the *time* of his death, which like everything else is subject to

God's decision – though again there are exceptional cases where certain human actions or proclivities can hasten death by attracting God's judgement (7:16, 17). Although some people attained a great age (6:3), Qoheleth spoke of human life as 'the *few* days that God has given us' (5:18; 6:12), a state of affairs that he describes as *hebel* (6:12; 7:15; 9:9). Life is 'passed like a shadow' (6:12; 8:13).

Qoheleth expressed his conviction of God's absolute control over the duration of human lives with his doctrine of the 'time' (*'ēt*) or 'times' that have been fixed by God. In 3:1–8 he states that God has ordained 'a time for everything'; and among these is 'a time to be born and a time to die' (3:2). We cannot, then, foresee our future: 'everything has its time' (8:6), but this time is hidden from us. 'No-one has … power over the day of death' (8:8). He constantly reiterates this teaching in different words, e.g. 'Time and chance happen to all' (9:11), and 'No-one can anticipate the time of disaster' (9:12). Human beings are 'ensnared' in a time of calamity 'when it suddenly comes upon them' (9:12; cf. 10:14; 11:2). Qoheleth advises his readers to be constantly aware of their mortality: 'It is better to go to the house of mourning than to go to the house of feasting; for this is the end of everyone and the living will lay it to heart' (7:2). This thought was rarely absent from his mind. Nevertheless the thoughts of the inevitability of our death and our ignorance of the moment when it will come should not prevent the enjoyment of life while it lasts. To ignore these things is folly; but for Qoheleth life remains a gift of God, and it would be equally folly to ignore that fact. 'Enjoy life with the wife whom you love all the days of your life of *hebel* that are given you under the sun, because that is your portion in life … Whatever your hand finds to do, do with your might; for there is no work or thought or knowledge or wisdom in Sheol, to which you are going' (9:9–10).

In 12:1–7 Qoheleth has given us the fullest picture in the Old Testament of the advance of old age. His purpose was a positive one – not to dwell morbidly on death but to encourage his young readers (11:9) to make the most of their youth and to enjoy life to the full by depicting the 'time of trouble' which will inevitably be their lot when they gradually lose their faculties and sink into decrepitude which will immediately precede the 'days of darkness' which will be many – that is, death. The process of decay will begin with the recognition that the things that used to give pleasure no longer do so (12:1 – cf. the words of the aged Barzillai in 2 Sam. 19:34–35). The stages of physical and mental decline are depicted (12:2–5) partly by means of poetical imagery which is not easy to interpret in detail but of which the general meaning is clear. Eventually (v. 6) 'the silver cord is snapped, the golden bowl is broken, the pitcher is smashed at the spring and the wheel broken at the well', and death ensues. Verse 7, which states that 'the dust returns to the earth from which it came and the breath returns to God who gave it' is reminiscent of Gen. 2:7, and makes sense of the admonition at the beginning of this section (12:1) to 'Remember your Creator': the young man should be aware, even from his youth, of his creation as a mortal being. It is noteworthy that Qoheleth is here portraying a person whose life has come full circle and who dies a natural death. Whether early or late, death will come at the end.

In 3:20 he echoes 12:7: 'All are from the dust, and all turn to dust again'. But these verses (3:20–22) speak of another aspect of the human situation: the question of life *after death*. They express Qoheleth's scepticism – or at least agnosticism – about the possibility of existence after death; but it is again characteristic of him that he uses this reflection to draw a positive conclusion: since we do not and cannot know what will follow our death when our body has returned to dust, there can be nothing better for us than to enjoy our activities in this present life. In 9:9–10 he makes his disbelief in a future life quite clear: he says that we are all destined to end in Sheol, the realm of the dead, reminding the readers of a belief that he shares with almost all the other Old Testament writers: Sheol is a place where there is 'no work, no thought, no knowledge and no wisdom', Sheol is the negation of all that is worthwhile, a shadowy world with no positive qualities. But once again Qoheleth uses this thought to give a particularly emphatic piece of advice to enjoy this life as much as possible, with good food and drink, fine clothes and precious unguents and the companionship of a beloved wife, and to go about one's activities with joyful enthusiasm. He uses the word 'portion' or 'lot' here as elsewhere to indicate that this kind of life meets with God's approval.

Family

In contrast with the authors of many of the books of the Old Testament, where the possession of a wife and children is regarded as an extremely important aspect of life, Qoheleth has little to say about this. About his own family, if he had any, he says nothing at all. Yet his references to himself especially in his use of first person singular verbs and of the personal pronoun 'I' ('*ănî*) constitute one of the most striking features of his book. However, his concern in this regard was with his *intellectual* processes, particularly with his search for wisdom and his reactions to the world and society. His reticence about his personal life does not necessarily mean that he had no wife or family; these are matters which may well have seemed to him to be irrelevant to his task as a teacher.

In one passage, however, he gives advice to his readers which includes a reference to a wife (9:9). He recommends a life-style of which one of the features is the possession of a wife, and a wife who is beloved. There is no reference in this passage, however, to children. The only other reference to women in the book (apart from a possible allusion to Solomon's concubines in 2:8) is 7:26, 28. This is a notoriously difficult passage, but can hardly, in view of 9:9, be taken as an indication that Qoheleth was a misogynist.

There are a few references in the book to sons, but these are all related to the question of inheritance – a matter which Qoheleth evidently regarded as extremely important. In three passages he deplores the situation of persons who have no heirs to whom they can leave their property. In 2:18–20 it is 'Solomon' who apparently has no legitimate heir and laments that he will have to leave all his great possessions to a stranger, who may be either wise or a fool, and who in any case had not worked to acquire them.

Similarly in 6:2 Qoheleth deplores the plight of persons who have to leave their wealth to be enjoyed by strangers. In 4:7–8 he cites the case of a man living alone with neither sons nor brothers, who deprives himself of an enjoyable life by devoting himself entirely to the acquisition of wealth and never understands the absurdity of his way of life in that he has no one to inherit.

It is in this context and this context alone that Qoheleth refers to the possession of children. In 5:14–16 he cites a case in which parents lose all their money in an unsuccessful business venture and have nothing to leave to their children, and 6:3 mentions a hypothetical case of a rich man who although he has many children – all presumably potential heirs – does not enjoy his life and is not even accorded a proper burial by them. These meagre and somewhat formal references to children cannot be said to reveal a genuine interest in family life; only the reference in 9:9 to a beloved wife reflects any warmth of feeling on this subject.

Justice

It is clear that Qoheleth lacked confidence in the judicial practice of his time. Whether he is alluding to the situation in his own country (5:8) or to human justice in general (what is done 'under the sun', 3:16; 4:1; 10:5), it is noteworthy that he mentions only cases of injustice; he never speaks in praise of impartial decisions by the courts. However, it should also be noted that he sometimes qualifies his comments, perhaps implying that the cases to which he refers may not be entirely representative. So in 7:15 and 8:14 he states merely that 'there are' (yēš) instances when the innocent are convicted and the guilty acquitted; in 3:16 and 10:7 he does no more than to note that he has *seen* similar cases; and in 5:8–9 he tells his readers not to be surprised *if* they see the poor deprived of their rights. The last of these passages may imply that such instances were frequent; but we are probably not justified in supposing that he has given his readers a full account of the judicial practice of his time.

At the same time Qoheleth knew that the miscarriages of

justice that he had observed had their origin in the actions and policy of an absolute ruler who permitted them – 10:5, though sometimes translated otherwise, probably has this meaning. It was the ruler who was responsible for the actions of his subordinates described in vv. 6–7. Under his rule the conventional norms of society were reversed: he gave the highest offices to fools and slaves, and as a result such people were empowered to exercise tyrannical power over others to their detriment (8:9). In 10:16–17 Qoheleth comments on the irresponsible behaviour of unworthy kings and, he implies, longs for a more capable monarch under whose rule the ministers of the crown ('princes') would act responsibly.

But Qoheleth recognized political realities. Above all it is supreme folly for anyone to curse the king or other influential individuals even in private or in one's thoughts, as there may be spies who would report the matter to the authorities (10:20). Qoheleth deplores the severe injustices that he has observed (4:1–3), but does not suggest how they might be remedied. He is an observer and not a reformer, and, as is often the case with those suffering under tyrannical regimes, appears to have thought that discretion was the better part of valour.

In some passages Qoheleth finds comfort in the thought that God himself will intervene to rectify or compensate for the unjust decisions of human courts. His lament in 3:16 that the innocent often fail to be acquitted is followed in the next verse by 'I said in my heart, *God* will give justice to both the innocent and the guilty, for he has appointed a time for every matter and every deed'. This opinion is in conformity with the general Old Testament belief that God is a just judge of human conduct, a belief that is frequently expressed in the book of Proverbs which insists that the wicked will sooner or later be overwhelmed by disaster. His association of this belief with God's fixing of the 'times' will have given reassurance to his readers, who might otherwise have concluded from some of his other statements that God's treatment of human beings is arbitrary. Similarly in 8:12–13 Qoheleth assures his readers that those who do not fear God will eventually be overtaken by God's judgement even though this may be delayed, while those who fear him will be spared.

Wisdom

Ecclesiastes is a book of wisdom *par excellence*. Unlike Proverbs which contains a collection of very brief sayings on various subjects of which wisdom is only one, it is the work of a single-minded author whose aim is to report his personal search for wisdom and the extent of his success or failure in this enterprise. Already in the introductory chapters 'Solomon' states that he had aimed 'to search out by wisdom all that is done under heaven' – in other words, everything that happens in the world (1:13) – an enterprise embracing the whole of human experience. Qoheleth gives a fuller account of this aim in 7:23, 25. He had already '*tested* all this by wisdom'; 'I said, I will be wise' (v. 23). What he meant by 'all this' is explained in v. 25, where he wrote: 'I turned my mind to know and to search out wisdom and the sum of things' (*hešbôn*, 'the reckoning, reason in things') and further in v. 27, where he stated that he had 'added one thing to another to find the sum'. These verses seem to offer an explanation of what 'Solomon' meant in 1:13 when he spoke of searching out by wisdom all that is done under heaven. No other Old Testament writer made such an ambitious attempt.

However, Qoheleth admits that his attempt to 'find the sum' has ended in failure. In 7:23–24 he explicitly confesses that the wisdom he sought was beyond his grasp: 'It was far from me. Reality (literally, 'that which is') is far off, and deep, deep; who can discover it?'. In asking 'Who can . . . ?' (cf. also 'who knows', 3:21; 6:12) he maintains that his failure is not due simply to his personal lack of ability. In fact, he believed himself to be, in the ordinary sense of the word 'wise', a wise man and wiser at least than most. That his view of himself was justified is demonstrated by the existence of the book itself, and was confirmed by the disciple or pupil who wrote 12:9 at the conclusion of the book. Qoheleth came to realize that '*no-one* can discover what happens under the sun.

However much they may toil in their search they will not discover it; even though those who are wise claim to know, they cannot find it out' (8:17). The reason for this lies in human nature itself: when he created men and women God deliberately made them incapable of doing so (3:11). This understanding of the unbridgeable gap between the divine and human natures led Qoheleth to exclaim, when giving advice about prayer, 'God is in heaven and you on earth; therefore let your words be few' (5:2). He failed to discover those things that God had reserved for himself, simply because he was a human being.

But Qoheleth recognized the existence of a more practical and everyday wisdom and encouraged his readers to acquire it. This was a kind of shrewdness that helped a person to make his way through life's ordinary problems and difficulties and so promote the enjoyment of the good life. Like the book of Proverbs Qoheleth divided human beings into two classes: one was either wise or a fool. He contrasts the two in a series of brief sentences:

> Wisdom excels folly as light excels darkness. (2:13)
>
> The wise have eyes in their head but fools walk in darkness. (2:14)
>
> It is better to listen to the rebuke of the wise than to the song of fools. (7:5)
>
> The quiet words of the wise are more to be heeded than the shouting of a ruler among fools. (9:17)
>
> Words spoken by the wise win them favour, but the lips of fools procure their ruin. (10:12)

In 5:4, in urging his readers who have made a vow to God not to anger him by failing to fulfil it, he states baldly: 'God takes no pleasure in fools'. He himself has no time for them. He refers to the disastrous consequences of idleness: 'The fool folds his hands and starves himself to death' (4:5). He notes the propensity of fools to inane mirth: 'Like the crackling of thorns under a pot, so is the laughter of fools' (7:6); yet he also deplores their tendency to harbour resentment: 'Do not

be quick to anger, for anger remains in the bosom of fools'
(7:9). But the fool is easily recognized: 'Even when a fool is
out walking, he cannot behave sensibly but shows everyone
what a fool he is' (10:3), and: 'Effort tires fools, who do not
even know the way to the city' (10:15). Such folly was
evidently intolerable to Qoheleth, who did not hesitate to
point out its inevitable consequences: for the fool there was,
in his opinion, no good life to be had.

Some of the advantages of wisdom according to Qoheleth
have already been mentioned. One of the most important of
them is that it leads to worldly success: 'Words spoken by
the wise bring them favour' (10:12). Qoheleth insists that by
the use of wisdom a person can bring success to an
enterprise that cannot be attained by other means: 'Wisdom
gives strength to the wise more than ten rulers that are in a
city' (7:19). He cites the case of the poor wise man who by
means of his wisdom saved, or *could* have saved, from
destruction or conquest a small underdefended city that was
being besieged by a powerful king with his army (9:14–15),
and commented that 'wisdom is better than brute force' (v.
16) and 'better than weapons of war' (v. 18). This kind of
wisdom will have consisted in giving good advice (cf. 9:17).
But it was also an example of 'knowing the time'. Although
Qoheleth maintained that we cannot know the times that
God has set for the future events of our lives or for the day
of our death (3:11; 8:8; 9:12), he conceded that there is a
place for the operation of wisdom in human situations where
people are free to make their own decisions. So in dealing
with the whims of an arbitrary monarch, the courtier or
minister if he possesses wisdom may be able to exercise
influence over him: 'the wise man will know the time and the
way' (8:4, 5). Also in more everyday and quite trivial
situations such as the splitting of logs, the application of
wisdom to the situation will prove efficacious (10:10); here
'wisdom' (ḥokmâ) means no more than common sense or
perhaps expertise. In general, 'wisdom protects the life of
those who possess it' (7:12).

Yet for Qoheleth even the possession of ordinary,
practical wisdom has its limitations and its failures. When
'Solomon' deplores the fact that the same fate will befall

both the wise man and the fool and that both will be
forgotten after their deaths (2:14b–16) and so qualifies his
previous praise of the superiority of wisdom given in the
preceding verses, he was probably referring to his practical
achievements listed in vv. 4–10 rather than to his grand
design to master the secrets of the universe. Elsewhere (6:8;
9:11) Qoheleth echoes these sentiments. In 9:13–16, the
story of the poor wise man whose advice would have saved
the city, he reflects that 'the poor man's wisdom was despised and his words not heeded' (v. 16). He reflects that
wisdom is vulnerable and that its effectiveness can be
undone by the stupidity of those to whom sound advice has
been given (9:18) and that even a little folly of this kind can
outweigh its force (10:1). In 7:16 he seems to suggest that it
is dangerous to be *too* clever!

We may sum up Qoheleth's thinking about the contribution of wisdom to the living of the good life in terms of the
need to be aware of the limitations that God has imposed on
his human creatures. Within those limits the good life is
possible for those to whom he has given the gift of wisdom,
though not for those whom he has deprived of it. Qoheleth
does not directly say whether it is possible to *acquire*
wisdom; but it is significant that he was a teacher whose aim
was to persuade his readers. His frequent and varied
exhortations to the young men whom he addressed – e.g. to
exercise caution in approaching God in the temple (5:1); to
avoid provoking God to anger (5:2); to fulfil one's vows
(5:4); to fear God (5:7); to obey the king (8:2); to spread
one's investments (11:2); to remember one's Creator (12:1) –
show that he believed that wisdom could be taught, at least
to the untutored mind. But he also warns that there are real
limitations to the effectiveness of wisdom. To attempt to
penetrate the mysteries of the universe only leads to
frustration; and although practical wisdom is a valuable asset
in life, one must expect to encounter frustrations in an
imperfect society in which folly often predominates.

Joy

Qoheleth makes frequent use of the word *śāmaḥ*, 'to enjoy', and *śimḥā*, 'joy, pleasure, enjoyment'. Even more frequent is his use of *ṭôb*, 'good' in the same sense. In 9:9 he also employs the phrase *rā'â ḥayyîm*, literally 'to see life', in the sense of 'to *enjoy* life'. He stresses that enjoyment of life is a divine gift (2:26; 3:13; 5:19), and he commends enjoyment to his readers (8:15; 9:7; 11:8, 9). Elsewhere he maintains that there is nothing better for human beings to occupy them-selves with than to 'eat and drink and find enjoyment' (2:24; 3:12–13; 5:18; 8:15; 9:7; cf. 3:22). This, he says, is God's intention for those who fear him and with whom he is pleased (2:26; 9:7). It is true that some of these passages occur in the context of comments on life's limitations and frustrations (human ignorance of the future, 3:12–13; the brevity of human life, 5:18; the existence of injustices in society, 8:14–15; the inevitability of death, 9:5–7; 11:8). But these are simply indications of Qoheleth's realism: life has its limitations and its evils. Nevertheless his confidence in the possibility of enjoyment is not thereby dimmed. It would not be correct to say that his attitude was one of escapism or of *carpe diem*. His remark that 'Light is sweet, and it is pleasant for the eyes to see the sun' (11:7) is sufficient test-imony to his own *joie de vivre*, and 9:7–9 with its robust advice to the young reader to eat and drink with a cheerful heart, to wear festal apparel and anoint himself with oil, enjoying life with a beloved wife in the knowledge of God's approval cannot be mistaken.

On the other hand Qoheleth made a clear distinction between genuine joy which is the gift of God and the thoughtless self-induced frivolous merrymaking of the fool. His solemn pronouncements in 7:1–4, that the day of death is better than the day of birth, that it is better to enter the house of mourning than the house of feasting, that sorrow is better than laughter, may seem to contradict his commenda-tion of joy elsewhere, but in fact they are intended to drama-tize a call to reflect on the folly of behaving as if pleasure will last for ever and that death is an irrelevance about which one need not think. Verses 5 and 6 at the conclusion of this passage make his point clear: he was warning his readers against the mindless attitude of fools who sang and made merry without a thought for the future. The same caution manifests itself elsewhere in the book: there will be no joy (he implies) in Sheol (9:10), and even the young must remember that they will be subject to the judgement of God (11:9).

God

The good life as conceived by Qoheleth depends entirely on the will of God. He is the creator of all that exists (11:5); he gave us our lives (5:18; 8:15), and he controls the events of our lives and fixes the time of our deaths. When we die our spirit, which he gave to us, returns to him (12:7). We have a duty to remember even from our youth that we are his creatures (12:1).

It is thus God alone who can give human beings the power to enjoy themselves (2:24, 26; 3:13). He is the only source of wealth (5:19), possessions and honour (6:2) and also of the ability to enjoy our work (5:19); but he gives these things only to those who please him (2:26) and who fear him (7:18; 8:12, 13). We must therefore be careful how we approach him in prayer (5:1, 2), for he takes no pleasure in fools (5:4), and if we anger him he may ruin our lives (5:6). It is also important to realize that what he has given he may also take away: so we should enjoy our prosperity when we have it but recognize that he has the power to change it to adversity whenever he wishes (7:14). The good life in Qoheleth's eyes is not something on which we can rely, because God's will is inscrutable. His message is that we should make the most of the good life which he has given us when it comes our way and for as long as it lasts. Whatever happens to us is our lot or portion (ḥēleq) and it is God who has determined it (3:22; 5:18, 19; 9:9).

Summary

Qoheleth's thought is complex. It would be possible to see him as a convinced pessimist because he does not disguise the unpleasant aspects of human life and society; yet his message to his readers was a positive one in that he envisaged for them the possibility of enjoying the good life. In fact he is best described as a realist. The key to his realistic attitude to life is to be found in his *doctrine of God*. He taught that the creator of the world is intimately concerned with the details of human lives and determines the fate of every individual one of his human creatures. But at the same time he remains utterly incomprehensible, and his actions are unpredictable. To those who 'fear' him, however – that is, those who do his will – he offers the possibility of the good life.

Qoheleth was aware of the prevalence of *injustices* in society. These arose from the fact that those in power did not fear God. He himself was not in a position of power, and he took the side of the poor and oppressed. But his realism led him to advise obedience to the rich and powerful. However, he saw his role as that of an observer and teacher rather than a reformer.

He was not opposed to the acquisition of *wealth*, but he pointed out the folly of making this one's principal goal in life, as its continuance cannot be relied on and the wealthy are never free from anxieties. He recommended a more modest style of life as a means to happiness, though poverty he regarded as a grave misfortune.

He held a positive view of God's *gift of life*, though there were people whose wretchedness threw doubt on its value for them. But life should be lived with an awareness not only of its precariousness but also of the fact of mortality. It was within such limits that life could and should be enjoyed. The thought that one must die ought to be no impediment to enjoyment; on the contrary, it should be a spur to making the most of life while one could. The idea of a meaningful life after death was not to be entertained; the probability was that there was no such thing, and after death there would be unending 'days of darkness'.

Qoheleth had little to say about the joys of *family life*, though in one passage he commended a joyous existence with a beloved partner. He had even less to say about children as a contribution to family life and referred to them only as potential heirs to the family wealth.

The subject of *wisdom* was a special preoccupation of Qoheleth. He described his own attempt to 'find the sum' — that is, to comprehend the mysteries of the universe and of human nature — and confessed that despite his pretensions to wisdom he had failed, not because of personal intellectual deficiency but because God had deliberately concealed this knowledge from all his human creatures. On a more mundane level he discussed the practical wisdom employed by men and women to guide them through life and commended its usefulness in many situations, but concluded that it was both limited and vulnerable to the actions of fools.

15

The Song of Songs

More than any other Old Testament book, the Song of Songs presents difficulties for an attempt to discern how it would have been interpreted by the first generation of those who read it in its final form. One of the difficulties is that there is no present consensus on the date either of its initial composition or of any subsequent final redaction. Like Proverbs and Ecclesiastes (Qoheleth) the book claims (1:1) to be Solomonic, and there is no reason to doubt that the connection with Solomon would have been credited by its earliest readers, as indeed it was by later interpreters up to the present time. But in the course of the history of its interpretation it has been understood in two quite different ways: the literal and the metaphorical. From the rabbinic and early Patristic periods Jewish and Christian exegetes alike found it difficult to interpret the book literally because of its erotic character, and have traditionally treated it metaphorically as an allegory representing respectively God's love for his Jewish people or Christ's love for the Church; but how early this practice began is not known. There is no hint of an allegorical intention in the Hebrew text itself or in the earliest of the ancient Versions, the Greek Septuagint, which rendered the Hebrew text literally. Read without presuppositions the Song is simply a book about human love. That it should have come to receive an allegorical interpretation after its reception into the scriptural canon is understandable, since on the literal level it appears to lack a religious message and so to be inappropriate as part of a canonical collection. But there is no convincing evidence that its earliest readers already attributed to it a spiritual meaning beyond the plain meaning of the text, and the following pages will be based on the presumption that this is a book whose theme is love between a man and a woman.

The concept of the good life is conveyed to the reader entirely through the words of the lovers which occupy virtually the whole of the book. Their love for one another is their only concern: for them it *is* the good life, and some of the aspects of the good life with which other books are concerned are entirely absent. This is even true of the notion of God's protection of human lives: although in the allegorical interpretations of the book the male lover is consistently identified with God, there is no mention of him at all in the text.

Security and Place

There is, however, a concern with *place* and *security*. References to places are generally of two kinds: places in the countryside to which the lovers resort and which they regard as their own, perhaps secret places, and the city, which holds danger for them. In 1:16–17 they speak of their couch surrounded by trees as being *their* couch, and in 2:4 the girl speaks of a 'house of wine', perhaps a vineyard into which her lover has led her to share its fruit with her. In a similar way 4:16–5:1 and 6:2 refer to a garden to which the two repair. In 6:11–12 there is a reference to an orchard of nut trees. All these passages are full of erotic imagery; and in 8:12 the girl refers to a vineyard which is her own and which is hers to give.

References to the city, however, are of a quite different kind. In contrast to the scenes in the country, the city is an unsafe place, whose streets and walls are regularly patrolled by guards or watchmen (3:3). But these, rather than ensuring the safety of the citizens, beat and wound the girl lover and take away her mantle (5:7). Moreover, even the relations between the lovers are not without anxiety: in 3:1–3 and 5:5–8 she is desperately looking for her lover but cannot find him. Only in their country retreat, it seems, can they live securely together.

Power and Wealth

As the incident with the watchmen shows, the lovers have no *power* in the ordinary sense: they have no redress against the violence of the powerful. As far as they are concerned it is their mutual love that constitutes real power. Love is as powerful even as death and passion as fierce as Sheol (8:6). It cannot be quenched or drowned by floods of water as humanity was once drowned in the great Deluge (8:7a). Moreover, love is true *wealth*, and cannot be bought at any price. The lovers' speeches are full of allusions to *sustenance*, especially fruit that is sweet to the taste, and to wine. But these are mainly not ordinary comestibles but poetical images of sexual love and its enjoyment. Their love is 'better than wine' (1:2, 4; 4:10). The 'fruit' of the beloved is like raisin cakes and apples (2:5). She is compared to an orchard of fruit trees (4:13) and to fruit in a garden (4:16); her cheeks are likened to the two halves of a pomegranate (6:7) and her breasts to clusters of grapes (7:8).

Health and Death

The lovers do not greatly concern themselves with *health*, *old age* or death. They are young and vigorous, full of life and, at least in each other's eyes, in full physical health. This is specifically said of the young man who is compared to a gazelle or young stag which comes bounding over the mountains (2:9, 17; 8:14); but it is implied that his lover whose beauty is so often extolled must also be radiant with health. The two are too completely absorbed in one another to look at anything beyond their present love. The word 'death' occurs just once (8:6), and the verb *hālâ* 'to be ill' only twice, in a phrase repeated by the girl lover, who says 'I am faint from love' (2:5; 5:8).

It is difficult for a modern reader to be sure what the original readers will have made of the sentence 'Love is as strong as death'. They may have taken it to be no more than a kind of superlative expression, the girl's intention being to make an impassioned declaration that the power of love was comparable to that of death, who has universal power over all human beings. It is unlikely that vv. 6b and 7a are serious statements that human love, like death, persists into eternity. Similarly the two statements by the girl lover that her love has made her ill or faint would not have been taken as a serious comment on the general state of her health, but rather as an allusion to a well-known psychological condition from which the victim soon recovers.

The explicit references to *family life* are restricted to the girl's relations with her mother and brothers. There is no reference to her father. There is also no indication that the lovers were intending to become man and wife: the words 'my sister, my bride' with which the man addresses the girl (4:8–12; 5:1) are both terms of endearment with no further implications. There is equally no suggestion of an intention to have children and found a family. This is a surprising deviation from the Israelite normal practice. With one possible exception (8:5) all the allusions to family relationships are to those of the female lover. She probably had a sister or sisters; this may be deduced from the statement that she was her mother's favourite (6:9). In 1:6 she refers to her 'mother's sons'; these may have been her half-brothers. It is to her mother's house in the city that she brings, or would like to bring, her lover (3:4; 8:2). The expression 'mother's house' is very rare in the Old Testament, but its use does not necessarily imply that the girl had no father living: it is probably natural that she should think primarily of her mother as likely to be the more sympathetic parent when she introduced her lover to the house. Her brothers (or half-brothers) are mentioned in two passages, 1:6 and 8:8–9. Both refer to their concern for their younger sister: in 1:6 they are angry because she has not sheltered her face from the sun and so has become sunburnt, and in 8:8–9 they speak of their intention to protect the younger sister from sexual harassment in view of her extreme youth – though her reply in v. 10 probably indicates that they are speaking of an earlier time.

There are no references to *law* or *justice* in the book. Apart from the brief references to the city and its watchmen, which may indicate that the *girl* – and possibly also her lover – was subject to a disapproving public authority, the book revolves on the level of the private, even secret, relationship between two individuals, which they believe to be of no legitimate concern to society. Nor can it be said that either *wisdom* or *God* plays any part in their thoughts or actions. It is *pleasure* and *enjoyment* that dominate their minds.

Pleasure

The tone of the book is set by its opening lines in which without any prelude the girl passionately declares

> Let him kiss me with the kisses of his mouth!
> Your love is more delicious (*ṭôb*) than wine. (1:2)

There is no need to point out all the passages in which the lovers express the intensity of their mutual love: in spite of the obscurity of some of the terms employed the book speaks for itself. Much of the text, for example, consists of descriptions of the physical charms of the girl by her lover (e.g. 1:9–16; 4:1–7, 10–15; 6:4–7; 7:1–7) with corresponding eulogies of the male lover by the girl (e.g. 2:8; 5:10–16). The rich imagery which is characteristic of the whole book suggests (but sometimes explicitly indicates) the erotic nature of their relationship. For them the good life takes the form of their loving feelings and the physical attraction of the partners one to the other.

But there is a further important dimension to the topic of joy and pleasure in the book. This is the love of nature, shown in the speeches of the lovers. Although nature in its more appealing aspects – flowers, trees, fruit, deer etc. – is a relatively frequent subject of the poetry of the Old Testament, none of the poetical books is so replete with the topic as the Song of Songs, which has been described as the most exuberant manifestation of a love of nature in literature prior to the beginning of the Romantic movement in Europe from the close of the eighteenth century AD. It is unlikely, however, that this kind of language had no precedent in the common usage of the ancient Israelites, especially in connection with love poetry which is no longer extant. It can be found to some extent in other ancient Near Eastern literature, especially from Egypt.

Much of the nature imagery in the book not unnaturally

takes the form of similes and metaphors applied to the
physical charms of the lovers as perceived by the other
partner. Eyes are compared to doves (1:15; 4:1; 5:12) and
pools (7:4), hair to a flock of goats (4:1–2), cheeks to
pomegranates (4:3), female breasts to fawns (4:5); honey is
associated with the tongue (4:11), the teeth are ewes (6:6)
and the belly a heap of wheat (7:2). In a dialogue (2:1–3) the
girl describes herself as an asphodel and a lily and compares
him to an apple tree growing in the wood. She also sees him
as a gazelle and a young stag (2:8–9, 17; 8:14), while he
compares her to a date-palm which he will climb in search of
its fruit (7:7–8). Again she is seen as being herself a garden
(4:12; 5:1) and a spring of running water (4:15), and he as like
a cedar of Lebanon (5:15).

The lovers' interest in nature and the countryside is of
course partly connected with their occupations. The man is a
shepherd (1:7–8; 2:16; 6:3) and the girl the keeper of a
vineyard (1:6; 8:11–12). But there are passages which seem
to reflect a joy in natural beauty for its own sake. In 2:10–14
the man urges the girl to accompany him into the countryside because spring has come:

> Arise, my love, my fair one, and come away;
> for now the winter is past; the rain is over and gone.
> The flowers appear on the earth;
> the time of bird song has come
> and the cooing of the turtle dove will be heard in our
>   land.
> The fig tree is putting forth its fruit
> and the vine blossoms shed their fragrance.

There is of course a connection here between young love
and the joys of spring; but there is also a genuine appreciation of the beauty and attraction of the countryside. In
6:11 there are expeditions in order to see the vine-blossoms
and the pomegranate flowers.

Summary

The concept of the good life in the Song of Songs differs from that of the other Old Testament books. Interpreted on a literal basis and before the subsequent introduction of allegorical interpretations, it will have appeared to its first readers as a dialogue between two young lovers. The book depicts the good life exclusively in terms of their love for one another which is all-absorbing, unaffected by considerations either of religion or of morality – a love which they believe to be 'as strong as death'. It is a celebration of the delights of erotic love and exists, as it were, on a plane of its own. Illness and mortality are far from the lovers' thoughts, and the only mundane aspects of daily life to which allusion is made are an element of insecurity represented by an unattractive picture of city life in which danger may lurk and the positive aspects of family life represented by the girl's mother and her protective brothers. But there is a genuine appreciation of the beauty of a beneficent natural world.

16
Isaiah

In common with some other prophetical books of the Old Testament, the book of Isaiah contains a mixture of prophetical messages about the good life – a mixture, that is to say, in the sense that some passages are addressed to those who are at present enjoying the good things of life but to whom the prophet announces a divine judgement which will deprive them of them, while others are addressed to those who have already lost them; to them the prophet promises their restoration. The question of the nature of the good life is frequently raised: all human lives come under God's scrutiny and judgement, and those whose mode of life does not correspond to God's requirements are living in a false security. The good life will be given to those who recognize and live by God's standards of righteousness. The second half of the book (from chapter 40 onwards) consists mainly of God's promises of a good life in the future, while in the first half promises and judgements alternate, sometimes even in adjacent passages. To the first readers of the completed book, who lived in hope of better things than those which they were currently experiencing, the message of the book would have been seen as both a future hope and a warning of the demands made by God of their faithfulness to his word.

Place and Security

The heading of the book (1:1) defines its contents as the vision of Isaiah son of Amoz which he saw concerning Judah and Jerusalem. In fact it is with the city of Jerusalem itself and its inhabitants that the author is mainly concerned. The names Jerusalem and Zion, its equivalent, occur to-gether more than a hundred times in 66 chapters, and are distributed throughout the book.

The book's interest is in the inhabitants of the city; but the lives of individual citizens are rarely singled out for mention. Sometimes the author's concern is with the population as a whole, considered as a single entity; at other times groups of persons are distinguished, e.g. the leaders (1:23; 3:14); the women (daughters of Zion, 3:16); the drunkards (5:11); the prophet's disciples (8:16); the scoffers (28:14); the poor and needy (41:17); the eunuchs (56:3–5); the righteous (57:1–2); the wise (29:14).

Chapter 1 is a characteristic example of the mixture of positive and negative assessments of the security or otherwise of Jerusalem. It begins with a picture of desolation resulting from the people's sinfulness: Zion has been left in isolation like a besieged city, and only a few survivors have been left in it (vv. 8–9). In vv. 16–20 a choice is given to these: if they turn from their sins they will again 'eat the good of the land', but if they refuse to do so they will be devoured by the sword. This announcement is then followed by a promise that if they repent Yahweh will restore the previous ordered life of the city: Zion will be redeemed, and will become once more a city of righteousness (vv. 26–27). In the first verses of the next chapter (2:1–4) a glorious picture of the city is presented: the temple mount will become a place of pilgrimage for many nations, who will stream to Jerusalem, which will become a world centre in which they may learn from Yahweh the ways of peace.

This double pattern of security and insecurity recurs frequently throughout the first part of the book (chapters 1–39). Only a few examples can be given here. In 3:1–8 Yahweh announces that he is about to deprive Judah and Jerusalem of the staff of life – bread and water – and also to bring about the collapse of ordered society. In 5:1–7 the prophet denounces the nation using the figure of an unproductive vineyard which must be destroyed by its owner (Yahweh) and in 5:8 he prophesies a failure of crops which will lead to depopulation of the countryside. In some passages it is predicted that the land will be lost to its present inhabitants altogether: there will come a time when 'cities will lie waste without inhabitant ... until Yahweh sends everyone far away' (6:11–12). In 39:5–7 this fate is interpreted more precisely: Isaiah tells Hezekiah of a future deportation to Babylon.

The promises of a redeemed and secure Jerusalem are frequent in both parts of the book, though they are often conditional. In 4:2–6 there is envisaged a purge carried out by Yahweh in which he has 'washed away the filth of the daughters (i.e., inhabitants) of Zion'; but he will then create a 'glorious canopy' over the whole city for all the survivors. In 28:16 he promises that he will lay a precious cornerstone in Zion which will give the city a sure foundation, perhaps suggesting a previous destruction; but it will offer security only to those who put their trust in him. In 32:1–2 the coming of a righteous king is prophesied, one who together with other leaders of the community will restore the security of the city, ruling justly. In 35:1–10 it is assumed that the exile spoken of in 6:12 has already taken place; it promises a glorious return of the exiles to Zion. They have been redeemed by Yahweh and will have everlasting joy, relieved from all sorrow (v. 10).

The emphasis on God's promise is intensified in the second half of the book in that the tone is now entirely positive. In these chapters the prophet's vision (1:1) is projected into the future. He foresees a time when Judah has been exiled from its land, and comforts them with a promise of their imminent glorious return (an early commentator, Ben Sira, spoke of him as one who 'saw the future and comforted the mourners in Zion', Ecclus. 48:24). Jerusalem-Zion now occupies all his thoughts, whether he addressing the exiles in Babylon or the deserted and forlorn city itself. Jerusalem will be rebuilt and repeopled (44:26–28); it will again become a place of joy and thanksgiving (51:3); the exiles will return with singing (51:11) and Yahweh himself will return to the city to reign there as its king (52:8–9). In the final chapters (56–66) the thought of Jerusalem as the place which is the true home of God's people is continued and even intensified. Jerusalem will be victorious over the nations, whose kings will come in procession bringing tribute (60:10–12), and will be known as 'the city of Yahweh, the Zion of the Holy One of Israel' (60:14). It will be a place of universal peace (60:17–18) and Yahweh will make it 'renowned throughout the earth' (62:7). Also in 65:18–25 Jerusalem is described as the place where future generations will live long lives in prosperity and security enjoying God's blessing in perpetuity. The passage, one of the last in the book, concludes by repeating words spoken near the beginning (11:6, 7, 9) concerning the coming of a future descendant of David under whose rule there will be universal peace, shared even by the wild animals. Jerusalem is seen as the centre of that perfect world.

Power and Wealth

Power in the book of Isaiah belongs to Yahweh alone. He controls the whole world, and his power is directed terrifyingly against all who challenge it (e.g. chapter 2). All human power or claims to power is therefore subordinate to him. And in this book *political* power is a major concern – not for its own sake, but because of its effect on the people of Israel in their endeavour to find for themselves the good life.

Isaiah teaches that Yahweh not only controls the nations of the world; he manipulates them as he wishes. As Ps. 75:7 states, he 'abases one and raises up another'. Yahweh had sent Assyria as the 'rod of his anger' to punish Israel for its apostasy (10:5), but because of Assyria's arrogance and destructive intention (10:7) he now intends to break the power of Assyria and relieve Israel from its subservience to it (14:24–25; 30:31; 31:8). The same fate awaits other nations, Israel's neighbours, for the same reason (13:11; 14:4–6; 16:7; 19:17; 23).

When Israel has been sufficiently punished and has learned its lesson (40:1), Yahweh will transfer to it the political power that he had previously given to other nations such as Assyria and Babylon, and once they have received this power they will keep it for ever. These promises are already adumbrated in the first part of the book. Judah will conquer the Philistines and other neighbouring peoples (11:14) terrify the Egyptians (19:16–17). But in the later chapters the promise of domination and wealth is expressed in more universalistic terms: the Egyptians will come in chains and prostrate themselves before their former enemies (45:14); the nations who have taken Judah into exile as

captives will bring them back as suppliants (49:22–23);
foreigners will be employed to feed the flocks and till the
fields of the now triumphant Judaeans, who will enjoy the
wealth of the nations (61:6) which will flow to Jerusalem like
an overflowing stream (66:12) etc. Israel will saved by
Yahweh with a salvation that will be everlasting (45:17). It is
interesting to observe that this dramatic change in Israel's
fortunes will be brought about by God by the same means
that he had previously employed to punish them: by em-
powering a foreign monarch. He raised up the Persian king
Cyrus to power, and it was through him that the other
nations would be forced to give up their wealth to Judah and
that Jerusalem and the temple would be rebuilt (44:28–45:7).

According to the books of Kings, the monarchs of Israel
and Judah were powerful figures. With some exceptions
they were firmly in control of their kingdoms and of their
people until eventually their power was undermined and
destroyed by the pressure exerted by powerful foreign
empires. It is remarkable that in the book of Isaiah the kings
of Judah are rarely mentioned by name. In fact only two –
Ahaz and Hezekiah – merited mention; and they are not
represented as powerful figures. Ahaz is described in chapter
7 as uncertain and pusillanimous. With his people he was
terrified at the news that the Syrians and the northern
kingdom of Israel ('Ephraim') had formed an alliance to
attack Judah (vv. 1–2). Despite the reassuring message from
Yahweh conveyed to him by Isaiah (vv. 7b–9) he refused to
accept the challenge of a sign from Yahweh that the message
was true, and was told that his kingdom would be overthrown
by the king of Assyria whom Yahweh would send to bring
disaster on it.

Hezekiah's attitude towards the words spoken through
Isaiah was very different from that of Ahaz; but he also was
powerless in the face of the threat to his kingdom by the
king of Assyria (36:1; 37:1). He not only paid heed to
Isaiah's message of assurance but also went to the temple
and sought help directly from Yahweh (chapter 37). However, these chapters (36–39) make it clear that it was Isaiah
who was the dominant figure during the reign of Hezekiah,
healing him from his dangerous sickness (chapter 38) and

also warning him about the consequences of receiving an embassy from the king of Babylon and displaying his wealth to him (chapter 39).

The author of the book makes it clear that Isaiah's function was a subordinate one: to act as Yahweh's agent sent by him to make known his demands and intentions to the people (6:8–9). It was in conformity with this role that many of his oracular pronouncements are prefaced by the phrase 'This is what Yahweh has said' (kōh 'āmar yhwh) or 'Hear Yahweh's word'. Thus the reader was intended to understand that Isaiah was speaking the very words of Yahweh which had previously been spoken to him. But the original readers of the book, no less than modern readers, can hardly have missed the extent to which the figure of the prophet is thrown into prominence, especially in the account of the political crises that marked the period in which he lived and worked. That he – and no other person – was sent to give personal advice to Judah's kings is a sufficient indication of this; and it was thus through his intervention that the people were saved on two occasions and enabled to live, even though precariously, the good life. Equally it was through his visions that they were encouraged to look forward to a future renewal of that good life after they had suffered for their sins (40:1).

There were occasions when it appears that Isaiah, presumably because of his intimate relationship with Yahweh, nevertheless acted on his own initiative as a national leader without a specific divine command. For example, he dared to interrogate King Hezekiah about his reception of the ambassadors from Babylon: 'What did these men say? From where did they come to you?'; 'What have they seen in your house?' (39:3, 4). Only when he had received Hezekiah's answers did Isaiah pronounce the word of Yahweh to the king. It was also he who played the role of healer, curing a serious disease from which the king had been likely to die (38:21). In these incidents Isaiah is presented as a kind of national hero-figure, able to save the king, and so the people.

Family

In general the book of Isaiah does not refer to particular families: it is to be assumed that the future of the whole people, whether good or bad, will be also that of the families that compose it. The sole exception is the family of Isaiah himself. He refers to his wife, whom he calls 'the prophetess', who is the mother of his children (8:3), and names his two sons (7:3; 8:3). These are said to be, together with their father, 'signs and portents in Israel from Yahweh' (8:18). That is, the names that he gives them portend what will happen to the nation. Both names have a favourable import for the nation's life. The name of his son – Shear-jashub, 'a remnant will return' – is interpreted in 10:21 as signifying the nation's return to dependence on Yahweh, though the following verse makes a qualification of this. Maher-shala-hash-baz (8:3) signifies the defeat of the nation's enemies at the hands of the Assyrians. Another significant name, Immanuel ('God is with us'), that of a child who will be born to an unnamed woman (7:14), has an equally favourable meaning (v. 16).

The author frequently uses family imagery in speaking of the future redemption and restoration of the chastened nation. Zion is pictured as a mother bereaved of her children who have been taken from her but who will now be reunited with them. In 49:20–23 her former inhabitants, pictured as young children, are to be returned to their mother by the kings and queens of the nations who have seized them, carried on their laps and on their shoulders. In 54:1–3 Zion is a barren woman who will miraculously find herself the mother of innumerable children and be obliged to provide for an unexpected increase of her family. In 66:22–23 the prophet speaks in similar terms; and in 59:21 he speaks more literally of a new covenant which will be observed for ever by the children and descendants of the redeemed people. This family imagery is employed elsewhere in other ways. Israel is described as Yahweh's son whom he formed in the womb and whom he guided and protected (44:2, 24; 46:3–4; 63:16); Zion is his wife whom he momentarily rejected in the past but whom he now takes back and promises to love with an everlasting love (54:6–8; 62:4–5).

Other references to family life reflect a concern for the difficulties experienced by ordinary people with regard to the dangers of childbirth and the problems of bringing up children safely. In 11:6–9 the description of the coming era of universal peace in which animals and human beings will all live harmoniously together centres upon young children and babies. These will be able to play safely in the vicinity of dangerous snakes, and to be the herdsmen of wild beasts. More frequent are references to childbirth, some of which probably pick up and use common proverbs, for example 37:3 which refers to the dangerous situation in which a mother in labour has insufficient strength to bear her child. The other passages are more encouraging: in 42:14 Yahweh announces his intention to redeem his people by comparing himself to a woman in labour who suddenly breaks out into loud cries before a successful birth. In 49:15 he refers to the virtual impossibility that a mother should not be devoted to her babies, promising that his care for Zion will be even greater than that of a human mother. In 45:10–11 Yahweh speaks as a father, reproaching those who question his good intentions towards his children. Here the notion of the chosen people as God's family is clearly expressed; but this choice of imagery also reveals a concern for the lives of the individual families of which the nation is composed.

Finally mention may be made of another birth: the birth of a child who will be a saviour of the nation. Apart from the mysterious Immanuel of 7:14, 9:6–7 speaks of a child 'born for us ... given to us' who will sit on the throne of David and rule in justice and righteousness; and 11:1–5 similarly announces the birth of a descendant of Jesse, David's father. Although it is stated that he will be of the royal family of Judah, his own parentage is not given.

Longevity

Although the birth of a child was an occasion for rejoicing, the good life in the family was often overshadowed by infant mortality and by the possibility of an unforeseen premature death due to unexpected illness. A passage describing the coming era of salvation (65:18–23), when the inhabitants of the restored city of Jerusalem would enjoy a life free from sorrow, promises the elimination of these evils. Every citizen would live out his allotted span, and this would be extended beyond the normal maximum of 80 years (cf. Ps. 90:10) to no less than 100, so approaching the legendary age of the ancient patriarchs (Joseph died at the age of 110 years according to Gen. 50:26). As other passages indicate, the length of human life was entirely in the hands of Yahweh, who extended that of Hezekiah by 15 years in response to his prayer (38:5), and promised that his Servant would live to see his descendants and 'prolong his days' (53:10).

Justice and Law

The words *mišpāṭ*, *ṣedeq*, *ṣĕdāqâ* and *tôrâ* occur altogether more than 100 times in the book of Isaiah. They are frequently rendered into English by such terms as 'justice', 'righteousness' and 'law'; but these are not their only connotations. For example, *mišpāṭ* in Isaiah sometimes has the meaning of a legal case or judgement; *ṣĕdāqâ* can mean 'victory' or 'salvation'; and *tôrâ* sometimes means teaching rather than law. In this section we are concerned specifically with justice and law as features of the good life for Israelites.

The author frequently describes a present situation in which justice was denied to many of the people, especially those who were unable to assert their legal rights. In 10:1–2 he denounces unnamed powerful persons who make unjust laws that deprive such persons of justice. These law makers, however, are probably not to be identified with Israelite kings, since Israelite kings did not make new laws. In theory at least Israel was governed by the laws of Yahweh himself, promulgated at Sinai. The proximity of this passage to references to tyrannical Assyrian overlords in vv. 5–11 would perhaps be taken by the first readers of the completed book of Isaiah to refer to them. They may well have seen the passage as relevant to their own situation when they were ruled by a foreign empire which ignored the rights of the conquered people in enforcing their political will.

Condemnations of current injustices are frequent in many parts of the book. For example, 1:21–23 describes a state of affairs in Jerusalem, which had once been renowned for honesty and the equitable administration of justice, in which the citizens are now given to violence and whose rulers accept bribes and ignore the attempts of orphans and widows to obtain a just hearing. Similar conduct is attributed to the rulers in 3:14–15 and 5:7–10, and 59:9–15 is part of a lament complaining of the impossibility of obtaining redress for such crimes, but in which the situation is attributed to the magnitude of the people's sins which prevent Yahweh from taking action to put things right (vv. 1–2).

However, the book is also replete with passages in which Yahweh promises a future for Zion when these injustices will come to an end. In 59:15b–20 he answers the lament of the preceding verses, saying that he has observed the inability of any citizens to put things right, and has determined to intervene, to punish the criminals and to rescue those who repent of their sins. Similarly in 61:8–9 he proclaims his love of justice and promises an everlasting covenant which will transform the righteous members of the community into a people enjoying his blessing. Those who maintain justice and do what is right will enjoy his salvation (56:1). He will fill Zion with justice and righteousness (33:5), and Jerusalem will become a place to which many peoples will come to receive his laws (2:1–3). In 60:21 he promises that 'Your people shall all be righteous; they will possess the land for ever'. So the book teaches that despite the present lack of justice the good life will once more be enjoyed by the people of Israel as the result of Yahweh's saving activity. According to 9:7, 11:4, 16:5 and probably 32:1 this will be achieved through the just rule of the future king of the Davidic line whom Yahweh will raise up.

Apart from 10:1–2, which accuses the contemporary rulers of fabricating their own iniquitous laws, virtually all the references to law (*tôrâ*) and commandments (*miṣwôt*) are to the laws of Yahweh rather than to human laws. The people are accused of disregarding Yahweh's law (5:24; 24:5;

30:9; 42:4, 24) or are urged to obey it (1:10; 51:4). Such
disobedience will lead, or has led, to their punishment and
misery. On the other hand, those who have taken his
commandment to heart will enjoy his salvation (51:7). Zion
will become the place from which his law will go out to
instruct not only Israel but all nations (2:3). But the nature of
this law is never clearly defined. It may have been interpreted in the strict sense of the Mosaic law; but it seems to
have the more general sense of Yahweh's instruction or
teaching about the kind of conduct that he requires from his
people and of which they ought to have been aware; it is
sometimes simply equated with Yahweh's 'ways'.

Wisdom

There are very few references in this, the longest of all the
Old Testament books, to wisdom. The possession of wisdom by the people as a whole or by individuals is clearly not
regarded as an essential or even a desirable feature of the
good life. Only in one rather obscure verse (33:6), which
speaks of Yahweh's filling Zion with salvation, wisdom and
knowledge is wisdom said to be one of his gifts to its
citizens. However, according to 11:2 the 'spirit of wisdom' is
an essential quality of a *ruler*: the future Davidic king whom
Yahweh will raise up, who will fear him and rule justly, will
be endowed with the spirit of Yahweh, a gift which includes
the 'spirit of wisdom and discernment'. This kind of wisdom
is a reflection of the wisdom of Yahweh himself, also
mentioned only in a single verse (31:2) which he will display
when he demonstrates his invincible power over the
pretended might of Egypt (31:1–3).

   Human pretensions to wisdom are viewed as nugatory or
evil. In 5:21 the author denounces those in Israel who are
'wise in their own eyes', evidently persons of influence who
are described as taking bribes and depriving the innocent of
their rights. In 29:13–14 those who claim to be wise are
denounced as insincere in their worship of Yahweh; they will
be swept away. The arrogant claim to wisdom of the king of
Assyria is also denounced (10:13), and the supposedly wise

advisers of the king of Egypt are castigated as fools who lead Egypt to disaster (19:11–15).

Joy and Pleasure

Joy in Isaiah is a gift of God. It is frequently associated with peace and security (šālôm). It is reserved for the glorious future when Yahweh will have redeemed his people; the present is not a time when they can rejoice. There is wild rejoicing in the city when its citizens suppose that it has been spared from defeat (22:1–2, 13); but that is due to a failure to understand that there is fresh disaster to come: it is rather to mourning that Yahweh now summons his people. Those who practice injustice do not know the way of peace (59:8): for the wicked there will be no peace (48:22). Looking back at the past, Yahweh laments that if the people had obeyed his commandments there would have been peace and security, but they had not done so (48:18).

But there is to be a time for rejoicing in the future. While there are no pictures of the good life of individuals, joy is a constant feature of the many pictures in the book of the happy state of the people whom Yahweh will redeem. Chapter 65 speaks of his servants who will rejoice and sing for joy, while those who have rejected him will suffer punishment. But elsewhere the negative aspect is omitted, and the picture presented is one of unalloyed joy, peace and prosperity for a single united community. This takes a variety of forms. In some passages the joyful journey of the released exiles to Jerusalem is depicted (35; 51:11; 55:12); others speak of their arrival and of a new, or renewed Jerusalem (49;13; 51:3). In 29:19 the author refers especially to the joy to be experienced by the humble and needy; in 52:7–9 of the messenger who brings the joyful news of Yahweh's reigning in the city; in 54:9–10 of his promise to establish or confirm his irrevocable covenant of peace which will ensure that he will never again be angry with his people. In 9:2–4 he speaks of light for those who had lived in darkness, and of joy at the removal of the burdens laid on the people by their oppressors; in 9:6 of the everlasting era of peace to be inaugurated by the coming Davidic king. Many passages, like 66:10–13, speak in general terms simply of the future prosperity of the city of Jerusalem. It may be said that in the end joy is the keynote of the book, bringing comfort to those readers who had longed for it.

God

The attribute of Yahweh most frequently named in this book is his holiness. He is 'the high and lofty One dwelling in eternity, whose name is Holy' (57:15) who is the incomparable creator of the universe (40:25–26). But significantly, his holiness is specifically linked with Israel: 'The holy One of Israel' is the title by which he is most frequently known to Isaiah, and it is in the temple of Jerusalem that he manifests himself to the prophet, seated on his throne and greeted by the seraphim as 'holy, holy, holy' (chapter 6). His universal power is thus perceived as manifested in his particular relationship with Israel: he can be described in the same passage as both maker of the world and maker of Israel (45:11–12; cf. 43:15). Zion is called upon to praise him as One who is 'great in your midst' (12:5–6).

As the Holy One of Israel Yahweh presides over Israel's life. Whether Israel enjoys the good life depends entirely on his judgement. When they rebel against him (e.g. 1:4; 3:1–5; 5:18–25) he becomes their enemy and fights against them (63:10). But their punishment will not last for ever:

> For a brief moment I abandoned you,
> but with great compassion I will gather you.
> In overflowing wrath for a moment I hid my face from
>   you,
> but with everlasting love I will have compassion on you,
> says Yahweh your Redeemer (54:7–8).

Summary

The book of Isaiah presents two contrasting pictures of the life of the people of Israel: the sinful present and the glorious future which the prophet foresees. Living in the sinful present, he depicts the situation of his time. He places particular emphasis on the capital, Jerusalem or Zion, and describes himself as Yahweh's messenger sent to warn the people of a divine judgement on the injustices practised in his time and their lack of faithfulness towards God, and of the fateful consequences. The security that they suppose themselves to enjoy is a delusion, and exile at the hands of foreign conquerors will follow. All power belongs to God, and he will not hesitate to use it against them.

The second picture is of unalloyed happiness in the future and has been revealed to Isaiah in visions. The punishment of the exile will come to an end, and those who have remained faithful or have turned back to God will return to their land and enjoy his blessing. Little is said about individuals, but God's care for the humble and needy is emphasized. Longevity for the redeemed is promised.

Although individual families are not singled out for mention, the prophet uses imagery which shows familiarity with both the joys and the problems of family life. Unlike many of the Old Testament books human wisdom is not valued: only God is wise. He is the Holy One of Israel, and his holiness is closely linked with the lives of his people, who will eventually understand his love for them.

17
Jeremiah

Many of the themes of the book of Jeremiah are similar to those of Isaiah. Both prophets stood on the frontier between two eras: the present, in which the good life, though threatened, was still partly a reality, and the future in which there was hope that when the anticipated destruction had actually occurred the nation would be redeemed and restored. But the point at which Jeremiah stands in history is later than that described by Isaiah, and the urgency is still greater; indeed within Jeremiah's own lifetime the end came, and the later chapters describe this event not as one which he foresees as a prophet but as a fact which has already happened (chapter 39), of which he himself has been an eyewitness. It is a unique feature of this book that Jeremiah is not a mere observer of the life of the city of Jerusalem but is himself deeply involved in it. The book is studded with narratives about his personal experiences in many of which he describes the hostility that he encountered, and also his internal struggles when he confronted Yahweh himself with his doubts and misgivings about his vocation. In such passages he takes the readers inside the life of the city and shows it to them at first hand as an insider.

Security

Jeremiah's description of the state of the city before its destruction indicates that although it was apparently prosperous, the 'good life' as understood by its inhabitants was far from being the good life as Yahweh and his prophet Jeremiah understood it. No less than Isaiah he condemns a variety of specific kinds of sin perpetrated there. But the people seem to be unaware of the danger in which they stand despite the ever-present threat of the military might of Babylon. Although they are guilty of theft, murder, the swearing of false oaths and overt worship of other gods, they are convinced that because they also hypocritically offer worship to Yahweh in his temple he will protect them and they will be safe (7:9–10). This fatal complacency is due especially to their being persuaded by false prophets, to whom Jeremiah is particularly hostile: these promise 'peace' (šālôm) – that is, safety; but no peace will be available to them (6:14; 8:11) because Yahweh is in fact determined on their destruction. Jeremiah taught the same message to those who had already been deported to Babylon with Jehoiachin: they also had their false prophets who had been assuring them that their exile would soon be over. It would last 70 years, though if they repented and sought Yahweh with their whole heart they would eventually be restored to their land (29:1–14).

Power

In the Jerusalem described by Jeremiah the people as a whole were castigated and condemned by him as guilty in various ways. But he reserves a particular condemnation for its powerful leaders including prophets and priests. These were false prophets: they had not been sent by Yahweh but delivered messages of their own devising, successfully assuring the people that all was well (5:31; 14:13–16; 23:25–32). There were, however, genuine prophets of Yahweh besides Jeremiah such as Uriah, who was put to death by Jehoiakim (26:20–23). But these were not believed and were frequently persecuted.

More than any prophet known to us Jeremiah, whose activity covered the reigns of Josiah, Jehoiakim and Zedekiah (1:2–3) and other intermediate kings, speaks his mind about all of them. It is Yahweh himself who is the universal king (10:7, 10); but he has given power to the kings of Judah, David's successors, to rule his people justly and to care for their welfare. This they have failed to do. Of one of these kings only (Josiah) does he speak with approval and regret. Josiah had ruled justly and defended the rights of the poor and needy, and in his time all had gone well (22:15–16). His son Jehoiakim, on the other hand, the king who treated the written scroll of Jeremiah's prophecies with contempt, ordering it to be burnt and ordering the prophet's arrest (chapter 36), is condemned as an unjust ruler who made his workmen work for nothing in building him a palace to display his wealth (22:13–14). The last king of Judah, Zedekiah, is characterized as vacillating and weak, unable to prevent the persecution of Jeremiah (38:5). So power passed out of the hands of Judah's appointed ruler, and shortly afterwards the kingdom itself was brought to an end by Nebuchadnezzar, whom Yahweh had chosen as his agent of destruction (25:9).

In the restored Judah of the future, however, Jeremiah envisages a restored Davidic dynasty as essential to its well-being. The character of the king whom Yahweh will raise up corresponds closely to that which Jeremiah spoke in praise of Josiah; and he adds 'In his days Judah will be saved and Israel will live in safety' (23:5–6). This is repeated in 33:15–16, and the verses that follow add an allusion to Yahweh's promise to David in 2 Sam. 7:16: 'There shall never lack a man to sit on the throne of the house of Israel' (v. 17). In the same verse a similar promise is made about a future priest, presumably considered to be a kind of co-ruler with the future king. Verse 21 continues with a reference to Yahweh's unbreakable covenant which guarantees the promise.

Law and Justice

Usually when Jeremiah speaks of the 'law' (tôrâ) of Yahweh he does not give a clear definition of it but assumes that its meaning is generally known. The people are condemned for not obeying it or not 'walking in' it – that is, of failing to make it the basis of their conduct. In 44:23, however, Jeremiah is clearly speaking of a written legal code: they have sinned against Yahweh by not 'walking in his laws and his statutes and decrees' – language reminiscent of Deuteronomy. It is this law that he accuses the scribes of falsifying or misinterpreting so that they have 'made it into a lie' (8:8). In the same verse he states that the priests, who are its guardians and official interpreters (18:18) claim that because they are in possession of it they alone possess true wisdom.

It is to be presumed that the law to which Jeremiah refers included the principles of the equitable administration of human justice. These, he states, were not always observed in the Jerusalem of his time. However, it appears that this was not invariably so. Whether justice was upheld depended above all on the characters of the various kings in whose reigns he exercised his ministry. As has been said, Jeremiah praised Josiah for ruling justly but condemned Jehoiakim for his injustice (chapter 22). Whether a defendant was given a fair trial could also depend on the intervention of others than the king. The detailed account of the trial of Jeremiah on the charge of disloyalty and spreading false prophesies is a significant example of this.

In 26:10–19, 24 the author describes a criminal trial which took the form of formal accusation, arrest, demand for the death penalty, speech by the defendant in his own defence, speeches by participants in favour of the accused and the decision by the judges to acquit the defendant. The chief accusers are the priests and the prophets; the officials (*śārîm*) act as judges. However, despite the decision for acquittal it appears that Jeremiah would probably have been put to death had it not been for the action of an influential supporter, Ahikam the son of the royal secretary Shaphan (v. 24). The king, Jehoiakim, is not stated to have been personally involved in this trial; but as the interpolated passage in vv. 20–23 shows, he was capable of ordering executions without benefit of legal trial: he put to death the prophet Uriah who had delivered a message identical to that of Jeremiah. In Jeremiah's trial the issue was that of true and false prophecy: Jeremiah had claimed that his message in which he warned of the destruction of the city if the people did not repent had been dictated to him by Yahweh himself. This was accepted by the officials and by 'all the people', whose role in the affair is, however, equivocal. In this connection the defence speech by some of the 'elders' (vv. 17–19) is of particular interest. They cited a previous case, that of the prophet Micah, whose words are also preserved in the book of that name (Mic. 3:12). Micah also had prophesied the destruction of Jerusalem in terms similar to those of Jeremiah, but Hezekiah, the king of that time, had believed his claim to be a prophet of Yahweh and, rather than putting Micah to death, had by turning to prayer saved the city. Jer. 26 is of particular interest in that it shows that in Jeremiah's time there was a judicial system which was not in itself corrupt, but which could be corrupted or set aside by an arbitrary and evil monarch.

Apart from the officers who defended Jeremiah at his trial (26:16) there were others who supported him against Jehoiakim's murderous intentions. Some of these were persons of influence who believed him to be a true prophet and were determined to see that he was justly treated.

Of special note was a prominent family whose members are frequently mentioned in the book, and who are also known from 2 Kings. The first of this family to be mentioned there was Shaphan the son of Azaliah and grandson of Meshullam. he had the important post of 'secretary' (*sōpēr*) – that is, secretary of state – to Josiah (2 Kings 22:3). Other members of his family to be mentioned are his sons Ahikam, already mentioned as Jeremiah's protector, and Gemariah; also Ahikam's son Gedaliah and Gemariah's son Micaiah. This family served several successive kings. It was Shaphan who read to Josiah the book of the law found by the priest Hilkiah in the temple (2 Kings 22:8–10); his grandson Gedaliah was appointed by the Babylonians as governor of Jerusalem (2 Kings 25:23).

In the book of Jeremiah several members of this family actively support and protect the prophet. When Micaiah heard Baruch, Jeremiah's secretary, reading the scroll that Jeremiah had dictated to him in which he warned of Yahweh's intention to destroy the unrepentant city, he reported this to the officials, including his father Gemariah, and they decided that this was a matter which ought to be brought to the notice of the king; but they advised Baruch and Jeremiah to hide from Jehoiakim's anticipated anger (36:19); and when the king burned the scroll they tried to prevent him from doing so (v. 25). Later, when the Babylonians had captured the city it was Gedaliah that they entrusted with the custody and subsequently the release of Jeremiah (39:14; 40:5–6).

An example of arbitrary imprisonment is found in 20:1–3, when Jeremiah was put in the stocks on the orders of the priest Pashur, the superintendent (*pāqîd*) of the temple, for prophesying Yahweh's intention to destroy Jerusalem and the cities of Judah. Later in the reign of Zedekiah, when the city was undergoing its final siege by the Babylonians and Jeremiah was regarded as a pro-Babylonian traitor and again arrested, imprisoned and ill treated (chapters 37, 38), the legal system seems to have broken down altogether; Zedekiah admitted the loss of his authority and his inability to prevent the officials from arresting Jeremiah and demanding the death penalty (38:5), even though he himself believed the genuineness of his message, sought his prayers and sent secretly to consult him (37:3, 17).

One incident at that critical time, however, shows that private legal transactions were still possible (32:6–15). Jeremiah went to Anathoth, his native place, to exercise his right as near kinsman to buy a field from his cousin, although as Yahweh's prophet he knew that the country would be shortly overrun by the Babylonian army and that claims to private ownership would soon be null and void. He caused the deed of the transaction to be sealed in a jar and kept for a long time in order to demonstrate his confidence that there would come a time when such transactions would once again be possible when the land was eventually restored to its former owners.

In a moment of despair Jeremiah had lamented that in Jerusalem there was not a single person, rich or poor, who acted justly (5:1–5). Yet from the account in the book of his career it is clear that in fact there were many citizens who deplored the injustices that took place especially during the reigns of Jehoiakim and Zedekiah, and who sought to rectify them. The impression given by the book as a whole is that there were two (perhaps more) opposing parties in the Jerusalem of his time, and that Jeremiah was by no means without allies who believed that he was a true prophet and that to ignore the law of Yahweh would lead to disaster. But, like Isaiah, he was not only a prophet of doom: he was as confident of the coming of a new age of prosperity and of justice as he was of the imminent destruction that Yahweh would bring upon the nation through the action of the Babylonians. This is the meaning of his double commission given to him by Yahweh at his call to be a prophet: 'to destroy and overthrow, to build and to plant' (1:10).

Like Isaiah, Jeremiah was inspired to foretell a renewal of Israel's fortunes when the exiles would return to their land. Among the characteristics of this new age would be the proper administration of justice and a general knowledge of God and his laws by the people. So in 23:4, immediately following a denunciation of the present rulers of whose unjust rule, he and others were the victims, he predicts the appointment by God of 'shepherds' – that is, rulers – who will ensure that in the future the people will no longer be afraid. The verses that follow (vv. 5–6) more explicitly, again as in Isaiah, announce the coming of a king of the line of David who would rule justly and give his people a much needed security. This promise is repeated in 33:15–16.

The basis of this new situation is expounded in a remarkable passage in 31:31–34. It will take the form of a new covenant that Yahweh will make with Israel and Judah by which the nature of the whole people will be transformed. He will put his law into their hearts so that they will all without exception possess a true knowledge of him. They will no longer need instructors to teach them, but will truly be his people, free from the fear of divine punishment.

Wisdom

Like Isaiah, Jeremiah had little good to say about those in his time who claimed to be wise. The only true wisdom was that of Yahweh himself, who had established the world by his wisdom (10:12 = 51:15), and compared with whom no other nation could lay claim to its possession (10:7). True *human* wisdom consists in knowing Yahweh and in understanding what he is doing and why he is bringing disaster on the land – that it is because the people have forsaken his law (9:11–14). The self-styled wise men who claim to possess the law but have falsified it are destined to share the

general punishment (4:22; 8:9; 9:23). Although they conspire
against Jeremiah and attack him for attempting to undermine
their authority (18:18), it is they who share the responsibility
together with the priests and prophets for misleading the
whole people.

Joy

In view of what has been said above it is hardly surprising
that the possibility of joyous celebration of the good life in
the final days of the city was severely restricted. Jeremiah
makes few references to it; and when he does so it is only to
predict that it will shortly come to an end. There are occasional references to ordinary occasions for rejoicing: a
father's joy at the birth of his child (20:15) and the happiness
of a newly married couple (7:34; 16:9; 25:10). But the
newborn child in question is Jeremiah himself, and the
reference occurs in a lament in which he curses his birth
because of his subsequent experiences of tension and
sorrow: it would have been better, he says, if he had not
been born (20:14–18). And the happiness of bride and bridegroom is mentioned only to prophesy that all such mirth
will shortly be brought to an end.

Indeed at Yahweh's command Jeremiah himself became an
ominous symbol of the *absence* of joy which would charac-
terize the coming fate of the city. In 16:2–4 he is commanded not to marry, because if he had children they would
be struck by famine, disease and premature death; and in
16:8 he is forbidden to participate in feasting. Again in
15:16–17, although he states that he had found happiness in
receiving Yahweh's word, he had not joined in communal
merrymaking but had remained a solitary figure because of
the burden and sorrow that that word had imposed on him.
Whatever of the good things that remained in the life of the
city, which during much of Jeremiah's career was under the
threat of foreign attack or the reality of foreign rule and
even witnessed a first siege and deportation (2 Kings
24:10–17) before its final destruction, is hardly touched on
by Jeremiah, who foresaw a terrible end to it. Joy would

only come again when Yahweh at last reversed the city's
fortunes:

> Then shall the young women rejoice in the dance,
> and the young men and the old shall be merry.
> I will turn their mourning into joy;
> I will comfort them and give them gladness for sorrow.
>   (31:13; cf. 30:19; 31:7)

God

Jeremiah was personally involved in all that happened in
Jerusalem in the course of his life and so was able to give a
full account of God's attitude towards it. Also, perhaps more
than any other prophet, he stood in a very personal relationship to Yahweh. This relationship was often one of great
tension; some passages show how he resented the mission
that he had been given and reproached him for placing him
in an intolerable position (e.g. 11:18–20; 12:1–4; 15:15–18;
17:14–18; 20:7–12, 14–18). But after some of these laments
he received replies from Yahweh which gave him an
unparalleled insight into the working of his mind.

The frequency and violence of Yahweh's destructive
threats reported by Jeremiah may have given the impression
to the reader that he is a vindictive God. But this is not the
message conveyed by the book as a whole. There are many
references to Yahweh's love for his people. In 3:19, for
example, he refers to his original hopes for them; in 31:3 he
speaks of his love and faithfulness to Israel which is eternal;
and in 2:2–3 he remembers how Israel as his bride had once
been his holy and devoted people. In 2:21 he describes Israel
as a vine which he had lovingly planted. Subsequently Israel
had turned against him, and since he was a God of justice he
was bound to inflict severe punishment on them. However,
he frequently appeals to them to return to him before it is
too late (3:13–14; 4:14; 6:16). Their salvation will depend on
his repentance (7:5–7). Furthermore, even before he has
inflicted his punishment on them he promises that he will
not *totally* destroy them (5:18; cf. 46:28). In 31:20, speaking
at this point of Ephraim – that is, the former northern Israel,

long conquered by the Assyrians – he speaks as a loving father who is deeply moved on behalf of his child, and promises to have mercy on them as well. For Jeremiah, therefore, the promises of a renewed good life for God's people after their punishment does not indicate a change in the nature of God, but attest to his nature as one who is both just and loving.

Summary

Jeremiah stood on the brink of a great disaster for the capital city, Jerusalem, and the small state of Judah. The Babylonian power, summoned by Yahweh to punish its citizens for their apostasy, was ready to destroy the nation and to send many of his people into exile; this work had already begun, and was carried to completion within the life of the prophet. Jeremiah himself, sharing the privations of the beleaguered city, became a symbol of the coming tragedy. The good life, of which some remnants yet remained, was about to come to an end. The city had been guilty of both idolatry and a failure of justice. For this the mass of the population was responsible, though they had been misled and corrupted by their leaders. Prophets and priests together with some of the kings attacked the prophet on the grounds that he was spreading alarm and despondency and falsely claiming to be the messenger of Yahweh. He was treated as a traitor suborned by the Babylonians, and his life was endangered. But he had the support and protection of a minority of influential persons who believed his claim to be a genuine prophet of Yahweh preaching a genuine word from God.

That Yahweh was angry with his people and threatened their destruction was, however, only one side of his message. His close relation with Yahweh made him aware of Yahweh's love for his people and enabled him to announce that the forthcoming destruction would not be total and to foretell the emergence in the future of a new Israel that had learned its lesson and would live under a new covenant which Yahweh would establish, once more enjoying the fulness of the good life which had once been theirs.

18
Lamentations

This book consists of five separate complete poems each lamenting the national disaster that had been prophesied by Jeremiah and other prophets and had now occurred. The poems include many allusions to Jerusalem before the disaster, and lament the loss of the good life. They describe the magnitude of the sufferings of the citizens. Some had been slaughtered by the invading Babylonian forces during the siege of the city; others had been carried off into captivity; and those who had been left behind were in an even worse state. They were enduring oppression and humiliation and were faced with starvation, from which some had already perished. These poets also depict the good life that had been enjoyed in the past. There is no single account of this: the poets refer to it when they wish to emphasize the contrast. Thus in 5:14–15 they refer to the peaceful companionship of the old men in the city gate, the enjoyment of music by the young and the joy of the dance. Their feelings, so poignantly expressed, attest their deep love for the city of Jerusalem – a love also reflected in many of the Psalms.

However, not all had been well with the state of the city. It was because of its sinfulness that Yahweh had now punished it. Priests and prophets had committed murder (4:13), and the prophets had failed to give guidance to the people which would have saved them from disaster (2:14). Yahweh had therefore ceased to speak through them (2:9). Nevertheless these poets also remember the good things. The city had been prosperous and well organized, providing *security* for its citizens. The king is singled out in particular as having provided protection for his subjects: he had been 'the breath of our life', and it had been believed that 'under his shadow we shall survive among the nations' (4:20). Other leaders, the 'princes' (śārîm) and the elders, also evidently enjoyed general respect. The poets also look back to the joyful time when the festivals were regularly held and the sabbath observed, when the temple with its altar was central to the life of the city. They also show concern for the ordinary citizens, the old, the young, men and women, and also the wealthy nobility who had been accustomed to a good life and had been brought up 'in purple', but were now reduced to the lowest level of existence. They also deplore the loss of a system of justice when human rights (*mišpaṭ-gāber*) had been protected (3:35).

It is possible that the poets' picture of the former good life was to some extent over-stated; but that life had now certainly been destroyed. The citizens had been reduced to slavery and even starvation; the city itself had been largely destroyed and its walls and gates broken down. Some citizens had been deported. But could the good life be restored? Much of the book is given over to lamentation and seems to exclude any possibility of such restoration. What saves the poets from total despair, however, is that they still cannot dismiss from their thoughts the conviction that Israel is and continues to be Yahweh's own people. Yahweh is central to this book as he is to virtually every book of the Old Testament. The poets' assessment of the meaning of the present and also his view of the future are therefore both entirely conditioned by what he believes about God's nature. It is because they perceive a tension here that they oscillate continually between despair and hope.

On the one hand the poets are in no doubt that it is Yahweh who has brought destruction on the city and its people. They recognize his omnipotence as ruler of the world, and that the good life that he had given he could take back (3:38) and has now done so. The human conqueror is only his instrument, sent and encouraged by him in his work of destruction; the poets do not hesitate to say that it is Yahweh himself who has carried out the slaughter (2:21). But they also recognize that his anger was fully justified: he is *ṣaddîq*, free from blame (1:18), and those who have suffered at his hands have no reason to complain about their fate (3:39).

In another mood the poets find it difficult to believe that Yahweh is fully aware of the extent of the suffering that he has caused. They ask whether he even perceives it (1:20;

3:36) and wonder whether he has forgotten that the sufferers are his own people (2:1; 5:20). In a mood of despair they lament that all hope is gone (3:18), and although they still appeal to God for mercy (1:20) they envisage the possibility that he has rejected his people for ever (5:22).

Yet in one passage at least the poets can still find grounds for hope. They find it in their recollection of Yahweh's past love for his people. In 3:22–26 they remember that his generosity (ḥăsādîm) is unbounded and concludes that his love is not exhausted. The exclamation 'Yahweh is my portion' is a way of asserting the permanence of the relationship between Yahweh and his people, and this gives grounds for hope (v. 24), because it remains true that 'Yahweh is good to those who wait for him' (v. 25). When they remember these things they are confident that Yahweh will not reject for ever but will show mercy since he has no pleasure in punishing (vv. 31–33).

Summary

In his anger Yahweh has deprived his people of the good life that he had formerly bestowed on them. The authors of these lamentations confess that, harsh though that punishment is, it is the consequence of their sinfulness and fully justified. They depict with nostalgia the good life enjoyed in the past, and poignantly contrast it with the people's present plight which affects all members of society. At times they feel that there is no hope – that Yahweh will never again restore what they have lost. But at other times, remembering past experiences of him as a God of love and mercy, they find grounds for hope that judgement will after all be succeeded by mercy. So for later generations of readers still to a large extent deprived of the joys of the good life the book will have been seen as combining a realization of God's terrible, though deserved, judgement on sinners with hope of a better future.

19
Ezekiel

The political situation in which Ezekiel lived was not the same as that experienced by either of his predecessors Isaiah and Jeremiah. For him the exile had already begun: he had been taken captive and transported to Babylonia together with King Jehoiachin and part of the population of Jerusalem in a first exile when Nebuchadnezzar first besieged the city (2 Kings 24:10–16), and it was from there that he saw his first vision of 'the appearance of the likeness of the glory of Yahweh' and was given his commission (chapters 1–3). It was thus as an exile that he uttered his prophecies and saw his visions; nevertheless like his predecessors his main concern was to warn Jerusalem and its inhabitants of the imminent fall of Jerusalem itself, an event which he recorded.

Like the other prophets whom we have considered Ezekiel is mainly concerned with the fate of the nation as a whole and makes few allusions to the everyday lives of individuals. On the other hand he makes a radical distinction between two types of members of the community, the 'wicked' (rāšāʻ) and the 'righteous' (ṣaddîq) and the respective destinies in store for them (e.g. 3:16–21), and also and most notably puts forward a doctrine of individual responsibility according to which each person will be judged by his actions and dis-positions (so especially chapter 18).

Place and Security

Unlike Jeremiah (chapter 29) Ezekiel says little about the conditions of life among those who have already been exiled to Babylon, even though he was living in their midst. The fact that in his place of exile, however, he is able to receive visions given to him by God (chapters 1–3) shows that God was with the exiles and revealed himself there. But his entire concern is with the fate of those who have remained in Jerusalem, of which he predicts the total destruction which in fact took place and was reported to him by a refugee (33:21). For them the good life was at an end and the whole of the region would be laid waste (33:28–29). In a vision he sees its inhabitants fall by the sword to the heavenly executioners whom Yahweh has appointed (9:1–11). This fate will be the result of the people's sins which include violence and murder but above all idolatry (chapter 8) and the refusal to obey Yahweh's commandments.

But even in the midst of these events there would be those who escaped the general slaughter. While Yahweh's executioners are ordered to make no distinctions in their work between men, women and little children (9:6), some would be saved: these were those who 'sigh and groan over all the abominations that are committed' in the city. On these Yahweh's angel-scribe, the 'man clothed in white linen', was to put a special mark; and they were not to be touched (vv. 3–6). This distinction is further elaborated in chapter 18, where the lives of righteous individuals will be spared while the wicked are to die.

What proportion of the inhabitants of Jerusalem were actually killed in the capture and pillaging of the city by the Babylonians we do not know; there was a second deport-ation of survivors to Babylonia by Nebuchadnezzar at that time (2 Kings 25:11–12). For Ezekiel the fall of the city is symbolized by the departure of Yahweh's presence. He sees Yahweh's 'glory' (*kābôd*) leave the city (11:23) and settle on a nearby mountain. It was in Babylonia that he saw it again (3:23): Yahweh was still with his people, but with the exiles, no longer with his holy city Jerusalem. But he was to return to the city (43:4–5) and to the temple.

Like the prophets previously discussed, Ezekiel believed that Yahweh had not irrevocably abandoned his people or his city, and especially in the last part of the book (chapters 40–48) he pictures the return of the exiles and the restoration of Jerusalem. But – and this is characteristic of Ezekiel's teaching – Yahweh will restore his people not for their sake but for his own sake: 'for the sake of my holy name' which they had profaned (36:21–22). It is only then that they will come to 'know Yahweh'. In this way it is emphasized that Yahweh's forgiveness of his people is not contingent on their repentance but is due to his concern that his reputation among the nations of the world should no longer be besmirched.

This principle is further elaborated in passages in which Yahweh promises to make a new covenant with his people to replace that which they had broken (16:59–63; 37:24–28), and especially when he speaks of giving them a new heart and a new spirit (11:19–20; 18:31; 36:22–32). These promises of a new heart and a new covenant are reminiscent of a similar passage in Jer. 31:31–34; but in Ezekiel the thought is carried much further. In 36:22–32 the prophet begins with the statement that Yahweh will do these things not for Israel's sake, but for his own, continues with a promise by Yahweh that he will take the exiles from the countries to which they have been driven, and a declaration of his intention to perform on them, as it were, an act of surgery in which he will cut out their heart of stone (i.e. of stubbornness and rebellion) and substitute for it a 'heart of flesh' (v. 26), so that they will from henceforth be obedient to his laws. This is followed by a further promise of their return to their ancestral land and to the security of knowing that they will be his people and he their God. The renewal of the good life will take the form of the renewed fertility of the land and the removal of the disgrace of famine (v. 30). Only then will Israel repent of its evil deeds. Thus it is strongly emphasized that this reversal of Israel's fortunes will be due solely to the initiative of Yahweh, who will unconditionally and irreversibly transform the character of the people. In this way Ezekiel finds a way to solve the apparently insoluble problem that Israel cannot by itself repent and deserve a reversal of its fortunes.

In the final chapters of the book Ezekiel sees a vision of a restored city and the renewed occupation of the land. The distribution of the tribal territories formerly carried out on Yahweh's command by Joshua will be repeated (48:1–29), and the city itself will receive a new name signifying Yahweh's perpetual presence within it: it will be called *yhwh šāmmāh*, 'Yahweh is there' (48:35).

Power

The kings of Israel, sometimes called 'prince' (*nāśî'* or *śār*) are unreservedly condemned by Ezekiel, who accuses them of such crimes as defiling Yahweh's holy name by whoring (43:7) and murder (22:6). The real earthly power in his day is that of the all-conquering Nebuchadnezzar of Babylon, whose harsh treatment of the last king Zedekiah who had rebelled against him was fully deserved (17:11–21). For the new restored community Ezekiel envisages the appointment of a new king who will be of Davidic descent and who will faithfully 'feed his flock' (34:23). He will be king of a reunited Israel, not of Judah only (37:24, 25); but in chapters 40–48 there is no suggestion that he will exercise real power like that of his predecessors. In these chapters he is never called 'king' (*melek*), but 'prince' (*nāśî'*). His duties are confined to honorific ones such as providing for certain sacrificial offerings in the temple (45:17) and joining with his people in sacrificial worship (45:16, 17). It is specifically stated that he will not oppress his people as his predecessors had done (45:8), and that he will not have the power arbitrarily to seize property for his own benefit or that of his sons (46:18). Ezekiel thus envisages an entirely new kind of state centred on the temple, whose only true ruler will be God himself and whose laws will be directly incumbent on the people as a whole.

Sustenance and Family Life

Ezekiel's two pictures of exilic hardship and life after the return from exile do not substantially differ from those of the other prophets whom we have considered. He prophesies famine, accompanied by pestilence and the sword, for Jerusalem (4:9–17; 5:17; 6:12) and an ideal life of plenty for the returned exiles. These will enjoy the benefits of good grazing land (34:14) and fruitful orchards and crops (34:27); indeed, the land which had remained a waste during the exile will now become 'like the garden of Eden' (36:35), and the ruined towns will be rebuilt. In 47:1–12, however, there is a vision of the restored temple in which a river flows from the city to give miraculous fertility.

One thing that is almost entirely lacking in these descriptions is any substantial reference to family life. This is one reason why the book gives the impression of harshness. Most of the few references to *children* are to monstrous crimes: cannibalism within the family, due to the acute sufferings from famine (5:10) and the practice of parents sacrificing their children (16:20–21). In 9:6 Yahweh commands his 'angelic' executioners not to spare mothers and children in their work of slaughter. A rare passage in which Ezekiel shows human emotion is that in which Yahweh announces that he is about to take away the life of Ezekiel's wife, who is described as 'the delight of your eyes' (24:15–18).

Law and Justice

For Ezekiel the good life was available to those who obey Yahweh's laws – his 'statutes and ordinances', the nature of which was supposed to be known to all. These laws were partly concerned with true worship, but also comprised Yahweh's moral demands. Among other things they included commercial honesty, and Yahweh appeals to the rulers to enforce this (45:9–12). The prophet was commissioned as Yahweh's 'watchman' to warn the people to abandon their criminal behaviour (3:17–27). The book contains a number of lists of his moral commands in which justice plays a leading role; the most comprehensive of these is in chapter 18. There it is made clear that obedience to these is literally a matter of life and death: the obedient will live, the disobedient will die. There it is laid down that one does 'what is lawful and right' if one

> does not eat upon the mountains or lift up his eyes to
>   the idols of the house of Israel,
> does not defile his neighbour's wife
>   or approach a woman in her menstrual period,
> does not oppress anyone

but returns to the debtor his pledge,
commits no robbery,
gives his bread to the hungry
   and covers the naked with a garment,
does not take interest on a loan,
withholds his hand from iniquity,
executes true justice between contending parties

and, in general, obeys Yahweh's laws (vv. 6–9). 'Such a man is righteous; he shall surely live.'

All these requirements apart from the initial ones about avoidance of idolatry concern respect for others and just treatment of them, especially the weak or oppressed; and they conform to what is prescribed in the Old Testament laws. Many passages contain condemnations of those who practice such injustices – e.g. rulers (34:7–10) and officials who murder (11:1–6). The whole land is filled with violent crimes (ḥāmās, 8:17).

In Ezekiel's portrayal of the coming new age the question of these moral requirements is not pursued in detail. But in 11:18–20 and 36:26–29 the observance of Yahweh's laws in the new dispensation is seen as the consequence of the possession of the new heart and the new spirit that he will give to the whole people; in the latter passage (v. 31) it is stated that they will remember their former abominable deeds and hate themselves for these. In the passages that refer to the future Davidic king (34:23, 24; 37:24–25) also it is either implied or specifically stated that under his rule (or his successors?) universal justice will prevail; elsewhere this is presupposed as a feature of the new covenant that Yahweh will establish (16:60–62; 37:26).

But judgement in this book generally means the direct and utterly effective judgement of Yahweh himself rather than human justice administered by his appointees. That Yahweh will judge his people both as a whole and with regard to particular classes – priests, prophets, elders, etc. – is a commonplace of Ezekiel's teaching; and his negative judgement involves the death penalty. The execution of this judgement on the people as a whole takes the form of the destruction of the city at Yahweh's command. But the divine judgement is operative also in a positive sense, and applies also to individuals (18:30; 34:17–22): it means life even for the wicked if they repent (33:19). In this latter passage Yahweh finds it necessary to defend his justice against the accusation that he has acted unjustly in punishing the nation, asserting that individuals will be judged according to their righteousness or their repentance, and will be permitted to live, while the irredeemably wicked will die.

Wisdom

It is remarkable that wisdom is not seen by Ezekiel as a desirable element in Israel's life. The only references to wisdom in the entire book (apart from 27:8–9, where 'skilled men' are mentioned) occur in chapter 28, which is a denunciation of the prince of Tyre, who in his pride declares himself to be a god (v. 2). He was indeed 'wiser than Daniel' (v. 3) but used this wisdom to become immensely rich (vv. 4–5). Although he had originally been placed by God in Eden, the garden of God' (v. 13) he was thrust out because he corrupted his wisdom (v. 17); and he is to die (v. 10). This passage is clearly a warning to the readers against inordinate pride. Wisdom plays no part in Ezekiel's conception of the good life.

Joy

Ezekiel, although he foretells a future of unalloyed peace and prosperity for those who have been deemed worthy to live under the dispensation of the new covenant or who have been transformed by the gift of a new heart and a new spirit and will thus enjoy the good life in its fulness, does not specifically speak of their joy. Apart from 7:12, where the prophet alludes to the joy that buyers have, the only references to joy in the book concern the joy of their enemies, who maliciously rejoice at the fall of Israel and who will receive their due reward. The true happiness of the restored Israel is, however, most clearly implied in the frequently repeated refrain 'They will be my people and I will be their God' – that is, the good life of former days preceding Israel's apostasy, when Israel enjoyed the intimacy of its loving and intimate relations with God, will be fully restored. For Ezekiel the most important specific aspect of this seems to have been the restoration of the temple and its sacrifices (40–48) in the city which will be renamed 'Yahweh is there' and when the waters of fertility and healing will miraculously flow from the temple.

God

Ezekiels's God is an exigent and uncompromising God. Much of the book consists of prophecies that the whole people is doomed to destruction because of its rebellion and refusal to obey the laws that he has imposed on them: there is no doubt that the fall of Jerusalem to the Babylonians with its aftermath is meant, or that Yahweh, who controls events, both can and will carry out his threats. Ezekiel himself was aware that this had in fact happened during his own time. There appears to be no 'good life' envisaged in these passages. However, Yahweh's action was not carried out without due warning, which it was part of Ezekiel's mission to give, 'whether they hear or refuse to hear' (2:5).

Ezekiel taught that some individuals in the community would escape death. He divides the nation into two groups, the righteous and the wicked. For the latter there is no hope of survival; but of the former it is promised that he 'will live'. Since Yahweh is the giver of all life, it may be presumed, though this is not directly stated, that the verb 'to live' here is shorthand for 'to enjoy the good life'.

Sometimes Yahweh speaks, through his prophet, of the benefits that he had conferred on Israel in the past. Thus in 16:6–14 Jerusalem is described as a girl baby abandoned by her mother who had been rescued and brought up by Yahweh who lavished on her every luxury and adornment appropriate to the good life. In this passage God speaks in erotic terms of his love (*dōdîm*) for her: she became his lover or his bride (we may compare Hosea 1–3 here). Such language, however, is very rare in Ezekiel. The chapter continues with an account of her subsequent sexual promiscuity, for which he had severely punished her; but it ends with a promise of her rehabilitation and restoral to his good graces.

However, the future good life for Israel in the book is predominately expressed in terms of the restoration of God's presence with his people centred on a restored temple in which they will worship and offer acceptable sacrifices. Thus in 37:26–28 Yahweh promises that

> I will make a covenant of peace with them ... and will bless them ... and *will set my sanctuary among them for evermore*. My dwelling place shall be with them; and I will be their God, and they shall be my people. Then the nations shall know that I Yahweh sanctify Israel, *when my sanctuary is among them for evermore*.

It is characteristic of Ezekiel's notion of the good life that most of the final eight chapters of the book is devoted to a detailed description of that temple.

Elsewhere, however, Yahweh speaks in more general terms of his care for his people. In 34:15–16 he assumes the character of a true shepherd: 'I myself will be the shepherd of my sheep, and I will provide them with a place to lie down ... I will seek the lost, and I will bring back the strayed, and I will strengthen the weak ... I will feed them in good measure.'

With all this it must be taken into account that Yahweh frequently speaks as if his only concern was his reputation in the world: he states that his concern was not for the well-being of his people as such but for his holy name, which they had defiled, and which must be rehabilitated for his sake. This reveals an aspect of God's character which, at least when expressed so openly, is hardly to be found elsewhere in the Old Testament.

Summary

Ezekiel foresaw the collapse of all good life in Jerusalem with the fall of the city to the Babylonians; he was himself an exile and shared the grief of the second and apparently definitive deportation. But he also believed that some individuals would escape this divine judgement. He divided the mass of the inhabitants of the city – and perhaps, of all Jews or even, by extension, all human beings – simply into two groups: the wicked and the righteous. The latter were those who had abjured the sins of the others – especially disobedience to God's laws, violence, and idolatry. They and only they would save their lives in the general destruction. All were subject to divine judgement.

For Ezekiel it was the presence of Yahweh among his people, manifested in the temple in Jerusalem, which made possible the good life. Because the temple had been polluted by the sinfulness of the people Yahweh withdrew his presence, to return only when the temple had been rebuilt and had been cleansed by a radical change of their nature. This would be effected by Yahweh himself, who would cleanse them with water and, by a violent operation, give them a new heart and a new spirit. But in his revelations to Ezekiel Yahweh surprisingly and frequently disclaims the notion that he performs these actions for their sake: rather, his motive is to defend his 'holy Name' and to protect his reputation among the nations. Nevertheless in some passages he reveals a more tender disposition, showing that he is in fact motivated by a love for his people which had its beginnings long ago.

The main impression probably intended to be made on the minds of the first readers of the completed book, who looked for encouragement in their less than enviable condition, was that Yahweh is an austere and demanding God who brooks no affront to his divine nature through disobedience to his moral laws and punishes severely those who transgress, but who – whether for their sake or his – is able and ready to bring about a radical change in the nature of his people and then to lavish again on them all the benefits and joys of the good life.

20
Daniel

In some respects the book of Daniel has close affinities with Esther. Its first six chapters consist of stories which depict essentially the identical situation: among the Jewish population living within a foreign empire there is a small group who attain high positions in the government by reason of having gained the favour of the king. These narratives will have been perceived by their Jewish readers as conveying a similar teaching as that of Esther, in particular that while on the one hand it is open to Jews to have successful careers in a foreign land, they cannot rely on the toleration of their rulers. These empires are ruled by absolute monarchs whose good will may evaporate at any time and who can decree a sentence of death without reason on any of their subjects including the Jews.

But the similarity between the two books ends there. Daniel is a very different kind of book from Esther. The tone of the book is profoundly religious: the real protagonist is God himself, who is seen to operate through the faith and courage of his chosen servants. Great emphasis is placed on the universal power of the God of the Jews in contrast to the powerlessness of the gods of the heathen rulers; on God's gift of wisdom to his faithful servants; on the power of prayer to him; on his ability and willingness to save them from the attacks of those who would destroy them; on his protection of the humble and his punishment of the arrogant.

Topics related to the good life are not entirely absent from the book. The *insecurity* of the Jews and their lack of a secure *place* in the world are already mentioned in the opening verses with the report of the siege of Jerusalem by Nebuchadnezzar and the defeat of king Jehoiakim of Judah resulting in the deportation of some of the population to Babylon. Chapter 1 is the story of the king's command to bring some of the young Jews of royal and noble descent to the court to be trained in the Babylonian language and customs. Among these were four young men named Daniel,

Hananiah, Mishael and Azariah, to whom were given Babylonian names: Belteshazzar, Shadrach, Meshach and Abed-
nego. The topic of *wisdom* is also introduced at this point: it
is stated that this, which was to play a crucial role in the
subsequent chapters, was one of these young men's accom-
plishments (1:4). At this stage, however, wisdom meant no
more than a quality which would make them suitable for
service in the royal court. Another topic of this chapter is
that of *sustenance*. The young men, led by Daniel, decline the
rich food and drink offered to them, requesting and
obtaining a plain diet of vegetables and water, so avoiding
the defilement that the Babylonian food offered to them
would entail by the breaking of the Jewish food laws (v. 8).
The salutary effect of this diet (vv. 14–15) is perhaps connected by the author in some way with the statement in v. 17
that God gave Daniel another kind of wisdom – the ability to
interpret visions and dreams, a wisdom superior to that of
the court magicians (v. 20). (Cf. Joseph's interpretation of
dreams in Gen. 40 and 41.)

Daniel's God-given wisdom is then illustrated in chapter
2, where Daniel was able to reveal to the king the contents
of a dream which had disquieted him but whose details he
could not now recall, and also to explain its meaning. For
this service he was richly rewarded and promoted, with his
companions, to the highest offices in the empire. The king
recognized that Daniel's God is 'God of gods and King of
kings' even though Daniel had interpreted the dream as
foretelling the destruction of his and the various empires
that would succeed his by God's eternal and indestructible
kingdom.

Two of the following chapters recount persecutions of the
four Jews in the reigns of Nebuchadnezzar and the Persian
king Darius respectively: Daniel's companions are thrown
into a blazing furnace (chapter 3) and Daniel himself into a
lion's den (chapter 6). Each of these chapters ends with the
rescue of these men by divine power from certain death and
with a declaration by the king of the unparalleled power of
the Jewish God, who alone deserves to be worshipped.
Chapter 4 is a sequel to chapter 3. The now 'converted'
Nebuchadnezzar makes a public declaration to his subjects in

which he recounts yet another dream which Daniel interpreted as meaning that the king's pride will be punished: he
will be deposed and reduced to the status of an animal until
he learns that God is able to appoint and humiliate kings at
his will. Nebuchadnezzar recalls that this punishment was
immediately carried out, and that he had been reinstated
after learning his lesson.

Chapter 5 is set in the reign of another king of Babylon,
Belshazzar. This king gave a great feast at which he committed blasphemy (in Jewish eyes) by sending for the sacred
vessels that Nebuchadnezzar had seized when he captured
Jerusalem and had placed in his treasury, using them as
drinking cups from which he and his guests drank while
praising the gods of Babylon. Terrified by the sight of a
mysterious hand writing on the wall which his wise men
could not interpret, he sent for Daniel who interpreted the
words as meaning that Belshazzar's time had come and that
his kingdom was to be destroyed. This story concludes with
the dramatic statement that on that very night Belshazzar
met his death and his empire fell into the hands of a foreign
conqueror, Darius the Mede.

The narratives concerning the adventures of Daniel and
his companions at the royal courts of Babylon and Persia
end with chapter 6. The second half of the book (chapters 7–
12) consists of a different kind of narrative relating the
dreams and visions not of the human rulers of those kingdoms but of Daniel himself. Despite their different literary
form, they are closely related to chapters 1–6 in that they
set out in greater detail the fundamental message that
Daniel's God is the undisputed ruler of the universe at
whose decree human empires and their rulers are established
and at whose decree they perish. In particular, they elaborate
the lesson of Nebuchadnezzar's dream in chapter 2 about the
future – that God will establish his everlasting kingdom,
bringing to an end the successive human empires. This
message is now conveyed to Daniel by angelic beings.

Chapter 7 refers again to the successive empires, at first
under the figure of a succession of animals of which the real
identity is given later in the chapter. But it differs from
chapter 2 in that the last of these is described in greater

detail, as fiercer than its predecessors. There follows a picture of God's judgement. The last empire is destroyed, and power is given to a new figure 'like a son of man' who 'comes on the clouds of heaven'. In the interpretation that follows the fourth animal, which has ten horns, is seen as ten kings and the 'son of man' as 'the people of the saints of the Most High' – that is, the Jewish people – whose reign will be eternal. It will now have become clear to the readers that the dream describes the future of the world which will end with the complete triumph of the Jews; and the remaining chapters are figurative accounts of present and future history. In the final chapter there is a promise of a glorious future beyond the present world for those who are endowed with wisdom and are 'written in the book' of life (12:1–3).

Summary

In every chapter of Daniel the author has in mind his suffering people who long for a good life. His purpose is not only to encourage them to believe that as God's people they will eventually triumph, but also to help his readers individually to have confidence that God is able and ready to help them in their distress.

1. In face of the temptation to believe that the gods of the powerful empires in which they live must themselves be powerful, the readers are presented with stories which show that it is their God alone who exists and who has supreme power.
2. They learn that it is he who is able to give both wealth and worldly power to faithful Jews, and also wisdom to those whom he chooses to be their leaders. But the good life consists not in wealth and power but in the rewards of faithfulness and in confidence in his supreme power.
3. Empires and their rulers are in the hands of God, who will exercise his judgement on them and punish their inordinate pride.
4. God is a saviour who rescues those who trust him (chapters 3 and 6).

5. When they are in danger he sends an angel to be with them, walking with them in the fire (3:24, 25) and stopping the mouths of the lions who would devour them (chapter 6).
6. God knows and has fixed the future history of the world. He will establish his eternal kingdom and put it into the hands of the Jewish people for ever (12:1–4).
7. God gives his help to those who pray to him daily (6:10). The book is full of instances of prayer and praises uttered by Daniel and his companions, so encouraging the readers to imitate them.
8. But all are sinful. The Jews and their forefathers have committed many sins, and they must confess their sins and repent, calling on God to forgive their sins as did Daniel (chapter 9).

21
Hosea

Like some other prophets Hosea makes virtually no differentiation between individual Israelites but treats the whole nation together as a single unit. Although he occasionally refers to particular groups — king, princes, priests, etc. — he generally addresses or refers to the people corporately as 'Israel', 'Ephraim', even 'they' or under the figure of wife or child. The impression given to the reader is that the nation — specifically Ephraim or the northern kingdom — is united in living its life, whether that life should be described as 'good' or 'bad'.

The nation that Hosea addresses is wealthy and self-satisfied (12:7–8). Yet in no real sense can it be said to be living the good life. In 4:1 Hosea describes its moral and religious condition in absolute terms: 'There is no faithfulness ('ĕmet) or loyalty (ḥesed) and no knowledge of God in the land'; and in the following verse he specifies perjury, deceit, murder, theft and adultery as crimes regularly committed.

Much of Hosea's rhetoric is couched in sexual imagery. In chapters 1–3 the relationship between Yahweh and Israel is portrayed in terms of a marriage, Israel being Yahweh's unfaithful wife (in chapters 1 and 3 the prophet's own marriage is represented as a symbol of this). Sexual imagery is frequent in the book; Israel is accused of 'whoredom' and adultery (cf. Ezekiel). It is not always clear in those passages whether the reference is to actual sexual irregularity or whether it is to be taken as an indictment of the unfaithfulness of the 'wife' Israel to her husband Yahweh. Elsewhere — notably in 11:1–4 — the nation is represented as Yahweh's son, saved from slavery in Egypt and lovingly raised by him, but who has turned against his father and resorted to the worship of other gods, specifically 'the Baals'.

Yahweh's love for Israel as husband and father is a prominent feature of the book, and Yahweh is represented as torn between his duty to punish them for their sin and his reluctance to do so. On the one hand he declares his intention to destroy them; but in a poignant passage (11:8–9) he reflects that because of his intense love for them he cannot do so and will restrain his anger.

In 6:1–3 and 14:1–3 there are appeals to Israel to return to Yahweh. But there is in fact no evidence at all in the book that this occurred in Hosea's time. Although the book contains a number of passages giving assurances of a reversal of Yahweh's plans to destroy the nation, for Hosea this destruction is still in the future; so also is the coming restoration to which he refers. This restoration appears to be motivated solely by Yahweh's enduring love, usually with no hint of a previous repentance by the nation.

Chapter 2, verses 14–23, express Yahweh's intention to lure his faithless wife Israel into the wilderness where she had lived after her release from Egyptian slavery, to receive a favourable response and to restore her to him as her husband. Similarly in 3:4–5 he speaks of his intention to impose a severe discipline on Israel after which they will return to seek him. In 1:10–11 and 11:10–11 there are simple prophecies of their return to Yahweh without any apparent cause save the good will of a loving God: 'In the place where it was said, to them, "You are not my people", it shall be said, "Children of the living God"' (1:10); and so they will once more be given possession of the land. A similar promise is made in 11:10–11. Following the appeal of vv. 1–3, 14:4–7 contain the most lavish of Yahweh's promises to Israel which will once again enjoy the good life in all its fulness under idyllic conditions, 'living under Yahweh's shadow'. But there also there is no statement that Israel had responded to the appeal: what Yahweh promises is an act of pure grace.

Summary

The book of Hosea is dominated by the portrayal of Yahweh as husband and father. In this presentation Yahweh is seen as torn between his need, in accordance with his righteous nature, to punish Israel for the sins in which the whole nation is involved, even to the extent of its total destruction, and his yearning, based on his enduring love for it, which moves him to compassion. The latter does not cancel the former, but will ultimately triumph over it in a movement of pure grace that will follow the punishment, restoring to the people the enjoyment of the good life even though there is no indication that they have repented. Thus although most of the book speaks of severe punishment for the nation's many and grave sins, its ultimate message for the readers will have been one of hope.

22
Joel

Despite its brevity this is a complex book whose structure is not easy to discern. The problem is not that it contains a mixture of judgement and of announcements of future joy: that is also true of other prophetical books of the Old Testament. It is rather that it oscillates between different kinds of speech – for example between straightforward depictions of disastrous situations and of cosmic catastrophe, between calls to lamentation and calls to arms together with promises of an idyllic future with no obvious connections between these, and that its language is sometimes plainly descriptive and at other times highly symbolic and allusive. Whether it presented problems to the original readers it is difficult to know; but like other prophetical books it has a positive message and will have given hope and encouragement to those looking for signs of a positive future. In its portrayal of a particular community it has much to say about the various groups that compose it and about both the absence and the enjoyment of the good life.

The book begins (chapter 1) with a vivid description of a natural disaster which is threatening the community's very existence. A dread plague of locusts has fallen on the countryside, consuming the crops and destroying the vines and the other fruit-bearing trees on which the life of the community depends, causing famine and drought, affecting both people and livestock. The good life to which the community is accustomed has come to an end. This situation is described as entirely unprecedented, and the readers of the book are called to wonder at it and to hand down the story of the event to future generations (vv. 2–3). Its effect is summed up in v. 12 with the words 'Joy has come to an end [literally, 'has withered away'] for the people'.

The writer takes it for granted that the plague has been sent by Yahweh: he concludes that it has come 'as a devastation from the Almighty' and that 'the day of Yahweh is near' (v. 15). But he also believes that Yahweh is able to redress the situation and calls for the proclamation of a solemn fast and a lamentation by all the inhabitants of the land in order to make an appeal to him to be willing to act. Both here and in the following chapter the communal lamentation is to take place in the temple and to be led by the priests, who have been unable, owing to the famine, to make the customary offerings there (v. 13).

The relationship between chapter 1 and 2:1–11 is not clear. Joel 1:19–20 already appears to speak of a different kind of disaster caused by fire. In 2:1–11 again the cause of the trouble is described in terms of an invading army; but whether this is yet another terror or whether it is still mainly a poetical description of the plague of locusts can hardly be determined. In 2:10–11 Yahweh is represented as a general leading the invading army, whose advance causes an earthquake and a catastrophe of cosmic dimensions, with sun, moon and stars darkened.

The book of Joel differs from the prophetical books previously considered in that there is no specific indication that the disaster is the result of specific or persistent sins on the part of the people, even though they assume that such a disaster can only have been caused by their sin (2:12). Yahweh appeals to the people to repent and turn back to him, with the implication that he might relent. The people themselves express this hope in vv. 13–14.

The book gives what is in some ways a very full picture of the community, of which every member is directly affected by the disasters described in it and who are all summoned to intercede with Yahweh. The people ('am) is summoned in its capacity as God's congregation (qāhāl, 2:16). Reference is made to the priests, the staff of the temple (1:9, 13; 2:17); the elders (1:14); also the farmers and vinedressers (1:11); the aged, children and babies (2:16); the newly married bride and bridegroom (2:16); even the drunkards, who need to be roused from their slumbers (1:5). Curiously for a prophetical book there is no mention of prophets, nor any reference to a king or rulers. It seems to be assumed that, in contrast with other prophetical books, there are none in the community who doubt the efficacy of prayer to Yahweh, who deliberately remain impervious to the summons, or who worship other gods.

While 1.:2–2:17 present the above disasters as occurring in a dramatic present and as calling for urgent prayer, 2:18 marks a change of tense: it speaks of a past event. It states that Yahweh, moved by passionate love and pity for his people, answered their prayers. Then in 2:19–27 he promises that the 'invading army' will be removed and the fertility of the land restored. The good life will in fact be so abundantly restored that it will make up for the years of deprivation (v. 25), and there will be no repetition of the humiliation that the people have suffered (vv. 26, 27). The words of assurance of the divine presence familiar from other prophetical books (e.g. Jer. 31:33; Ezek. 37:27; Hos. 2:23; Zech. 8:8; 13:9) are here repeated:

> You shall know that I am in the midst of Israel,
> and that I, Yahweh, am your God and there is no other.
> (v. 27)

It is striking that in this second half of the book as (almost) in the first there is no reference whatever to the people's having committed sins that might account for their past distressful situation. All is pure grace: Yahweh has now acted with great kindness towards a people whom he had previously (apparently for no particular reason) afflicted.

There follows in vv. 28, 29 a further promise that affects all members of the community. There will come a time ('afterwards') when Yahweh will pour out his spirit on them all, on sons and daughters, old men and young, even on their male and female slaves. This outpouring of Yahweh's spirit is evidently an even greater gift from Yahweh to his people. Whatever the phrase may have been intended to mean – and the earliest readers, like the modern ones, may have interpreted it in various ways – it will probably have been seen as equivalent to the 'new heart' and the 'new covenant' of Jeremiah and Ezekiel, transforming the very nature of God's people for good, conferring on them the 'good life' at its highest level. The additional promises that its recipients will prophesy, dream dreams and see visions would have been seen as signs of this 'conversion'; we may compare Moses' wish (Num. 11:29), 'Would that all Yahweh's people were prophets, and that Yahweh would put his spirit on them!'

In the final chapters (2:30–3:21) the community of which the book speaks is identified clearly for the first time: it is Jerusalem (Zion). Much of these chapters is devoted to the coming punishment of the nations that have oppressed Judah and Jerusalem in the past. Among these the Philistines (Tyre and Sidon) are indicted for particular cruelty: they have sold the people into slavery; but now the situation will be reversed, and they in turn will become Judah's slaves – though 'every one who calls on the name of Yahweh will be saved' (2:32). 'Jerusalem shall be holy, and strangers shall never again pass through it' (3:17).

Summary

The book begins with a portrayal of an Israelite community suffering from a plague of locusts together with other phenomena which threaten its very existence. These have been sent by Yahweh, though the reason for his action is not stated: the victims assume that they are being punished for their sins, but no specific sins are mentioned. The people are summoned to fast and pray for deliverance. Yahweh replies favourably to their prayers, and promises the resumption of the good life that they had previously enjoyed. In 2:28–29 he makes the additional promise that he will at a later time pour out his spirit on all the members of the community, so effecting a transformation of their nature, causing them to prophesy and see visions.

23
Amos

Like the other prophetical books Amos contains both oracles of judgement (here not against Jerusalem and Judah but against the northern kingdom with its capital Samaria) and of restoration after destruction and exile; but the promises of restoration occur only at the very end of the book and occupy only a few verses (9:11–15); the rest of the book is devoted to denunciation of the people for their sins and threats of total annihilation. Amos was a Judaean, but was called to prophesy to northern Israel (7:15) at a time when that nation was enjoying a period of military success (6:13) and – for some – wealth and prosperity, in the time of Kings Uzziah of Judah and Jeroboam (II) of Israel (1:1).

Throughout the greater part of the book Amos prophesies a terrible end to the 'good life' of the kingdom of Israel and the violent death of many of its citizens. This will be brought about by an invading and conquering enemy – Assyria is meant – who will at Yahweh's command take them into captivity 'beyond Damascus' (5:27). They will thus be deprived of their *place* (the land) and their *security*. But unlike the citizens of Jerusalem at a later time (that of Jeremiah and Ezekiel) when that city had already experienced disruptive foreign aggression and real power had already seeped away from its kings and government, they were completely unaware of the fate of which the prophet warned them, and were living in a fool's paradise, glorying in the supposed security of their position (4:1; 6:1, 13; 9:10), even though Yahweh had already warned them by afflicting them with various indications of his displeasure – famine, drought, failure of crops, plague and sudden deaths (4:6–11). 'Yet you did not return to me, says Yahweh' (4:6, 8, 9, 10, 11).

In speaking about the criteria set by Yahweh for the living of the good life and of the fate of those who fail to meet these criteria, Amos does not distinguish between individuals or families who do or do not deserve punishment for their sins.

The nation as a whole has sinned, and the nation as a whole will be destroyed. This blanket judgement on human behaviour is already exemplified in the series of divine judgements on the surrounding nations with which the book begins (1:3–2:5). Here each of the peoples in question is designated by its corporate name (Aram, Philistines, Edom, sons of Ammon, Moab, Judah) and/or by the name of its capital city or other principal cities (Damascus, the Philistine cities, Tyre). The specific crimes for which they are indicted are attributed to a corporate 'they'.

It is noteworthy that for Amos the living of the good life, whether viewed from a material point of view (prosperity, land, security) or from a moral one is not a feature of Israel alone as God's people. Amos and his readers evidently took it for granted that there was an internationally agreed code of moral behaviour of which the named peoples – and presumably others – were aware; and as it was Yahweh who would punish them for breaching this code it must have been Yahweh who had established it in the first place. Indeed, it was Yahweh – whether they knew this or not – who had given these people their place in the world. Each had had its 'exodus'; in this respect Israel was on a par with the Cushites (Ethiopians) and other nations: it was Yahweh who had brought the Philistines from Caphtor and the Aramaeans (Syrians) from distant Kir to the lands in which they now lived (9:7).

The judgement on Israel is no less comprehensive. Total destruction is prophesied for them in many passages; for example, in 2:6 the same formula is used against Israel as is employed against the other nations: 'For three transgressions and for four, I will not revoke the punishment', and 8:1–3 speaks of the 'end' of Israel. The 'day of Yahweh' will be not light but darkness (5:18–20). The people will be taken into exile (5:27; 6:7) and the capital city will be destroyed (6:8). This final judgement will be implemented 'against the whole family that I brought up out of the land of Egypt' (3:1) because no heed has been paid to Yahweh's previous warnings (4:6–12; 7:1–9). He has appealed to the people urging them to 'seek me and live', to 'seek good and not evil that you may live', to 'hate evil and love good, and establish justice in the gate' (5:4; 5:14–15). The offer is made that if these admonitions are heeded 'it may be that Yahweh, the God of hosts, will be gracious to the remnant of Joseph'. This is an offer of the continued enjoyment of the good life for those who accept it; its rejection left Yahweh no choice.

Although Amos seems to treat the whole nation as irremediably corrupt and doomed to inevitable destruction, his denunciations are addressed almost exclusively to a wealthy, influential luxury-loving upper class, living in supposed security in a period of national success (6:1). Only two social classes are mentioned in the book: the wealthy, and the poor and destitute. The latter are never directly addressed by Amos: they are always presented as the victims of the former (2:6, 7; 4:1; 5:11–12; 8:4–6). These passages give a vivid picture of society in Amos's time, when some were living, in a material sense, the 'good life' while this was entirely denied to the remainder. But for him this 'good time' was in fact an 'evil time' (5:13). His sympathies are clear: he identifies the suffering poor as the righteous' (ṣaddîq, 2:6; cf. 5:12).

The luxurious life of the rich is fully described. They have built splendid houses in which to reside (3:15; 5:11; 6:11); they own vineyards (5:11); they possess beautiful furniture (6:4); they love wine (4:1; 6:6) and enjoy feasts at which they are entertained with music and songs (6:5, 6; 8:10); they anoint themselves with fine oils (6:6); they think themselves secure in their way of life (6:1).

Amos clearly disapproved of this way of life, perhaps because he himself before his call to prophesy belonged to a social class to which such things were unknown (7:14–15). The sins of which he accused the wealthy in Israel were, however, much more serious. It was not luxury in itself that caused him to announce the downfall of the nation. The main sins for which he denounced the wealthy – apart from a rare reference to the practice of idolatrous worship (5:25–26; 8:14) were of three kinds, all characteristic of a class that knew no restraints and could apparently behave as it pleased: unjust treatment of the poor (including robbery and violence), insincere worship and commercial dishonesty. These three were closely linked.

Justice

The accusations of unjust treatment of the poor by the rich are frequent and often detailed; they occupy a greater place in this book than in almost any other of the prophetical books. They make it clear that in Amos's time the poor were denied any access to the good life. Some of the accusations are general, though couched in extremely harsh terms: the rich 'oppress' and 'crush' the needy (4:1) and 'trample' on them (2:7; 5:11; 8:4). 'They sell the righteous for silver and the needy for a pair of shoes' (2:6b), is probably an allusion to the practice, probably not illegal, but devastating in its social effects, of driving poor debtors into slavery (they demand unreasonable interest from them in the form of 'levies of wheat', 5:11), and then selling those slaves to others for profits in money or land. The profits from such violent action were then stored in private depositories (3:10), or might be spent on drink (4:1) or on illicit sexual pleasure (2:8). Amos also claims that these people obtained immunity for their crimes by corrupting judges and witnesses: they 'turn justice to wormwood' (5:7; 6:12) and are hostile to those who witness in court (literally, 'in the gate') to testify to the true facts (5:10, 15). Their crimes are all the more heinous because of the uses to which they put their gains: sexual licence (2:7–8); luxurious living (4:1); building for themselves splendid stone-built houses and planting vineyards to increase their profits still more (5:11).

False Religion

It is recognized throughout the Old Testament that the worship of Yahweh is essential to the living of the good life, being the source of divine blessing. But in Amos the worship offered in Yahweh's sanctuaries by those who are guilty of such crimes as have been described above is blasphemous, because it bears no relation to the lives that they are leading: they are accused of an irredeemable hypocrisy towards God, which is made the more unforgivable by their very assiduousness in attendance at the temple. In 4:4–5 not only the rich but the whole 'people of Israel' is denounced for its frequent worship at Bethel and Gilgal with its offerings and sacrifices which 'they love to perform'. In 5:4–6 Yahweh urges the 'house of Israel' to 'seek me and live' rather than 'seeking' the great sanctuaries of Bethel, Gilgal – and also Beersheba across the frontier in Judah – sanctuaries which he intends to destroy. In 5:21–23 he declares that he loathes the religious festivals celebrated by the people because they are incompatible with the injustices that they practice in their daily lives. (In an ambiguous oracle Amos may even suggest that the worship offered to Yahweh by the nation long ago in the desert before they entered the land was false and not offered to him (5:25), although the more natural way of taking it is that the prophet is making the extraordinary claim that the Israelites did not offer sacrificial worship at that time.) Finally in 9:1 in a vision Amos sees Yahweh standing by the altar (of Bethel?), commanding the immediate destruction of the temple as he had previously threatened.

But apart from the somewhat problematic 5:25 the book contains no repudiation of sacrificial or other formal temple worship in itself, and it is unlikely that the earliest readers would have interpreted these strictures as a condemnation of such worship. Thus, for example, when Yahweh states that he *hates* the worship that is carried out in his name (5:21–24) it is only the immorality of its contemporary practice (in the time of Amos) that is being condemned.

Dishonest Commercial Practice

In 8:5–6 Amos castigates the wealthy landowners for dishonest practices. They 'make the ephah small and the shekel great', and 'practice deceit with false balances' – that is, they sell wheat to the poor at inflated prices; and they also 'sell the sweepings of the wheat', that is, the 'wheat' that they sell to them is not genuine wheat at all but only the useless chaff left over after the wheat has been threshed; the best they keep for themselves. These practices are yet another device by which the poor are deprived of an adequate livelihood; Yahweh swears that he will never forget them, and will therefore 'cause the land to tremble' – that is, he will bring about the ruin of the nation (vv. 7–8).

Prophecies of Hope

The denunciations of the nation's sins conclude with an uncompromising statement: 'The eyes of the Lord Yahweh are upon the sinful kingdom, and I will destroy it from the face of the earth' (9:8a). But there immediately follows a line which appears to contradict this: 'except that I will *not utterly* destroy the house of Jacob' (9:8b). There is not, however, an *absolute* contradiction here. This line does not negate the threat of destruction; but its form shows it to be a *mitigation* of that threat. Yahweh will destroy the nation, but not completely. What form the mitigation may take is not stated; but it seems to reflect a kind of hesitation in Yahweh's mind somewhat comparable to his self-questioning in Hos. 11:8–9, where he wonders how he can destroy the people whom he has loved and continues to love (though Amos never in fact speaks specifically of Yahweh's love for Israel). But to the first readers of the completed book there would be a degree of hope in this line, since for them the 'destruction' of the nation had already occurred, and 'I will *not utterly* destroy' would give at least some encouragement that having survived the threatened destruction they could claim still to be Yahweh's people. (For a somewhat similar teaching compare the notion of the remnant in Isa. 1:9; 10:20–22.)

In the final verses of the book Yahweh is represented as abruptly and unexpectedly announcing a total reversal of his preceding threats of destruction:

> I will restore the fortunes of my people Israel ...
> I will plant them upon their land,
> and they shall never again be plucked up
> out of the land that I have given them. (vv. 14–15)

The people, then, are already living in exile; and these verses do not suggest that the restoration will occur immediately. It is announced not for the present but for some future time: 'on that day', v. 11; 'the time will come', v. 13.

A feature that is strikingly absent from these verses is any indication that the people have in fact repented of their sins as Amos had urged them to do. These verses make no reference whatever to the present moral or religious state of the people who are now to be redeemed. Yahweh appears simply as a *deus ex machina* or fairy godmother dispensing largesse to an (apparently) unresponsive people.

The picture of the future life of the redeemed people in their land (vv. 13–14) is an idyllic one, comparable in some respects to passages in other prophetical books such as Isa. 44:3–4, 65:18–22, Jer. 31:4–5, Hos. 14:5–7 and Joel 3:18, but going far beyond those into the realm of fantasy. According to v. 13 the ripening of crops and the maturing of grapes will be miraculously speeded up so that

> the ploughman will follow hard on the reaper
> and the grape-treader on the planter of seed;
> the mountains will drip sweet vine.

(Ezek. 47:12 has somewhat similar imagery.)

The message conveyed by these verses is one of exceptional fertility of the land and of rebuilt cities. It is noteworthy that no mention is made of such notions as a new covenant or a new heart (as in Jeremiah and Ezekiel), of a new relationship with God or of a restored divine presence. The familiar pattern of sin–punishment–repentance–restoration is not observed here. Nevertheless, to a generation suffering the effects of exile and the burden of foreign rule this passage coming at the very end of the book will have radiated a message of hope, making the whole prophecy an essentially encouraging one like that of the other prophetical books which have been considered above.

Summary

The book of Amos depicts the corruption that was characteristic of northern Israel at the time when the prophet had

been sent by Yahweh from south of the border to prophesy
there. Amos fulfilled his mission to denounce the nation for its
sins and to announce its imminent destruction. There was to
be no distinction between the guilty and individual citizens
who might be innocent of these deeds. However, the
denunciations in the book are almost exclusively directed
against a particular class: the wealthy and influential upper
class which oppressed the poor in order to augment their
profits, making the good life an impossibility for them; who
indulged in dishonest commercial practices; and who angered
Yahweh by an assiduous attention to a public worship which
was totally at variance with their immoral lives. Towards the
end of the book, however, 9:8b marks a change of heart on
Yahweh's part: although he will not retract his intention to
destroy the nation, the destruction will not be a total one. In
the final verses of the book it is presupposed that the
destruction, followed by exile, has already taken place.
Although there is no indication that the nation has repented,
these verses foretell the restoration of the nation in idyllic
terms, so giving encouragement to the first readers of the
completed book.

24
Jonah

The book of Jonah is quite unlike the other prophetical books of the Old Testament. It does not consist of a collection of messages given by Yahweh to a particular prophet to proclaim to others, but is a story *about* a prophet. Its main human character is a single prophet, Jonah, who is commissioned by Yahweh to go and deliver a particular message, but who initially refuses to accept his mission. The message that he is commanded to deliver is that Yahweh will shortly destroy a great heathen city. When this message is nullified because on hearing it the whole city repents, Yahweh changes his mind and shows mercy to its inhabitants, Jonah is displeased. Though he knows that Yahweh is a merciful God (4:2) he is disappointed that he has not been allowed to witness the destruction of a city renowned for its wickedness. The story is told with great skill and humour, and at first reading may seem to be simple and straightforward; but the attempts that have been made throughout the ages to elucidate its purpose are so diverse that it is clear that it is not simple at all.

It is not possible here to refer to more than a few of the interpretations that have been proposed. There is nothing in the book itself or in the rest of the Old Testament that gives a positive indication of the way(s) in which it may have been understood by readers at the time when it was written. Some early (but not contemporary) Jewish interpreters concentrated on the character and behaviour of Jonah, seeing him as an unworthy prophet who resisted Yahweh's command to preach to the people of Nineveh because he did not want them to repent and so escape the threatened destruction. An early Christian interpretation (Matt. 12:41) somewhat similarly commended the people of Nineveh for having taken the warning to heart and repented. Other more recent scholars have understood the book as primarily an exposition of the nature of Yahweh as all-powerful creator and controller of natural phenomena yet as patient, merciful saviour. Another theory popular in modern times has been that the book was written to support the universalistic view that God desires the salvation of all peoples, against a narrow belief current in the author's time, that salvation is for the Jews only. And so on.

The other characters in the book, the sailors (1:5–16) and the king and people of Nineveh (3:3–9) are all foreigners and unbelievers yet their behaviour is exemplary, while the only Jew in the story, Jonah, is strongly rebuked by Yahweh, who patiently shows him the error of his ways. In his resistance to God's merciful treatment of Nineveh, his disobedience to his calling and his deliberate attempt to escape from Yahweh's presence (1:3), Jonah, though relatively a wealthy man (1:3), is clearly not living the good life that only God can give. As the only example in the book of an Israelite and a worshipper of Yahweh (1:9) he will presumably have been regarded with horror by the readers. However, at the end of the book Yahweh gives Jonah a lesson (to which Jonah's reaction is not recorded!) about the nature of the good life, which is that what he requires from his adherents is that they should act on their knowledge that he is a merciful God and follow his example (4:2, 11).

Summary

This book has been interpreted in many ways. Its contribution to the topic of the good life is the message that this can only be truly lived by those who not only recognize God as the creator and all-powerful controller of the whole world but also comprehend and practise in their own lives his infinite mercy and desire for the salvation of all human beings.

25

Micah

Like some other prophetical books, Micah is greatly concerned with the notions of *security* and *place*, both in a negative and a positive sense. The feeling of security on which the people of both Israel and Judah is at present priding itself (2:6; 4:11) is illusory; Jerusalem will be reduced to rubble because of its sins. But this will not be the end of the nation: there will be survivors from the disaster, and Yahweh will gather these like a flock of sheep and protect them (2:12). Indeed, Micah goes on to paint a picture of the good future in store for Jerusalem which is as impressive as any in the prophetical books. Jerusalem, on Mount Zion, will be raised up above all the surrounding hills and will become a place to which the nations of the world will flock in order to receive instruction about Yahweh's ways (4:1–2 – this passage is virtually identical with Isa. 2:2–3). The passage continues with a prophecy of the cessation for all time of warfare between the nations (v. 3, reversing the militaristic words of Joel 3:10). Finally comes a picture of future ideal domestic happiness, when every *family* will enjoy security from fear, tending its own property and enjoying the fruits of labour (v. 4).

Chapter 5, verses 2–5a refer to the means by which, humanly speaking, this universal peace will be achieved. These verses, like Isa. 9:6–7 and 11:1–9, hint at the future appearance of a 'new David' coming from Bethlehem, to whom will be given *power* over his 'flock': he will give them security, and will himself 'be peace'.

In describing the sins of his time, Micah, like Isaiah and other prophets, denounces the present rulers, especially for the *injustices* which they commit. Among other instances of this he refers to their seizure of property and disregard of property rights (2:2) and acceptance of bribes to pervert the judicial process (3:9–11a). Such practices are not, however, confined to the political and judicial authorities: both priests and prophets are equally guilty (3:11). The prophets are also accused of uttering false prophecies of peace when sufficiently supported by the people but of threatening war when they are not (3:5). In 5:12–14 it appears that the people as a whole are also guilty: they are accused of forbidden religious practices including sorcery and the worship of images. It is for such open disobedience to Yahweh's requirements that all classes will be made to suffer.

In contrast with this propensity to wickedness (the prophet speaks of those who 'devise evil on their beds' and put it into effect as soon as they get up in the morning, 2:1–2; of the rulers, who hate the good and love evil, 3:2; and of the citizens in general who are 'skilled to do evil', 7:3), the question of the nature of the good life is specifically raised. The inhabitants of the village of Maroth may hope for good ($t\hat{o}b$) – that is, for the continuance of their peaceful life (1:12), but this will be denied them when the Assyrian is at the door. The 'good' that the rulers hate is again the welfare of their subjects, which they make impossible when they strip them of their possessions and livelihood (3:1–3).

Finally in 6:6–8 the question 'What is the good?' – that is, what must be done to obtain the good life – is specifically posed and answered. The implied questioner is already aware that it can only be attained by an acceptable approach to God – that is, by satisfying his requirements; he enquires what these are. In vv. 6–7 he asks, in a series of rhetorical questions, whether it is more numerous and more expensive animals for sacrifice that will satisfy him; but the final question reveals the absurdity of the question: it asks, as a climax of the series, whether what God really wants is a human sacrifice like that which Abraham was prepared to offer of his most valuable possession (Gen. 22). Then in a sudden switch, the hypothetical questioner is reminded of what he ought already to know because he had already been told by God himself: that his requirements are far simpler, though far more difficult to fulfil because they involve a change of heart: justice ($mi\check{s}p\bar{a}t$) and kindness ($hesed$) to others and a life of humble submission to God in close companionship ('walking') with him. Here, then, is Micah's definition of 'what is good' – what is the source of the good life.

Like some other prophetical books, notably Amos, the book ends on a positive note. In 7:18–20 the readers are assured that Yahweh is essentially a merciful and forgiving God whose word may be utterly relied on: he does not retain his anger for ever but will 'cast all our sins into the depths of the sea'. The final verse of the book is a reminder of the unbreakable oaths that he swore in ancient times to Jacob and Abraham. In this way the book will have been seen by its first readers as one of encouragement to those who had already suffered God's wrath but who, if they now fulfil his requirements, can now look forward to a better future.

Summary

Following a pattern common to other prophetical books, the book of Micah moves from an indictment of the present sinfulness of the prophet's own time through a prophecy of dire punishment to a promise to the survivors of disaster of a renewed good life lived in obedience to God's demands.

26
Haggai

Haggai, like the first chapters of Ezra, is primarily concerned with the need to rebuild the temple in Jerusalem after the destruction of the city by the Babylonians. The two principal officials of the Jerusalem community under the more favourable regime of the Persian king Darius, Zerubbabel the governor of Judah and Joshua the high priest, are urged by Yahweh through the medium of the prophet Haggai to carry out the work of rebuilding and are given the assurance that Yahweh will be with them and will give them his support (2:1–5); the author records that they obeyed his commands and began the work (1:12–15).

The building work had of course to be done by the ordinary members of the community, who were reluctant to undertake it, claiming that the time had not yet come to do it (1:2). These also are urged to begin the work. It is a characteristic of this book that the blessings of the good life are regarded as entirely dependent on the construction of the temple: unless it is built things will continue to go badly with the community. Yahweh's honour is entirely bound up with the possession of a temple (1:8), and until it is built he will withhold his blessing on the products of the soil on which the lives of the people depend (1:10–11). Once the foundations of the temple have been laid he promises that they will enjoy his blessing and continue to enjoy it in the future (2:19).

The omission from the book of mention of any of the other features of the good life – security of place, power, wealth, family, justice, etc. – may seem strange; but this extremely short book was evidently written, and will have been so understood from the outset, with a particular and urgent contemporary concern in mind. It was not designed as a complete picture of the good life, and some of those other concerns, though they may have been real enough, are not relevant to its purpose.

The material situation of the community described in the

book is not entirely clear. On the one hand the people are busy building houses for themselves; they are reproached for doing this instead of repairing the ruined temple, which lies neglected. On the other hand, the harvests are poor and they do not have enough to eat or the means to clothe themselves adequately (1:6, 11; 2:15–19). Yahweh has caused drought and other calamities to fall on the land. All that they do, including the offerings that they make to Yahweh (presumably on the site of the now ruined altar) is adjudged unclean and so not acceptable to God (2:14).

The blessing on the community promised on condition that the temple be rebuilt (2:19) is further elaborated in two passages, 2:6–9 and 2:21–23. In both of these Yahweh announces that he is about to 'shake' heaven and earth and the nations of the world. In 2:6–9 this event is associated with the rebuilt temple: it will be more splendid than its predecessor, and the nations will spill their treasures over into it; so 'on this place' (perhaps meaning the temple-centred territory of Judah) Yahweh will give peace (*šālôm*, prosperity). Verses 20–23 go further: Yahweh when he shakes the world will destroy the power of the other nations (the primary reference must be to the Persian Empire with its contemporary king Darius). The book closes (v. 23) with an astonishing promise to Zerubbabel the governor of Judah, the leader under whose authority the temple is to be built. This Zerubbabel son of Shealtiel is stated elsewhere (1 Chron. 3:19) to be of royal descent, the son of Jehoiachin (Coniah), the king of Judah who was deprived of his throne by the Babylonians and deported to Babylon. Here he is given the title of 'my servant' and designated by Yahweh as the one whom he has chosen – two titles frequently used elsewhere in the Old Testament of kings of Israel; moreover, with an allusion to Jer. 22:24, where Coniah is compared to a signet ring on Yahweh's hand but destined to be torn from it and cast away, Yahweh now promises that that situation will now be reversed, and that Zerubbabel will now be made into a signet ring. This appears to be a covert allusion to the restoration of the Davidic monarchy to rule over the dis-empowered nations; and it will certainly have been so interpreted by the book's first readers.

Summary

In Haggai the good life, at least in the material sense, is entirely dependent on the rebuilding of the temple after its destruction by the Babylonians. If Zerubbabel together with the people of Judah undertake the task of rebuilding it the divine blessing that is now lacking will be restored. The author envisages a coming age of prosperity for the people of Judah in which after a cataclysmic cosmic upheaval the new temple will be miraculously furnished and adorned by the treasures of the nations, the foreign powers will be reduced to impotence and a descendant of David will reign.

27
Zechariah

Like that of Haggai, the first part of the book of Zechariah is much concerned with the rebuilding of the temple after the exile. In fact, both of these prophets are held to have been chiefly responsible through their prophecies for persuading the people, and especially the governor Zerubbabel, of the urgent necessity to do so. Although neither book refers to the prophet after whom the other is named, they are mentioned together elsewhere as collaborating to achieve this (Ezra 5:1; 6:14). But the book of Zechariah is not only much longer than that of Haggai but also much more complex; it also fills out the details for the Jerusalem community of the good life that is now in store for them.

Zechariah 1–8 consists mainly of an account of a series of eight visions seen by the prophet together with explanations of their meaning by an angel, and a number of oracles and narratives. The visions themselves are mysterious, but their general meanings as interpreted by Yahweh's angel are clear. Yahweh is now full of good will towards his formerly sinful people who have been adequately punished. He will return and dwell in their midst, and will empower Zerubbabel to build the temple: Jerusalem and the other cities of Judah will be inhabited once more; the former wickedness of the people will be miraculously removed. The nations that have oppressed them will be destroyed, though many individual foreigners will come and seek to join God's people (8:20–23). The authority of the high priest Joshua will be confirmed, and he will rule together with Zerubbabel.

Specific details of the coming good life in these chapters are few but significant. The people will no longer be afraid of what might happen to them, for, by referring to the precarious existence of the earlier period before the foundation of the temple was laid, Zechariah implies that they will now enjoy *security* (8:10). Their lives will be peaceful and prosperous (8:11–12) and marked by God's blessing. With regard to *family*, Zechariah uses the same imagery as Micah (Micah 4:4) – that of the vine and fig tree, to indicate domestic contentment: each family will possess its own land and orchard, and families will invite each other to take their rest in these surroundings (3:10). They will also enjoy remarkable *longevity*: old men and women will once again sit peacefully in the streets of Jerusalem staff in hand because of their great age (8:4). There will again be an abundance of healthy and happy children: the streets will be full of boys and girls playing (8:5). There are not many Old Testament books that so picture the details of domestic life.

This idyllic prospect, however, remains conditional on continued obedience to God's moral law. In 3:6–8 the high priest Joshua is reminded of the behaviour incumbent on those who exercise *power* in the community. Joshua is to be given charge over the all-important temple complex only if he observes what God requires of him. The phrase 'your companions who sit before you' (v. 8) possibly extends this admonition to other prominent officials. In 7:8–14 it is made clear that these commandments must also be observed by the whole people. Although these verses refer to the past, they are clearly a warning for the present generation, who are reminded that it was a previous sinful generation who by refusing to maintain *justice*, turning a deaf ear to their duty to care for the weak and poor, and hatching plots against their fellow-citizens had brought upon themselves the horrors of the exile and the ruin of the land. A further warning in 5:3–4 singles out thieves and those who swear falsely, announcing that their houses will be utterly destroyed.

The remaining chapters of the book (9–14) contain many obscurities, some of which appear to refer to specific events occurring in the community. The precise allusions in such passages will probably have been forgotten soon after they were written. Much of the language employed is symbolic rather than literal. There is little allusion to the details of the good life; the welfare or otherwise of the people is described only in very general terms. But despite the frequent obscurity certain principal themes can be discerned.

One of the most prominent of these concerns the internal governance of the community. In these passages its rulers are referred to under the figure of shepherds — a usage frequent in ancient Near Eastern literature and in the Old Testament: compare, for example, Ezekiel. It is clear that the state of things is bad. The warnings in the first part of the book, that the divine blessing is dependent on the obedience of both governors and people to God's laws have evidently not been heeded, at least by the rulers. The 'flock' — that is, the bulk of the people — is suffering from the oppressive rule of wicked 'shepherds', who do not care for its well-being (10:3; 11:4–9), or even lack a 'shepherd' altogether (10:2). Yahweh's reaction to this situation is ambiguous and confusing — so confusing that it can hardly have made sense except to those who originally composed these passages. On the one hand he threatens to raise up for them a worthless and rapacious shepherd (11:15–16) in order to punish them. In 11:4 he appoints the prophet Zechariah to be the shepherd of the flock, but only in order to arrange for its slaughter; he, however, refuses to act as shepherd and abandons the people to judgement (11:9). In 13:7 God commands the sword to strike down the shepherd so that the flock will be scattered. On the other hand Yahweh states that he cares for them (10:3) and that though two-thirds will perish he will purify the remainder from their sins and accept them again as his people a (13:9). As in 8:20–23 the survivors of the nations will be converted and will journey to Jerusalem year by year to worship Yahweh and celebrate the feast of Tabernacles, though this time their conversion does not appear to be entirely voluntary, since if they do not do so they will be afflicted with drought and plague (14:16–19).

On a quite different level there is a second main theme similar to that of chapters 1–8: Yahweh will save his people and punish the nations that oppress them (9:1–8; 10:6–12; 12:1–9; 14;1–19). Also in this part of the book there is a remarkable passage prophesying the coming of a king — there is no mention of 'shepherds' at this point — who will inaugurate an era of peace when war will cease, and who will rule over a united Israel (9:9–10). This passage is very much in the line of similar prophecies in Isaiah 9 and 11. Other passages suggest that this king is to be identified with David or a descendant of David. The community is called 'the house of David' (12:7, 8; 13:1), and the inhabitants of Jerusalem, even the feeblest will be 'like David', while the house of David will be 'like God, like the angel of Yahweh' (12:8).

Another theme in the book which is, however, confined to a single passage (13:2–6), is a condemnation of prophecy. Elsewhere in the book prophets are highly regarded as Yahweh's spokesmen, conveying his message to the people. Zechariah himself is described as a prophet (*nābî'*) to whom the word of Yahweh came (1:1, 7), and great respect is shown to his predecessors, the 'former prophets' (1:4; 7:7, 12) who had in the past warned the people of coming disaster but who had not been heeded. In one oracle (1:6) Yahweh is recorded as referring to them collectively as 'my servants the prophets'. Yet in 13:2–6 prophets are seen as hostile to the good life. They are associated with idolatry and the unclean spirit, and Yahweh promises to remove them from the land. Prophets will henceforth be regarded by the people as liars worthy of death; they will be ashamed of their *métier* and will be obliged to conceal their identity from the people.

This incongruity constitutes an unsolved problem for modern scholars, and may have been also for those who read the completed book for the first time. That it would have been understood by them as an announcement that henceforth true prophecy will be at an end is improbable. It is more likely that they would have seen the passage as referring only to *false* prophets, who had been active in earlier times – notably in the time of Jeremiah, who had denounced them – and were still active in the time of Zechariah.

Summary

Zechariah, like Haggai, urged the importance for the life of the Jerusalem community of the rebuilding of the temple; but this book describes in much greater detail the internal problems that they faced. The prosperity of the citizens together with the destruction of the nations that had oppressed them is prophesied, and the coming of an ideal Davidic king who will bring peace is promised; but this desirable state of affairs will be conditional on their continued obedience to Yahweh's commands. The present internal problems of the Jerusalem community are dealt with in detail, and some passages seem to indicate that Yahweh's patience is at an end. The first readers of the book, however, would have been able to take the more positive assurances of a good life to come as the true message of the book.

28
Malachi

The book of Malachi is set in a later period than that of Haggai and Zechariah. The temple has been rebuilt; but all is not well in the Jerusalem community. Most of the book is devoted to listing the many ways in which the people have dishonoured Yahweh and so are deprived of the good life that he is ready to confer on them. In 3:7, for example, he reproaches them for having failed to obey him 'ever since the days of your fathers' (that is, their ancestors), and urges them to 'return to me, and I will return to you'.

The book is unique in that it consists mainly of a series of disputations between Yahweh and 'Israel' in which Yahweh accuses his interlocutors of their failures and dismisses their attempts to justify themselves. Yahweh is represented as addressing them through (literally, 'by the hand of') Malachi, though it is not stated that Malachi is a prophet. The people's defence takes the form of a series of questions with which the book is liberally punctuated. Most of these are introduced by the phrase 'Yet you say ...'. They reply to Yahweh's statement 'I have loved you' by asking, 'How have you loved us?' (1:2); they ask, 'How have we despised your name?' (1:6) and, when he accuses them of offering polluted food on his altar, they ask, 'How have we polluted it?' (1:7). When he states that he no longer accepts their offerings they ask, 'Why does he not?' (2:14). He accuses them of wearying him with their words, and they ask, 'How have we wearied him?' (2:17); he replies that they have rejected him, saying, 'All who do evil are good in Yahweh's sight', and 'Where is the God of justice?'. When he urges them to return to him they enquire, 'How shall we return?' (3:7), and to his accusation that they are robbing him they ask, 'How are we robbing you?' (3:8). To his charge that they have spoken harsh words against him they reply, 'How have we spoken against you?', and are told that they have said, 'It is vain to serve God' and 'What do we profit by keeping his commandments?' (3:14).

The indictment is a severe one – as severe as that which the earlier prophets had pronounced on the nation before the exile. The main accusation concerns the person of Yahweh himself and his honour. The people have turned against him, denying that he has loved them, accusing him of injustices and of favouring evil rather than good, declaring that it is pointless to serve and obey him. The priests are singled out in particular. As in Ezra and Nehemiah the proper service of God in the temple is clearly of paramount importance. The priests have become slack and greedy, choosing inferior animals for sacrifices (1:6–10); but the laity seem to be equally involved, in such matters as the payment of tithes (3:8). The accusations also include such sins as sorcery, adultery, oppression of the weak (3:5), and divorce (2:14–16).

The presence or absence of the good life is to be determined entirely by the people's attitude towards Yahweh. On the one hand there will be a divine judgement – a 'great and terrible day of Yahweh' (4:5). Yahweh himself will come in judgement, having previously sent his messenger to prepare the way for him; this messenger will purify the temple cult and its practitioners (3:1–4).

On the other hand Yahweh assures the people of his own unchangeable nature. He has not altered his attitude towards his people: if he had, they would already have perished. The explanation of this dual proclamation about the people's fate is to be found in the making of a radical distinction between two groups within the community: the righteous and the wicked. A brief narrative fragment (3:16) records that some persons took seriously the accusations that had been made in their hearing. These were a group who 'revered Yahweh'; their names were to be recorded in a 'book of remembrance', and they would be spared the judgement (3:16–19; 4:3). But the evildoers would be consumed (4:1–2). This making of a distinction between obedient and disobedient was not new; it is found also in other prophetical books from the period of the monarchy.

In 3:10–11 the prophet announces a time when those who obey Yahweh (here defined as those who regularly pay their tithes!) will enjoy also the material benefits of the good life:

a bounteous rain from heaven ensuring abundant crops and fruitful vines, when 'all nations will count you happy, for you will be a land of delight' (3:12).

Summary

The picture of the Jerusalem community after the rebuilding of the temple as represented in the book of Malachi is a dismal one. The people do not prosper because they have turned against Yahweh, refusing to admit the benefits that he has conferred on them, dishonouring him by failing to offer him the worship that he requires, even asserting that serving him is pointless because it brings them no advantage. Those who behave in this way will be annihilated in the coming judgement. But there is another group within the community who sincerely honour Yahweh and have taken heed of the accusations that he has made. These will be spared the judgement, will be accepted as his people, and will once more enjoy the good life with its material delights.

29
Summary and Conclusions

Despite their astonishing diversity of genre, form and contents, the books of the Old Testament are in agreement about some essential features of the good life. With few exceptions their authors recognize that as life itself depends entirely on the good will of the one God, so also does the quality of that life. Life is good or not at his pleasure; and although his nature is perceived as inscrutable and may at times appear capricious, in the main he desires the well-being of his people Israel and, although his displeasure is severe indeed, his mercy is even greater than his displeasure. There are few books of the Old Testament that do not offer some kind of hope of an eventual enjoyment of the good life based on his good will. In many of the books the present is depicted as a time of misery and judgement; but in their final form the scriptures will have been valued by their readers for their promise of a future life of peace and prosperity guaranteed by God himself.

It is within this expectation that the other features of the good life have their place. The most prominent of these is that of *security*, expressed above all in the secure possession of the *land*. This theme pervades the whole of the Old Testament; but it assumes very different forms. It is present in Genesis from the very beginning. The whole of the Pentateuch assumes the form of a journey with the sole goal of the possession of the land that has been promised; the theme from Joshua to Samuel to Kings is of the fulfilment of those promises; but the later chapters of Kings record the progressive and eventually total loss of the land to foreign conquerors owing to divine displeasure with a corrupt and disobedient people. Exile is the theme of such books as Esther and Daniel 1–6; but with Ezra and Nehemiah a glimmer of hope reappears, with a limited return to Jerusalem, though under foreign rule. The thought that God has after all not abandoned his people then led to a revival of confidence in a complete restoration of the land for those who turned back to God after a period of apostasy. The ancient promises would at last be fulfilled, and the people would never again be exiled from the land.

Other themes also have their place in the Old Testament concept of the good life. Israel encountered *power* in various forms during the course of its history. Ultimately, of course, the authors of these books recognized that all power belongs to God, and that therefore all human power that sets itself against God is doomed and finally void. This applies both to the political empires and to Israel itself. God was prepared to use the foreign rulers to punish Israel, as according to Isaiah he used Assyria and also, in Jeremiah, Nebuchadnezzar. In the end, however, these foreign powers were doomed to destruction. Within Israel itself, human power could either promote or hinder the good life, as is shown in the history of the kings. But some of the prophets looked forward to the coming of an ideal king who would bring peace to the nation and rule over them with justice.

What is true of power is also true of *justice*. God is called 'lover of justice'. But the authority that he has given to human kings and judges was frequently misused and corrupted. In the Old Testament such misuse usually takes the form of denying their rights to the poor; and it is with these that God shows himself to be especially concerned. This was a perennial problem, attested both in Kings and in the prophets. God's reaction to injustice is sometimes represented as direct; but the true administration of justice, so essential to the good life, is made a chief characteristic of the ideal king whose coming is foretold in some of the prophets.

The treatment of *wealth* in the Old Testament is ambiguous. On the one hand it is a gift of God and so, both for the nation and the individual, a feature of the good life. The wealthy person (e.g. the patriarchs of Genesis) is often one who enjoys the special favour of God. On the other hand (for example in Proverbs and the Psalms) the wealthy are sometimes disliked as a class of people who are arrogant and use their wealth immorally to give them power over others. No doubt this was sometimes the case; but in general wealth is regarded positively as a sign of divine blessing, though Ecclesiastes in particular regards it as deceptive, ephemeral and so not conducive to the good life of those who possess it. Rarely is it regarded as an unmitigated evil.

There are few references in the Old Testament to *health* and illness, and even fewer to old age, apart from the excessive life-spans of the patriarchs in Genesis. *Death* in old age was taken for granted and not seen as in any way incompatible with the living of a good life, though premature death, especially by violence, was sometimes seen as a punishment for an evil life (especially in Proverbs). The death of Abraham at 175 is regarded as an appropriate ending to a virtuous and successful life. There are, however, some references to the evils of senility (especially Eccles. 12:1–5).

Other features of the good life are assigned only secondary status. Lineage was always a matter of importance to Israelites, as is attested by the numerous genealogies; according to Ezra the returning exiles were even required to provide proof of their family descent in order to be officially recognized as genuine members of the Jewish community (Ezra 2:59–63). But *family life* in the sense of an intimate community in which husband and wife, parents and children and brothers lived together is depicted only comparatively rarely. In some books, especially Genesis, Ruth and parts of Samuel, family relationships are an integral part of the ongoing story; but in others, where military or national concerns take precedence, they receive little or no attention; in some, indeed, individuals other than national leaders are hardly mentioned.

It is curious that in most of the books *wisdom* is not specifically identified as characterizing human actions, nor is the term frequently used of God himself (though there are exceptions to this in passages that praise him as the creator of the world). In fact there is evidence that the term 'wise' when used of human beings had a negative connotation. A notable example of this is the case of Jonadab, who planned Amnon's rape of his sister: he is called 'very wise' (*ḥākām mě'ōd*). To be 'wise in one's own eyes' is a pejorative term, especially in Proverbs and Isaiah. Wisdom, then, is an ambiguous term: Solomon's wisdom, for example, is a specific gift of God (1 Kings 3:12; 4:29–34) which enabled. him to rule his people in accordance with God's wishes and also gave him an international reputation. In Proverbs, wisdom is a goal to be sought by individuals above everything else. In Deuteronomy wisdom is a qualification for leadership, and in Deut. 4:6 the whole nation of Israel is described as wise through keeping God's laws. The actions of Israel's successful leaders might well so be described, but wisdom is very rarely attributed to them.

Finally, joy and *pleasure* are a feature of the good life that receives comparatively little attention. It is rarely attributed to individuals except in psalms of praise and thanksgiving in the Psalter, but rather to public rejoicing on great national occasions such as David's bringing the Ark to Jerusalem or the dedication of the temple. There were no doubt many occasions of private joy such as the birth of a male child, but these are not generally recorded. Joy is often a feature of the prophecies of the restoration of the nation, however; but much of the history of Israel recorded in the Old Testament is a tale of woe rather than of joy. Ecclesiastes distinguished between the inane laughter of fools (7:4) or of those who make pleasure their only goal in life (2:1–2) and the lasting joy which is given (to some) by God (2:26–28; 8:15).

It may reasonably be questioned whether the good life is a major topic of the Old Testament. This question should be answered in the affirmative. Ancient Israel was in many respects a materialistic people in the sense that it constantly sought to obtain the good things of life, though these were frequently denied it. The topic of the good life has been neglected in recent Old Testament study, and deserves more intense research.

In this book I have tried to set out as far as is possible the Old Testament concept of the good life as it would have been perceived by those who first read this literature in its present form. This has not been an easy task, and is inevitably somewhat speculative. The Old Testament, it seems to me, will have been seen by those readers as fundamentally an optimistic book, looking to the future despite its emphasis on the shortcomings of the past and the judgements on past sins. The attempt has been made here to avoid interpreting it in the light of the interpretations of modern scholars, as an exercise in the early history of exegesis. How far this distinction has been successfully made it is for the reader to decide.

Further Reading

Barton, John, ed., *The Cambridge Companion to Biblical Interpretation* (Cambridge University Press, 1998)

Barton, John, and Muddiman, John, eds., *The Oxford Bible Commentary* (Oxford University Press, 2001)

Childs, Brevard S., *Introduction to the Old Testament as Scripture* (SCM Press, 1979)

Clements, R. E., ed., *The World of Ancient Israel: Sociological, Anthropological and Political Perspectives* (Cambridge University Press, 1989)

De Vaux, Roland, *Ancient Israel: Its Life and Institutions* (Darton, Longman & Todd, 1961)

Deist, Ferdinand E., ed., with a preface by Robert P. Carroll, *The Material Culture of the Bible: An Introduction* (Sheffield Academic Press, 2000)

Janzen, Waldemar, *Old Testament Ethics: A Paradigmatic Approach* (Westminster/John Knox Press, 1994)

Kee, Howard Clark, Meyers, Eric M., Rogerson, John, and Saldarini, Anthony J., eds., *The Cambridge Companion to the Bible* (Cambridge University Press, 1997)

LaSor, William Sanford, Hubbard, David Allan, and Bush, Frederic William, eds., *Old Testament Survey: The Message, Form, and Background of the Old Testament* (Eerdmans, 2nd edition, 1996)

McNutt, Paula, *Reconstructing the Society of Ancient Israel* (Westminster/John Knox Press, 1999)

Metzger, Bruce M., and Coogan, Michael D., eds., *The Oxford Companion to the Bible* (Oxford University Press, 1993)

Miller, Patrick D., *The Religion of Ancient Israel* (SPCK / Westminster/John Knox Press, 2000)

Perdue, Leo G., Blenkinsopp, Joseph, Collins, John J., and Myers, Carol, *Families in Ancient Israel* (Westminster/John Knox Press, 1997)

Rogerson, John, and Davies, Philip, *The Old Testament World* (Cambridge University Press, 1989)

Sawyer, John F. A., *From Moses to Patmos: New Perspectives on Old Testament Study* (SPCK, 1977)

Wenham, Gordon J., *Story as Torah: Reading the Old Testament Ethically* (T&T Clark, 2000)

Whybray, R. N., *Job* (Sheffield Academic Press, 1998)

Whybray, R. N., *Wealth and Poverty in the Book of Proverbs* (Sheffield Academic Press, 1990)

Wright, Christopher J. H., *God's People in God's Land: Family, Land, and Property in the Old Testament* (Eerdmans / Paternoster Press, 1990)